ISBN 978-1-332-06610-0
PIBN 10279271

THE YORKSHIRE

Archæological Society.

RECORD SERIES.

Vol. XXXI.

FOR THE YEAR 1902.

YORKSHIRE INQUISITIONS.

Vol. III.

EDITED BY

WILLIAM BROWN, F.S.A.

Honorary Secretary of the Society.

PRINTED FOR THE SOCIETY,

1902.

PRINTED BY

J. WHITEHEAD AND SON, ALFRED STREET, BOAR LANE,

LEEDS.

INTRODUCTION.

T HIS volume contains 106 inquisitions, ranging from 1294 to the spring of 1303, in addition to two omitted from the earlier volumes, dated 1245 and 1282. The character of the inquisitions is much the same as those given in Vol. II. As regards the rank of the persons concerned, the most important inquisitions are those of the Earls of Lancaster (No. LIV.), the King's brother, relating to Pickering, and that of his uncle, the Earl of Cornwall (No. LXXXV.), lord of the Honour ol Knaresborough, this latter one unfortunately very imperfect. Some of the inquisitions are of considerable length, notably those of Roger Mowbray (Nos. LVI., CVII.) and John Bellew (No. CVIII.).

In addition to the usual *inquisitiones post mortem* and *ad quod damnum* there are three "Proofs of age,"—Geoffrey, son of Robert Luterel (No. XLVIII.), Thomas, brother and heir of John de Longevilers (No. LXXXIIa.), both from the *Curia Regis* Rolls, and of Henry, grandson of Henry, son of Conan of Kelfield (No. XCVIII.). Only the last of these was proved in Yorkshire.

Appended to No. XLII. is an extract from the *Curia Regis* Roll, which gives a curious account of the marriage service and of the subsequent endowment of the bride by her husband at the church door of lands still in his father's possession, but to which endowment his father at the time verbally agreed. Customs, obtaining the force of law, are sometimes proved by jurors in these inquisitions. At Scarborough (p. 93) it was shown that a testator when on his deathbed could devise realty: and from No. XLIX. it appears that it was lawful to behead, without any formal trial, a malefactor, pursued with hue and cry, as soon as taken.[1] No. LXIV. gives an example of

---

[1] A somewhat similar case is entered on one of the Yorkshire Assize Rolls (N-1-14-1, fo. 63) for the reign of Edward I., where Brother Henry of de Herternesse, a *conversus* of Fountains, and others, were indicted for beheading two

two hospitals, both at Scarborough, founded by the piety and generosity of the burgesses of the town, and not by the King or any private benefactor.

The matter of tenure is constantly referred to in these inquisitions. Some are very curious. The Meynells of Whorlton, near Stokesley, held their lands of the Archbishops of Canterbury, on the condition of acting as their butlers on the day of their enthronization (p. 115). The same family held the manor of Castle Levington, near Yarm (p. 114), by the tenure of providing a horseman for forty days with the Royal army. The lord of Hooton Paynel (No. XLVII.) was bound to find four men with horse and arms, apparently in the wars in Wales; and Roger Mowbray, as lord of the manor of Kirkby Malzeard, found five. Another peculiar military tenure was that of finding an arblaster or crossbowman for lands at Givendale, near Pocklington. Sometimes this service took the form of assisting in the guard of some castle, *Castelward*, as Tickhill (p. 84), or the castle in the Honour of Holderness, probably Skipsea (No. C.). *Waytemete*, payment for the food of the *waits* or watchmen (p. 84), was for a similar object.

One incident of tenure, which occurs on almost every page, is suit of court. This part of the service must have been most onerous and irksome. The ordinary manor courts, called at Hovingham (p. 76) Hallemote courts, were held once every three weeks, as at Dringhouses (p. 16), Harewood (p. 32), Thirsk (pp. 76, 78), Buttercrambe and Ripon (p. 153), and at all of these the tenant of lands within the manor was bound to be present in person or by his attorney. The courts of the chief lords, for the holders of manors, called at Skipton (pp. 48, 147) Knights' courts, were held at similar intervals, as at Pontefract (p. 15), Richmond (p. 30), Beverley (p. 34), Knaresborough (p. 43), Whitby (p. 82), Bishop Wilton (p. 94), and Sherburn-in-Elmete (p. 107). Burgesses, at least at Borough-

lads, both under age, for stealing bread, butter, and cheese, to the value of 3*d*. The jury found, "quod predicti latrones fuerunt de etate xiiij annorum, et quod burgauerunt quandam domum, et inde asportauerunt bona ad valenciam vij*d*., et cum manu opere capti fuerunt et decollati, *prout moris est in patria*. Ideo nichil."

bridge (p. 128), were only compelled to attend three times in the year. In addition to these courts there were the Wapentake courts, occurring in Holderness (p. 57) every three weeks, but in other cases, as of the Wapentakes of Harthill and Rydale (pp. 42, 76), the tenants had to attend only once a year. Courts for the Riding are mentioned three times (pp. 42, 76, 78), but in each case the North Riding is the one named. Here once a year was sufficient attendance. Courts for the County occur twice. In one place (p. 78) suit of court was to be paid once a year, and in another (p. 76) every six weeks. It was perhaps in connection with this court that the payment of *Schirefgeld* (p. 143), apparently the same as *Schirrefstuthe* (p. 84), was to be made. In boroughs the burgesses paid a tax on their houses, called housegabel, from the Old English *gafol*, a tax.

Mention is made of an unusual kind of grant in No. LXXXII., where the jurors found that the Priory of Thornton, in Lincolnshire, could, under a grant from one of the Earls of Albemarle, retithe the cheeses in the Earl's dairies in Holderness, that is, take a tithe of the nine parts remaining after the tenth had been taken by the parish priest. An unusual measure, a stang, equivalent to a pole, occurs in No. XXIII.

WILLIAM BROWN.

Northallerton,
    August, 1902.

CONTENTS.

————◆————

CONTENTS.

CONTENTS.

CONTENTS.

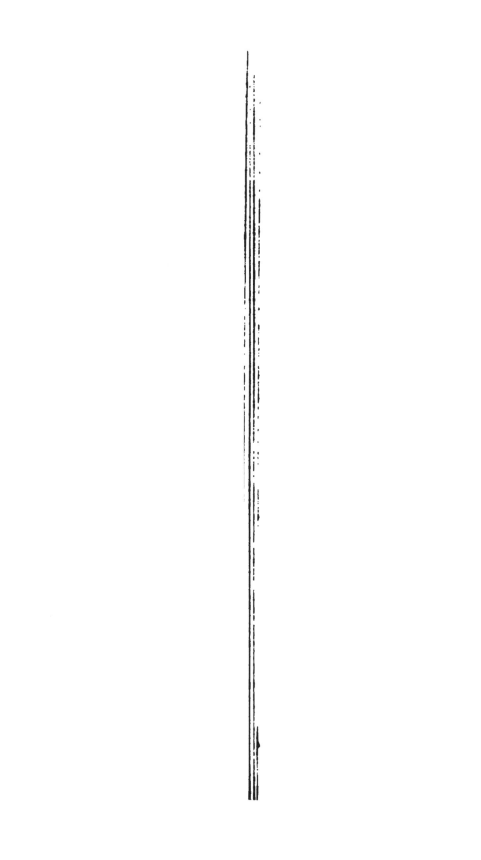

ABSTRACTS OF YORKSHIRE INQUISITIONS.

I. WILLIAM DE WERNEVILLE[a] *or* WENNERVILE. *Inq. p. m.*

[29 HEN. III. No. 40.]

Writ directed to the guardian of the lands of John, late Earl of Lincoln and Constable of Chester, and dated at Westminster, 21 Jan., 29th year (1244-5).

INQUISITION made on the land of Sir William de Wenner-vile[b] by John de Hoderode, John de Curtenay, John de Kyneslay, William *de Bosco*, William *de Assartis*, Robert Camberlan, Adam de Himleswrde, Hugh de Hundelay, Adam de Crigleston, Henry Forester (*forestarium*), Alan Steward (*dispensatorem*), Ralph son of William. W. de Wennervile held in demesne 12 score and 12 acres of land (4*d.*), the sum of which, £4 4*s.*; also 18 acres of meadow (2*s.*), the sum of which, 36*s.* He had in service of free tenants, 33*s.* 7*d.* In bondage (*bondagio*), 21½ bovates of land, of which 6½ bovates are in Himleswrde[c] (6*s.* 1½*d.* a bovate); in Kyneslay 15 bovates, 3*s.* 10½*d.* a bovate. Sum of the bonders of Himleswrde and Kyneslay,[d] £4 16*s.* 8½*d.* (*sic*). There are many cotters (*cotarii*), and they render yearly £4 0*s.* 10½*d.* Sum total, £16 12*s.* 1½*d.* A watermill and windmill, rendering this year twelve quarters of wheat (*siliginis*). Of all the abovesaid the lady[e] has her third part in the name of

[a] An account of this family, more usually Wannervile, is given by the late Mr. Richard Holmes in the *Yorkshire Archæological Journal* (xi., 437*n*). I am indebted to Mr. Holmes for calling my attention to the omission of this inquisition. As the official index makes the county *Castr'*, as though for Chester, and calls Himleswrde *Hunlesworde*, and speaks of the manor of Wennervill, there is some excuse for the omission.

[b] Wernevile in the writ.

[c] Hemsworth.

[d] Kinsley.

[e] Mr. Holmes (*loc. cit.*) says that William de Wannervile married one Margery. He gives no authority for this statement. If correct, he must have married again, as on Dec. 26, 1244, the guardian of the lands of the Earl of Lincoln was ordered to assign dower to Hawise, widow of William de Vereville (*Excerpta l Rotulis Finium*, i., 429).

dower. The same (*idem*) has an heir male,[a] and he will be thirteen years old at the feast of St. Giles next (Sept. 1). He has only as much pasture in the vill as goes with the demesne, and he defends his land by the service of one knight.[b]

1a. ROBERT DE GRELLE. *Extent of lands.*
[10 EDW. I. No. 20.]

INQUISITION[c] made at York on Tuesday in the octave of St. Michael, 10 Edw. (6 Oct., 1282), by John de Lithegr', sheriff of Yorkshire, by the King's writ, on the true value of the knights' fees which Robert de Grelle deceased held in chief in the county of York, by Nicholas de Ribston, John de Stockeld', Hugh son of Avice of Hauerton, Henry son of Luke (*Luce*) of Hoperton, William Wadiloue of Gelistorp', Alan de Gelistorp, Richard de Kerby, William de Blacbericroft, John son of Henry of Dicton, Nicholas Maynnrid', John son of Ralph of Thorneburg', and Henry Skot. John Mauleverer held of Robert de Grelle four carucates of land in Flasceby[d] by the service of ward and relief, where twelve carucates of land make a knight's fee. Robert did not die seised thereof. The land is worth 22 marcs a year in all issues.

1b. PHILIP DE COKEFELD. *Inq. ad q. d.*
[22 EDW. I. No. 113.]
Writ directed to the King's bailiffs of Kynggestone upon Hull, and dated at the Tower of London, 5 Nov., 22nd year (1294).

INQUISITION made concerning the lands and tenements which were of Ivo de Cotingham in the town of Kinggestone upon Hull by Robert de Barton, Hugh son of Isabel, Hugh Belle, Robert de London, Walter Celererman, Robert de Middelton, John Skayl, Robert de Dripol, Henry Danyel, Stephen *del Ker*, Robert de Aldeburg', and Robert de Paghel, who say on their oath that it is not to the

[a] Mr. Holmes says his name was Adam. William de Ebor, provost of Beverley, bought the wardship of the land and heir of William de Wenreville for four score marcs, and on March 4, 1244-5, the guardian of the Earl of Lincoln's lands was ordered to give the seisin of Wenreville's lands and heir to the provost (*Ibid.*, i., 431).

[b] Et tantum pasture quantum habet in villa sequitur dominicum, et defendit terram suam per servitium unius militis.

[c] No writ for Yorkshire. The writs to the sheriffs of Rutland, Norfolk, Lancashire, and Oxford, dated May 24. Thomas son and heir of Robert de Grelle was aged two . . . (*Inq. p. m.*, 10 Edw. I., No. 3).

[d] Flaxby, in the parish of Goldsborough.

damage or prejudice of the King, or of others, if Philip de Cokefeld hold a messuage with appurtenances which the said Ivo held of the King in the town of Kinggestone upon Hul on the day of his death. The said Philip may hold the messuage with appurtenances to him and to his heirs of the King and his heirs for ever by the services due and accustomed, without damage or prejudice of the King, or of others, because the said Ivo was a bastard. He had a son named Hugh, born in lawful wedlock (*de legittimo matrimonio procreatum*), who died two years ago and before his father, and also two sons and two daughters, who are yet alive and all bastards. Ivo did two suits at the King's court in the year, viz. at the next court after Easter and after Michaelmas; and he paid yearly 20s. at two terms, at Pentecost 10s. and at Martinmas 10s. The value beyond is 10s. a year. Dated at Kinggestone on Friday the morrow of the Epiphany, 23 Edw. (7 Jan., 1294-5).

II. WILLIAM DE ROWELEY *or* ROULEYE. *Inq. p. m.*
[22 EDW. I. No. 15.]
Writ dated at Westminster, 12 Nov., 22nd year (1294).

INQUISITION made of the lands and tenements which were formerly of William de Roweley in the town of Kyngestone upon Hul by Hugh son of Isabel, Hugh Belle, John Rotinharing, Stephen *del Ker*, Robert de Middelton, Robert de Dripol, John de Faxflete, John Skayl, John Rouchut, John Moubray, Roger *le Taverner*, and Henry Flemynge, who say on their oath that William de Roweley died on Thursday before the feast of St. Laurence, 22 Edw. (5 Aug., 1294), and all his lands were taken into the King's hand on Saturday after the feast of St. Laurence in the year aforesaid (14 Aug., 1294): and they are yet in the King's hand. He had on the day of his death in the town of Kyngestone four tofts which yield yearly to the King 29s. 4d., and held no other land of any other lord in the said town. The said tofts were worth to the use of the said William 43s. 4d. beyond a certain farm. As to his next heir they are altogether ignorant, because he was born in the town of Harwys, near London by ten leagues. As to the age of him who says he is the heir, they believe it to be about sixteen years. Dated at Brustwyke on Monday the eve of St. Thomas the Apostle in the 23rd year of the reign of King Edward, son of King Henry (20 Dec., 1294).[a]

---

[a] By endorsement a direction to wait until the so-called heir sues—"Expectet quousque ille qui se dicit heredem sequatur."

III. JOHN DE LOVETOT (LUVETOT) THE ELDER. *Inq. p. m.*
[23 EDW. I. No. 33.]
Writ[a] dated at Aberconewey, 28 Jan., 23rd year (1294-5).

INQUISITION upon the true value of the knights' fees and advowsons of churches which were of John de Lovetot deceased in the bailiwick of Thomas dc Normanvile, the King's Escheator beyond Trent, made at Pontefract on Saturday after the Annunciation of the B.V.M., 23 Edw. (26 March, 1295), by William son of Walter of Estoft, Thomas de Egmanton, John de . . . by, Robert Cortewys, William Godefray, Walter son of Agnes, John de Doffeld, John Steward, Stephen de . . . . . . de Heke, Adam de Preston, and Adam de Arnethorp, who say that he held nothing in the said bailiwick of the King in chief, but he held in his demesne as of fee a toft, twenty . . Athelingflet with the advowson of the church there. The toft is worth by the year 12*d.*, and every acre . . . . . . The church is worth 300 marcs[b] a year. He had the said lands and advowson . . . . of John Deyvile, who held of Sir Roger de Moubray. Upon great part of . . . . . . formerly controversy was moved between the abbot of Selby and the patron of the church.[c]

IV. WILLIAM DE FAUCUNBERGE. *Inq. p. m.*
[23 EDW. I. No. 34.]
Two writs directed to Thomas de Normanville, Escheator beyond Trent, and dated 4th and 8th of Feb. respectively, in the 23rd year (1295-6).

INQUISITION before Thomas de Normanville on Thursday before the feast of St. Gregory the Pope, 23 Edw. (10 March, 1294-5), at Brandesburton, by Walter de Flinton, Robert *de la More*, John de Fitling, Simon de Lunde, Henry de Wyueton, Amand de Surdevale, Walter de Dringhou, Robert Cance, Stephen de Drynghow, Nicholas Kyrkeman, William Barn, and Walter Northiby, who say

[a] A writ of the same date directed to Malcolm de Harlee, Escheator *citra Trentam.*

[b] The value of advowsons of churches is in all 368 marcs.

[c] By inquisitions taken in the counties of Cambridge, Huntingdon, Oxford, Suffolk, and Surrey, the heir is found to be John, son of John de Lovetot the elder, deceased. His age is variously stated to be 24 (Suffolk, 3 inq.), 25 (Cambridge), 26 (Essex), 27 (Suffolk), 30 (Essex, 3 inq.), and 40 years (Surrey). Dower was assigned to Joan, his widow, in the bailiwick of Malcolm de Harley (Escheator *citra Trentam*), on the 8 Feb., 23 Edw. (1294-5). On 29 July, 1295, the homage of John, son and heir of John de Luvetot, having been taken, the Escheator *citra* was ordered by the King, then at Wycombe, to restore to him his lands (*Rot. Fin.*, 23 Edw. I., m. 11).

on their oath that William de Faucunberge held nothing of the King in chief within the limits of Holdernesse, but he held of Walter de Faucunberge a capital messuage at Catfosse, worth by the year 10s. There are four carucates and three bovates of land (the bovate, 5s. a year), and in service 15 bovates; of which Robert de Faucunberge holds two, yielding yearly a rose; John Barn holds three by knight's service; Peter de Faucunberge, one for a clove (*clavum gariofili*); William son of William de Faucunberge, four for a penny; Henry, brother of the said William, three for a clove; the Prioress of Killinge,[a] two in pure almoign. William *le Taillur* held of him six acres of land with two tofts, yielding yearly a pound of pepper. The said William de Faucunberge held the wood of Killinge, worth 9s. 8d. a year. All the aforesaid lands and tenements were held by him of Walter de Faucunberge by knight's service.

John son of William de Faucunberge is his next heir, and aged twenty-three years.[b]

V. JOHN SON OF JOHN DE REDMAR *or* REDDEMERE.

Inq. p. m.

[23 EDW. I. No. 28.]

Writ dated at Aberconewey, 4 March, 23rd year (1294-5).

INQUISITION made at Ravenserodde on Thursday after the feast of St. Augustin the Archbishop, 23 Edw. (2 June, 1295), before Thomas de Normanville, Escheator, by William de Hoton, John de Risum, Stephen de Shyreburne, John de Holeym, William de St. Quintin, John de Ravenser, Nicholas de Thorne, Stephen Tryppoke, William de Carlton, Robert Julian, Robert Costantin, and John Fryboys, who say on their oath that John son of John de Redmar held in demesne of the King in chief a messuage with appurten-

---

[a] Nunkeeling.

[b] There are four other inquisitions, taken in the counties of Nottingham and Derby. By two of these the age of the heir is found to be twenty-three, and by the two others, twenty-one; all before the same Escheator (Thomas de Normanville). On 4 April, 1295, the King took at Aberconewey the homage of John, son and heir of William de Faucumberge (*Rot. Fin.*, 23 Edw. I., m. 16). The executors of Thomas de Normanville, the Escheator accounted for 39s. 10d. from the demesne lands which were William de Faucumberge's in Cokeneye, Barleburgh and Catefosse, from Sunday after the feast of the Purification of the B. V. M. (6 Feb., 1294-5) up to 4 April following, before livery to John, son and heir of the said William, who found as sureties for payment of his relief, William de Wallecote, William de Bubwithe, Peter de la Twyere, and Amandus de Surdeval (*Escheators' Accounts ultra Trentam* ⅜).

ances in Northorpe,[a] worth by the year 4s., and 4½ bovat
of land there (at half a marc the bovate). Of him Jol
de Northorpe held six bovates by free service of 10s. yearl
and William de Redmar, a bovate and a half by fr
service of a pair of white gloves. He also held in demesi
half a bovate of land in Esington, worth 7s. a year, and
the same town in a plot (*placea*) called Lokholm 10 acr
of land (at 6d. the acre). Of him John de Northorpe he
half a bovate and 41 acres by free service of 5s. a yea
and John de Redmar his father held 33 acres in Esingt(
for term of his life by the same service. All the aforesa
tenements the said John held of the King by free servi(
of 30s. yearly, (and nothing of any other). Alice l
daughter is his next heir, and she was half a year old
Pentecost in the year abovesaid (22 May, 1295).

Another writ dated at Aberconewey, 20 March, 23rd year (1294-5).

INQUISITION made at Ravens[er] before John de Lythegreyr
Escheator beyond Trent, on Saturday the morrow of tl
Epiphany of Our Lord (7 Jan., 1295-6), by William de Hoto
Henry de St. Martin, Ralph his brother, John de Ryso1
Stephen de Schireburne, William de St. Quentin, Peter
sea (*ad mare*), Stephen Tryppoke, John Freboys, Richa
Bucke, William de Carleton, and Stephen Brun, who say (
their oath that John son of John de Reddemer held of t:
King in chief on the day of his death, in demesne as of f
a messuage in Northorpe worth by the year 4s., and
bovates of land (at 6s. 8d.), also half a bovate in Esingt(
with 10 acres of land in a plot (*placea*) called Locholi
by free service of . . . s. a year. The half bovate is wor
7s., and every acre 6d. a year. John de Reddemer fath
of the said John is yet alive and held of his son 33 acr
of land in Esington for life by free service of 5s. Ea(
acre is worth 6d. a year. John de Northorpe held of Jol
son of John de Reddemer 6 bovates of land in Northor1
by free service of 10s. a year (the bovate 6s. 8d.), also ha
a bovate (at 7s.) and 43 acres of land (at 6d.) there 1
free service of 5s. a year. William de Reddemer held
him one bovate in Northorpe (at 6s. 8d.) by free service
a pair of white gloves. Whereas all these tenements us(
to be held of the Earl of Albemarle, of his barony

---

[a] In the parish of Easington, now swallowed up by the Humber (**Boy**
Lost Towns of the Humber, p. 49).

Holdernesse, by free service of 30*s.* a year, they are now held of the King in chief by the same service. Alice, daughter of the said John, is his next heir, and aged . . [a]

Writ of *certiorari*, directed to the treasurer and barons of the exchequer, and dated at York, 22 Feb., 24th year (1295–6). Whereas it is found by inquisition made by John de Lythegraynes that John de Reddemere held of the King in chief by service of 30*s.* a year only, wishing to be certified whether the tenure was by other service, so that the custody of the lands ought to be had by reason of the minority of the heir, the King commands the rolls of the exchequer to be searched, and the certainty in the premises to be stated in writing. The barons, after reciting the particulars set out in the King's writ, returned their answer (without date) to the following effect.

THE rolls and memoranda of the Exchequer being thoroughly searched (*perscrutatis*), it is not found in them, that John de Reddemere, or his ancestors, held anything of the King, or his progenitors in chief; nor is it found that the King, or his progenitors, had the custody of lands and tenements after the death of any ancestor of the said John. True it is that Isabel, late Countess of Albemarle, deceased, before her death caused to be extended all fees, which from any cause were held in England of William *de Fortibus*, formerly Earl of Albemarle, her husband, by writs of chancery (as it is said). It is expedient that these extents (which are returned to chancery) be seen in full; and then by these evidences, as well as by any memoranda in the Exchequer, certification might be made in the premises. It seems also very expedient for the Crown that the like extents made of lands, tenements, and fees, should be enrolled in Exchequer for perpetual memory of the thing, and for evidences to be had in a similar case.

VI.[b] THOMAS DE MULTON OF GILLESLAND.[c] *Inq. p. m.*

[23 EDW. I. No. 62.]

Writ directed to Thomas de Normanville and dated at Lammays, 23 April, 23rd year (1295).

INQUISITION made of the lands and tenements of Thomas de Multon of Gillesland, between U[se] and D[erwent], before Thomas de Normanwile on Tuesday after the feast

[a] On the back of this inquisition is a note that the land is to be restored to the heir, etc. "Reddatur terra heredi et faciat quod facere debet."

[b] Badly written, and parts difficult to read.

[c] Coram Rege. Hillary Term. 5 Edw. 3 (1330–1), m. 162. Cumberland. Ralph de Dacre and Margaret his wife claimed from the King the custody of the forest

of Holy Trinity, 23 Edw. (31 May, 1295), by Walter de . . . .
Philip son of Hawyse of Kelkefeld, Henry son of Thomas
of the same, Adam *le Lange* of the same, William Russell
of Naburne, Augustin Cook (*cocum*), Richard de Fyskergat
of Styvelingflet, Walter de Heulay of the same, Thomas *in
le Wylges*, Henry Kingesman, William Helewys, and Robert
Freman. The said Thomas held the manor of Thorgamby
save half a marc, also 74 acres of land in demesne (at 8*d.*),
7 acres of meadow (at 18*d.*), 19 acres of several pasture (at
a marc). The profit (*comoditas*) of wood is yearly 2*s.*; the
pasture in Smythefeld is worth 12*d.* a year.

Free tenants. The prior of Ellerton holds four bovates
of land for 4*s.* a year; Robert Freman, one bovate for 18*d.*;
Laurence Squier, a toft for 5*d.*; the prioress of Thicheued,
a toft and croft in pure and perpetual almoign; Nicholas
Clerk (*clericus*) holds a bovate of land for 4*s.*; Maurice
Cauncelu, a toft and 15 acres for 7*s.* 6*d.*, and 24 acres of
land for 8*s.* a year; Thomas Mel, a bovate for 14*s.*; William
son of Nicholas, a croft and 6 acres of land for 7*s.* 7*d.*; and
a horse-mill (*molendinum equorum*) for five quarters of hard
corn (*duri bladi*). In services of bondmen (*bondagiorum*),
£13 19*s.* 5½*d.*; also of cottagers (*cottagiorum*), £6 15*s.* 6½*d.*;
in hens, eggs and boon-works (*prayar*), 5*s.*

Geoffrey de Hertrepol holds five score and 6½ acres.
The same holds five acres and a half of meadow for term
of his life for a ginger-root (*pro una radice gingiberi*). All
this he held in chief of the King.

Thomas his son is his next heir and aged 14 years.[a]

of Inglewode, and gave this descent :—

Thomas de Multon of Gilleslande
|
Thomas
|
Thomas
|
Thomas
|
Margaret d. and h. = Ralph de Dacre.
(*Genealogist* (N.S.), x. 86).

[a] There are other inquisitions for Suffolk and Cumberland, in which latter county
Thomas de Multon had large possessions. The inquisition taken for Suffolk,
24 May, 23rd year (1295), finds that the heir will be 13 years of age at Michaelmas-
day following (29 Sept., 1295), while one of those for Cumberland, taken on Tuesday
after Pentecost (24 May, 1295) in the same year, gives the same age at an earlier
date, the first of August (*ad gulam Augusti*). In answer to a writ dated 4 July,
23rd year (1295), it is found by inquisition taken at Brampton on Tuesday after
the feast of the Translation of St. Thomas the Martyr (12 July, 1295), that
Sir Thomas de Multon, father of the Thomas now deceased, enfeoffed his son and
Isabel his wife jointly in the manor of Kirkeoswald, and that Isabel was yet living
at this date. In the accounts of the Escheator, Thomas de Normanville, for the
year commencing at Michaelmas, 20 Edw. I. (29 Sept., 1292), he renders under the
county of Cumberland account of the rents of lands which belonged to Thomas de
Multon of Gillesland, who held of the King in chief, from Monday after the feast

VII. JOHN DE STEYNGREVE OR STAYNGRIF. *Inq. p. m.*

[23 EDW. I. No. 54.]

Writ dated at Lammys, 25 April, 23rd year (1295).

INQUISITION taken at Nunnington on Friday before the feast of Holy Trinity, 23 Edward (27 May, 1295), before Thomas de Normanvil, the King's Escheator, by Sir John Jarpenvil, Walter Romayn, Robert de Sproxton, Thomas de Etton, Roger Raboc, Robert de Colton, James de Holme, Richard Mareschal, Adam *le Torny*, John son of Absolon, Thomas son of Ydonia, and Richard de Holthorp, who say upon their oath that John de Stayngrif held on the day of his death nothing in the county of York of the King in chief; but he held six carucates of land in Nunnington, worth by the year £16, of John Paynel by knight's service, whereof six carucates make a knight's fee. He also held there of the said John Paynel a messuage and five cottages which are worth 18s. a year; a mill worth 8 marcs; a meadow and a pasture in Waterholm which are worth £10. He held of William de Ros by the service of a pound of pepper, a messuage and half a carucate of land worth two marcs a year[a]; in Wesby[b], of the Abbot of St. Mary's, York, by the service of half a marc, a messuage worth 4s. a year, and a carucate worth 4 marcs a year; in Stayngrif[c], of John Paynel by knight's service, a messuage worth half a marc, three carucates worth £8, a watermill worth 20s., 10 cottages worth 20s., and a meadow worth

of St. Peter *in Cathedra* in the said year (23 Feb., 1292-3) to 27 March next following, on which day those lands were delivered up by the King's writ to Thomas, son and heir of the said Thomas (*Escheators' Accounts ultra Trentam ⅜*). 20 June, 1297. Westminster. Information given to John Lythegr', Escheator beyond Trent, that in consideration of a fine the King had pardoned Isabel, widow of Thomas de Multon of Gillesland, deceased, who held in chief, for entering without licence the manor of Kirkeoswald with the park and advowson of the church of the same manor, and also a salt-pan in the vill of Burgh-on-Sands (*salinam in villa de Burgo super Sabulones*), held in chief, of which Thomas, father of the said Thomas, enfeoffed the same Thomas and the said Isabel jointly, and that the King had taken the fealty of the same Isabel for the same, and also for 30s. of land in the said vill of Burgh and Fulwood', which William son of Michael of Wylmerley and Walter son of Walter *le Neyr* held immediately of the said Thomas, and which Thomas and Isabel acquired for themselves of the said William and Walter in fee (*Rot. Fin.*, 25 Edw. I., m. 11). On 9 Oct., 1298, the King at Jedburgh gave leave to Isabella, Thomas de Multon's widow, to marry John de Castre, but if she were not joined to the said John in matrimony, the right pertaining to the King of her marriage was to be reserved (*Calendar of Patent Rolls*, 1292-1301, p. 368).

[a] Perhaps the last vill of Ricall, near Nunnington, which was held by John de Staingrive of Robert de Ros in 1284-5 (*Kirkby's Inquest*, p. 117).

[b] Not identified, unless an error for Eseby, now Easby near Richmond.

[c] Stonegrave.

10 marcs, where 6 carucates of land make a knight's fee;
there also of Roger de Moubray, by yearly service of 2s.,
a carucate of land worth 4 marcs; and of the Prior of
Hexhilsam[a], by yearly service of one marc, two carucates
of land worth 8 marcs; and in Shouesby,[b] of Matthew
Lovayn by knight's service, a messuage worth 2s., two
cottages worth 3s., a watermill worth 20s., and 3 carucates
worth £6 a year, where 20 carucates of land make a knight's
fee; in Kelkefelde, of Arnald de Percy by knight's service,
a messuage and a bovate of land which are worth by the
year 14s.; and in Neuhaye,[c] of John Paynel by knight's
service, 20 acres of land, worth yearly half a marc; and in
Schotton[d] of the Abbot of St. Mary's, York, by service of
4s., a carucate of land worth 6 marcs a year.

Isabel, daughter of the said John and wife of Simon de
Pateshill, is his next heir, and aged 22 years and more.[e]

[a] Hexham.

[b] Skewsby.

[c] Newhay, par. Drax, part of the Paynell fee.

[d] Scotton, near Catterick.

[e] A writ of the same date (25 April, 1295) was directed to Malculm de
Harleye, Escheator this side Trent. By virtue of this writ other inquisitions were
taken for the counties of Essex (m. 2), Wednesday in Whitsun week, 23rd year
(25 May, 1295), Bedford (m. 3), Friday the morrow of St. Dunstan, the same year,
(20 May), and Lincoln (m. 4), Whit Monday, same year (23 May), by which the
heir was found to be 22 (Bedford), 23 (Essex), and 24 (Lincoln) years old. A
later writ dated at Luwell, 11 June, same year (1295), states, that the inquisition
(it does not appear which of the three) returned into Chancery is insufficient,
because no mention is made if Isabel, daughter and heir of John de Steyngreve,
is next heir of Ida, who was his wife, to the lands and tenements which he held
by the law of England after Ida's death. Further inquiry is commanded to be
made. A small fragment of an inquisition here follows in the file as stitched up;
but not enough to show its purport or date.

By the inquisition taken at Lincoln (before adverted to) on Whit-Monday,
23 Edw. (23 May, 1295), it is found that the said John held in Fryseby of Richard
Folyot 36 bovates of land and a moiety of a watermill, which Jordan Folyot,
father of Richard, gave to Simon de Steyngreve, father of John, in frank marriage
with Beatrice his daughter.

26 June, 1278. Writ from the King to the Sheriff of Bucks. and Beds.
informing him that he had caused to be assigned in his Court held before him at
Westminster to Roger de Munbray, John de Steynegryve and Ida his wife, John
de Horbiry and Elizabeth (sic) his wife, Michael Pihot and Joan his wife, and
William de Mountchensy (de Monte Caniso) of Edwardeston and Beatrix his wife,
heirs of William Beauchamp (de Bello Campo) of Bedford, their reasonable shares
which fell to them from the inheritance of the said William Beauchamp in the
manors of Broham and Lyncelade, which Amicia, William Beauchamp's widow,
lately deceased, held in dower, as in certain rolls handed to the heirs by the King
more plainly appeared. The Sheriff was ordered on inspection of the rolls, and
after retaining for the King's use and the use of the said Roger, under age and
in the royal custody, who was the eldest (de eynescia) of the said heirs, a third
part of the said manors, to cause the said co-heirs to have seisin according to the
tenor of their rolls of their properties without delay (Rot. Fin., 6 Edw. I., m. 9).
Westminster, 12 Aug., 1295. Homage taken of Simon de Pateshull, of Bedfordshire, who married Elizabeth, daughter and heiress of John de Steyngreve (Ibid.,

VIII. WILLIAM DE PERCY THE YOUNGER OF KILDALE.ᵃ *Inq.p.m.*

[23 EDW. I. No. 16.]

Writ dated at Lammays, 3 May, 23rd year (1295).

INQUISITION taken at York before Alexander de Ledes, keeper (*custode*) of the office of Escheatry in the county of York, on Sunday the eve of St. Peter *ad vincula*, 23 Edw. (31 July, 1295), by these twelve underwritten, viz. by Stephen Gouwer, Walter de Thorpe, William de Neuby, clerk, William de Moubray, Robert de Colleby, William de Hoton, clerk, William Tosty, Robert *le Bret*, John de Fymtres, Stephen de Erneclyve, William Gylyot of Lackenby, and Richard de Fenton, who say on their oath that William de Percy the younger, deceased, held on the day of his death no lands or tenements of the King in chief. He held Ormesby with Caldecotes,ᵇ and one carucate and a half of land with appurtenances in Crathorne of Arnald de Percy his brother for a penny a year, and as much foreign service as appertains to such a holding. The same William did homage only to Robert de Twenge deceased for Ormesby and Caldecotes, and no other services. He did all foreign services to William de Percy his father, and after his (the father's) decease to Arnald de Percy, son and heir of William de Percy the elder, his father. Ormesby and Caldecotes are worth £40 a year; the land in Crathorne, £4 a year.

Alexander, son of the said William the younger, deceased, is his next heir, aged fourteen years.

Writ dated at Westminster, 12 Aug., 23rd year (1295), referring to the inquisition lately returned as being insufficient, because it is not mentioned whether or not William de Percy of Kyldale held of the heir of Marmaduke de Twenge, deceased (who held of the King in chief), lately under age and in ward to the King. Further inquiry therefore is to be made without delay.

INQUISITION made at Stokeslee on Saturday before the feast of St. Bartholomew, 23 Edw. (20 Aug., 1295), before the keeper of the office of Escheatry by Robert de Colleby,

23 Edw. I., m. 10). The executors of Thomas de Normanville, the Escheator, accounted for £13 4s., issues of the lands of John de Steyngreve in Nonyngton, Steyngreve, etc., from St. Mark's day (25 April, 1295) to 12 August following, before delivery to Simon de Pateshille, who married Isabella, daughter and heiress of the said John. Pateshille's sureties for paying his relief were William de Shireburne, John de Butterwicke, and William Barde of the same, all of the county York (*Escheators' Accounts ultra Trentam*, ⅜).

ᵃ See Vol. II., p. 19. On 30 April, 1288, William de Percy of Kildale the younger, going to Jerusalem, had letters nominating Roger de Scotre and Richard de Wausand his attorneys in Ireland for three years (*Calendar of Patent Rolls*, 1292-1301, p. 158).

ᵇ Cargo Fleet, near Middlesbrough.

Walter de Thorpe, William Guer, William de Ebor., John de Fyntres, William *le Moubray*, William *le Clerck* of Hoton, William *le Clerck* of Neuby, Robert Brette, Robert de Salton, William Tosty, and William *del How*; who say that William de Percy held his whole land in Ormesby, Caldecotes and elsewhere in the bailiwick of Langb[arugh] of Arnald de Percy, and nothing of the heir of Marmaduke de Twenge, and he did no other service to the said heir.[a]

William died in Wales on Friday before the feast of St. Mark the Evangelist, in the year abovesaid (22 April, 1295); and Alexander, his son, is his next heir, and aged fourteen years.

IX.   ELIAS DE RILLESTONE.[b]   *Inq. p. m.*

[23 EDW. I.   No. 42.]

No writ.

INQUISITION taken at Skipton in Cravene before Thomas de Normanville on Saturday after the Ascension of the Lord, 23 Edw. (14 May, 1295), by Sir John Gyliot, Richard Tempest, William de Cestrehunt, Everard Fauvel, Constantine Fauvel, Richard de Eston, Ranulf de Oterburne, John de Kygheley, Elias de Stretton, Robert de Skothorpe, Adam son of William of Broghton, and Robert son of Geoffrey of Bradele, who say on their oath that Elias de Rillestone on the day of his death held of the King, lord of the Honour of Skipton Castle in Craven, as of barony and not of the Crown, a capital messuage in Rillestone,[c] and the herbage of the garden is worth by the year 3s. He also held there 70 acres and half a rood of arable land in demesne (at 7d. the acre), 40s. 11d.; also 21 acres of meadow in demesne (at 10d.), 17s. 6d.; 21 bovates and half an acre of land in demesne (at 4s. the bovate), £4 4s. 4d. He held there 4   of meadow (at 10d.), 3s. 4d.; 3 (at 7d.), 21d., and   in Crakehou[d] at (10d.).

He held the herbage in Holden in the field of Rillestone, worth 6s. 8d. a year; and a wood there, the dead wood of

[a] Idem Willelmus de Percy tenuit terram suam in Ormesby Caldecotes et alibi in balliva predicta die quo obiit de Arnaldo de Percy, et nichil de herede Marmaduci de Twenge, nec nullum aliud servicium predicto heredi fecit.

[b] 12 June, 1278. The lands of John, son of Elias le Rilleston, were ordered to be seised into the King's hand (*Rot. Fin.*, 6 Edw. I., m. 11).

[c] Rilston, par. Burnsall.

[d] Now Cracoe.

which is worth without waste 2*s.*; part of the watermill of Rillestone and Heton,[a] and his share is worth by the year 53*s.* 4*d.*; three cottages in Rillestone (at 18*d.*), 4*s.* 6*d.*

FREE TENANTS of the said Elias.

Simon son of Thomas de Bernelwike held of Elias a toft and two bovates of land in Rillestone by homage and service, and he owes a penny at Christmas; William de Lindale, a toft and a bovate by homage and service, and he owes a pound of cumin on Easter-day; the Abbot of Derham, a carucate of land in Skethorpe[b] by homage and service only; Robert de Skothorpe, half a carucate of land there by homage and service only.

TENEMENTS which he held of others.

Of Sir Hugh fitzHenry four bovates in Elslacke (at 3*s.* 6*d.*) by homage and service, 14*s.*; of lady Margaret de Neville by homage and service in Hoton[c] a carucate and a half which Robert Dealtry (*de Alta ripa*) and Walter de Hoton held of Elias by homage and service; of the same lady Margaret there by homage and service half a carucate which the Abbot of Furness held of Elias in almoign.

The next heirs of Elias are his two daughters, Emma and Cecily, of whom the elder is three years, and the younger three months old.

> Sum total, £11 12*s.* 3*d.*, of which 14*s.* are held of Sir Hugh fitz Henry.[d]

[a] Hetton, three-quarters of a mile west of Rilstone.

[b] Probably Scosthorp Hall, on the right bank of the Aire, par. Kirkby Malhamdale. The abbot of Derham held two bovates here in 1301-2 (*Kirkbys Inquest*, p. 201). West Dereham in Norfolk, a Premonstratensian Abbey, was founded in 1188 by Hubert Walter, Dean of York, and afterwards Archbishop of Canterbury. In 1199 King John confirmed the gift of Adam fitz Adam of the church of Kirkebi Malghedale to this Abbey. (Dugdale's *Monasticon Anglicanum*, vi., 899, 900).

[c] A misreading for Heton, Hetton, par. Burnsall, where Margaret de Neville held land (vol. i., p. 263). See also *Kirkby's Inquest*, p. 190.

[d] The foregoing inquisition is here in duplicate, with this difference, that one inquisition, probably that returned to Chancery, has the names of the jurors. The latter is much defaced (with a wash now turned dark brown), and these names are read with great difficulty. [*Endorsed.*] Consilium consentiat propter . . . . . . et fidele servicium si placeat domino Regi et adhuc sit in manu sua.

X. ROBERT LE GRAY (GREY) *or* DE GRAY (GREY).[a] *Inq. p. m.*

[23 EDW. I. No. 60.]

[m. 1]

Writ directed to the keeper of the office of the Escheatry in the county of York, and dated at Luwel (Lowell in co. Brecknock), 11 June, 23rd year (1295).

[m. 3]

ON Sunday after the feast of St. John the Baptist, 23 Edw. (26 June, 1295), inquisition was made at Rillistone before Sir Alexander de Ledes, keeper of the office of the Escheatry in the county of York, of the lands and tenements, rents and services which were of Robert *le [Gray]* on the day of his death in the wapentake of Stayncl[iff] by William de Cestrehunt, John de Kegelay, Robert de Schothorpe, Henry son of Beke, John de Heton, Walter de Heton, Thomas *le Longe* of Lytton, Alan *del Thwaytes*, Adam de Oulecotes, Richard Nunnefrere, Richard de Conistone, and Richard de Heton. Robert de Gray held nothing of the King in chief in the wapentake of Stayncl[iff], but he held a moiety of the whole town of Ketilwelle of Sir Walter de Faucumberge for homage and service and for a pair of gloves on Easter-day without other secular services, viz. eight tofts with eight bovates of land, of which every bovate with its toft is worth by the year 12s. 9d.; a cottage, worth 2s. a year, and a watermill, 20s. a year; except from the tofts, land and mill, dower which Isabel de Gray holds.

Sum of the extent, £6 4s.

John *le Gray* is son and next heir of the said Sir Robert *le Gray* and aged twenty-three years and more.

[m. 2]

Writ addressed to the same keeper and dated at Aberconewey, 4 July, 23rd year (1295). The writ by which the lands of Robert de Gray were taken into the King's hand, and upon which the inquisition was taken, has not been transmitted with the inquisition. The writ is now to be sent without delay.

[m. 4]

ON Saint Swithin's day, 23 Edw. (15 July, 1295), inquisition was made before the same keeper concerning the lands etc. of Robert de Grey in the wapentake of Hosgodecross by

[a] Son and heir of Walter de Gray, nephew of the archbishop of the same name. The above-named Walter married Isabel, daughter and co-heiress of William de Dustune (Vol. I., p. 282). On 8 July, 1295, the Escheator *citra* had notice that the King had taken the homage of John, son and heir of Robert de Gray, at Karnarvon. Mention is made of Robert's widow, Joan (*Rot. Fin.*, 23 Edw. I., m. 12). This renders it likely that the Robert Grey (*sic*) to whom the King at Norham forgave a fine of £10 for marrying Margaret, widow of Ralph de Gaugy, on 5 June, 1291, is a different person (*Ibid.*, 19 Edw. I., m. 12).

Robert de Scelbroke, William Belle of Elmesale, Richard *del Riddinge*, John de Went, Roger Noel of Ardington, Henry de Preston, William Pyrecoke of Went, Robert *del Heyle*, Robert Smith (*fabrum*) of Wpton, Jurdan del . . . , Hugh Nouel of Burge, and Stephen Snel. Robert de Grey held nothing of the King in chief in the wapentake of Hosgote-cross, but he held the manor of Upton[a] with appurtenances of Henry de Lacy, Earl of Lincoln,. for homage and doing suit at the Earl's court of Punfrayt every three weeks. The capital messuage is worth 13*s.* 4*d.* a year. There are sixty acres of arable land at 6*d.* the acre. There are free tenants, viz. Bernard Toffe holds a bovate of land, yielding yearly 3*s.*; Geoffrey son of Beatrice, a bovate yielding yearly 15*d.*; Roger Dringe, a bovate for 12*d.* He had in bondage ten bovates of land, of which every bovate yields yearly 10*s.*; a windmill worth 10*s.*; and a pasture called Bulker, worth 8*s.*

Sum of the extent, £8 6*s.* 7*d.*

John *le Grey* is son and next heir of Sir Robert de Grey, and aged twenty-three years and more.

[m. 5]

INQUISITION made before the same Alexander de Ledes on Thursday the morrow of the Apostles Peter and Paul, 23 Edw. (30 June, 1295), of the lands etc. of Robert de Gray in the wapentakes of Herthylle, Use and Derwent, Aynsty and Holdernesse, by Ralph de Douuay, Richard de Herle-thorpe, William de Burton, John de Fancurt, Adam de Estorpe of Boulton, William *de la Dale*, Philip son of Hawyse, Adam *le Lunge* of Kelkefelde, William Russel of Naburne, Augustin *le Cu* of the same, Robert Tyntteluue of the same, William de Kelkefeld, clerk, Henry of the Cross (*de cruce*) of Walton, William *le Cerue*, Robert Fox of Angrum, Henry *le Fraunceys* of Merstone, Nicolas Wyvile of Bykerton, and Michael de Knapton. Robert de Gray held nothing of the King in chief in the aforesaid wapentakes, but he held in Sculecotes of the Archbishop of York a capital messuage worth by the year 6*s.* 8*d.*; also twelve bovates of land (at one marc); four cottages worth 6*s.* 8*d.*; thirty acres of meadow at 2*s.*; sixty acres of pasture in severalty (*in separal'*) at 8*d.* the acre. He also held of the same a passage worth 4*s.* a year, and in Sutton[b] three bovates of land (at 20*s.*); two cottages worth 2*s.* a year. These tenements aforesaid are held of the Archbishop by knight's service.

[a] Upton, par. Badsworth.
[b] Not very clearly written.

He also held in Scoulecotes of John de Meux (*Melsa*) four bovates of land, yielding yearly to him 4*d.* and scutage when it falls; the bovate is worth 3*s.* 4*d.* a year; and of the Archbishop in Boulton[a] a cottage worth 12*s.* a year. He had in the same town rent of assize from Robert de Boulton, 3*d.*, and from William son of Walter, 6*d.*; also rent of assize in Gouthorpe[b] from Richard Bustard, 12*s.* 6*d.*, and from Alexander de Gouthorpe, 5*s.*; in Suthburton,[c] from William *de la Dale*, 24*s.* 6*d.*, of which he pays yearly to the church of St. John of Beverley a penny. He held in Morby, in the wapentake of Use and Derwent, of the heirs of Robert Greteheved, *i.e.* Agnes and Alice, a messuage worth 2*s.* a year, and eight bovates of land (at 10*s.*), sixteen acres of assart (at 6*d.*), ten acres of meadow (at 3*s.*); and he yields to them therefore 12*d.* yearly; in Drenghous, in wapentake of Hainsti, of the Treasurer of York, nine bovates of land with a moiety of a messuage; a bovate is worth one marc, and the moiety 2*s.* a year. He also held of the same twenty acres of *Forland* (at 12*d.* the acre), six acres of meadow (at 3*s.*); and he yields yearly to the said treasurer for these tenements, 5*s.* and suit of court every three weeks.

Sum of the extent, £36 16*s.* 5*d.*, of which he yields yearly (as above) 6*s.* 5*d.*

John de Gray is son and next heir of Robert de Gray, aged twenty-three years and more.[d]

XI. WILLIAM GRYVEL, *Deceased. Of the Bailiwick in the Forest of Galtres.*

[23 EDW. I. No. 69.]

William de Vescy, Justice of the King's forest beyond Trent, sends to John de Wyresdale a transcript of the King's mandate, directed to himself and dated at Aberconeway the first of July, 23rd year (1295), his writ bearing date at Barne near Chester, Sunday the morrow of St. Swithin in the same year (3 July, 1295).[e]

INQUISITION made at York on Monday after the Octave of the Apostles Peter and Paul, 23 Edw. (11 July, 1295),

[a] Bolton, par. Bishop Wilton.

[b] Gowthorpe, par. Blacktoft.

[c] Bishop Burton.

[d] The writ directed to the Escheator *citra Trentam* (Malcolm de Harleghe) is dated at Fennonoyr, 27 May, 23rd year (1295). The inquisition taken thereupon in the county of Oxford, 25 June, 23rd year (1295), finds that John de Grey, eldest son of Robert, is his next heir, and aged twenty-eight years.

[e] "Die dominica in crastino S. Swythini anno supradicto." Now, St. Swithin's day is usually reckoned as the Translation, or 15 July, as in No. CXLIII. Here we have the *Deposition* or 2 July, the morrow of which is Sunday, 3rd July. The morrow of 15 July was Saturday. Observe also the date of inquisition.

by the oath of Paulinus de Lillinge, Robert Hagget, Robert de Scuppeton, Simon Gunnays, John Maunsell, verderers; Walter *le Graunt*, Walter de Stokesby, Nicholas de Bossall, William de Baxeby, Walter Ysaac, Theobald de Tollerton, Walter son of Peter of Scuppeton, and Thomas Blaunefrunt, regarders; and by oath of the townships of Galtres Forest, that is to say, Esingwalde, Hoby, Sutton, Stivelington, Ferlington, Strensall, Haxeby, Wyginton, and Neuton, what manner of bailiwick William Gryvell, deceased, had in the Forest. They say that William Gryvell was a mounted forester (*forestarius eques*) with one horse and one groom only, to ride through the whole forest for attaching all trespassers whomsoever he might find. For the support of himself, his horse and his groom, he had nothing certain save out of the country, like any other forester there. He likewise had custody of the launds of Ingaldtweyt and Alwaldetoftes, for which he paid yearly to the King 100s.; which said launds (*lande*) are taxed at 40s. beyond his farm of 100s. a year; and to guard those launds he was to find two keepers at his own cost.[a]

XII. ROBERT LE CHAUMBERLEYN. *Inq. ad q. d.*

[23 EDW. I. No. 70.]

Writb directed to the keeper of the office of the Escheatry in the county of York and dated at Dinbegh (Denbigh), 13 July, 23rd year (1295).

INQUISITION made at York before John de Lithegreynes, Escheator beyond Trent, on Friday after the Octave of St. Michael, 23 Edw. (7 Oct., 1295), by Robert de Berley, John de Lascy, Roger de Riwile, Alan de Saxton, Robert Pavely, John de Schipwic, William de Hornington, Elias de Neuton, William son of the Master (*fil' Mag'ri*) of Tadecastre, Philip son of Hauwise, Adam son of Sewall of Ayreminne, and William Sibri, whether or not it be to the damage or prejudice of the King or of others if the

---

[a] At foot of the parchment is written :—" Johannes Hayward imponit premissa"; and at the top (over *Inquisicio*), " per J. Haywarde." This must be the John de Wiresdale of the writ, who was hayward of the forest and in that capacity held the inquiry. On 1 Sept., 1295, the King, then at Westminster, granted to his servant, John Hayward, the bailiwick of the forest of Galtres with the launds (*landis*) of Ingoldesthwaite and Alwaldecotes, which William Grivel, lately deceased, had by grant from the King. To have and to guard as long as the King should please, so that he answer as fully therefor to the King at his Exchequer, as the said William was wont to do (*Rot. Fin.*, 23 Edw. I., m. 7). See also *Calendar of Patent Rolls* (1292–1301, p. 145).

[b] On the back a memorandum that this writ was received on Monday before the Exaltation of the Holy Cross (12 Sept.).

King should grant to Robert *le Chaumberleyn* that he may give and assign his manor of Drax with its appurtenances to John Loterel, so nevertheless that afterwards the said John may enfeoff the said Robert and Parnell (*Petronill'*) his wife of the manor aforesaid, to have and to hold to them and their heirs for ever. They say that, if Robert *le Chaumberleyn* should have an heir and die, leaving that heir under age, the King by reason of the feoffment would lose the wardship and marriage. Robert holds his manor of Drax with appurtenances of the King for homage, 4*s.* 7½*d.*, and a certain fine to the wapentake, and it is worth by the year in all issues thirty pounds. Besides the gift and assignment aforesaid the said Robert has a carucate of land with appurtenances in Northdriffeld which is worth yearly 100*s.*, and he holds it of Gerard Salveyn and Arn[old] de Preston for the term of his life, yielding to them five marcs a year; and so there remain to him two marcs and a half.

XIII. German Hay *for* the Prior and Convent of St. Oswald's, Nostell. *Inq. ad q. d.*

[23 Edw. I. No. 115.]

Writ directed to the Sheriff, and dated at Westminster, 18 Aug., 23rd year (1295).

INQUISITION taken at Suthe-Kyrkeby before John de Byron, Sheriff of Yorkshire, on the morrow of the Exaltation of the Holy Cross, 23 Edw. (15 Sept., 1295), by Robert Tylly, John Harynggell, Thomas de Barvynge, John de Treton, John de Langeton, William son of Jordan, Hugh Perunell, William de Bernethorpe, William Paynell, Robert de Schyrbarw, Henry son of William, and Ralph *de la Wodhall*, whether or not it be to the damage of the King, or of others, if the King grant to German Hay that he may give and assign 100*s.* of land and rent in Sudkyrkeby to the prior and convent of St. Oswald, to have and to hold to them and their successors for ever. They say that by chance it might be to the damage and prejudice of the King, because, if the heir of Henry de Lacy, Earl of Lincoln, were under age at the time of the Earl's death, and in ward to the King, and the said German should then die, the King would lose the custody or relief of the land and rent, for the said German holds of the Earl by knight's service that land and rent, which are worth by the year in all issues seven marcs and 3*d.* Beyond the gift and assignment aforesaid there remain to the said German £40 in land

and tenements, which suffice to sustain all charges to which he was before liable, so that the country will in no wise be charged or aggrieved. The prior and German have been warned by the Sheriff to be before the King at the day and place named by Richard de Broddeswurthe and Gilbert de Clayton

---

XIV. RICHARD DE GAYTIL *for* THE ABBOT AND CONVENT OF COVERHAM. *Inq. ad q. d.*

[23 EDW. I. No. 102.]

Writ directed to the Sheriff, and dated at Westminster, 20 Aug., 23rd year (1295).

INQUISITION made at Rychemund on Saturday before the feast of St. Michael, 23 Edw. (24 Sept., 1295), by John de Hunton, Stephen de Coverham, Thomas de Swynigthwayt, Richard Cook (*cocum*), Helyas *del Gyle*, John de Clesseby, Walter Gylle, William de Ellerton, William de Rokeby, Thomas de Preston, Robert *de Fornas'*, and Nicholas de Wendeslay, whether it be to the damage and prejudice of the King, or of others, if it be granted to Richard de Gaytil [Geythill *in writ*] that he may give and assign half a carucate of land with appurtenances in Walebrune [*Walebr'*] to the abbot and convent of Coverham [to have and to hold to them and their successors for ever]. They say that it is not to the King's damage, except Richard commit felony, whereby the King might lose the year and waste for a year and a day; and not to the damage or prejudice of others, except that Richard could not be put in assizes, etc. The said Richard holds the half carucate of the abbot and convent by foreign service, and yields yearly 18*d.* The abbot and convent hold and ought to hold by foreign service of Sibil de Horneby and Emma her niece, heir of Eufemia (*nepta ejus hered' Eufemie*); Sibil and Emma hold of the lady Sibil de Thorneton by foreign service, where eighteen carucates of land make a knight's fee. The lady Sibil de Thorneton holds and ought to hold the land of Sir John of Britany, Earl of Rychemund, by the same service; and he of the King in chief. The half carucate is worth by the year in all issues 18*s.*

The said Richard has beyond the gift and assignment aforesaid other tenements in the county of York in a certain town called Minskyp, to provide for services, etc., in the room of the half carucate so given. He may be put in juries as

before, notwithstanding that gift. The country is not thereby
charged or aggrieved more than customarily because that
Richard is in holy orders.[a]

INQUISITION made at Rychemond on Saturday before the
feast of St. Michael, 23 Edw. (24 Sept., 1295), by John
de Hunton, Stephen de Coverham, Thomas de Swynigthwayt,
Richard Cook (*cocum*), Elias (*Helyam*) *del Gyle*, John de
Clesseby, Walter Gylle, William de Ellerton, William de
Rokeby, Thomas de Preston, Robert *de Fornas*', and Nicholas
de Wendeslay, etc. [*A repetition of the foregoing inquisition.*]

XV. WALTER LE BOTILLER *for* THE CHAPEL OF ST. MARY, RIPON. *Inq. ad q. d.*

[23 EDW. 1. No. 97.]

Writ directed to the Sheriff, and dated at Westminster, 28 Aug., 23rd year
(1295). Inquiry to be made whether or not it be to the damage or
prejudice of the King, or of others, if it be granted to Walter *le Botyller*
that he may give and assign for ever two carucates of land with
appurtenances, to two perpetual chaplains and their successors, to
celebrate daily for the souls of the Kings of England and for the souls
of his (Walter) ancestors in the chapel of St. Mary, Ripon.[b]

INQUISITION taken before J[ohn de] Byroun, Sheriff of
Yorkshire, on Friday after the feast of St. Matthew the
Apostle, 23 Edw. (23 Sept., 1295), by twelve jurors, namely,
John de Stodlay, Roger   , William de Cloutherum,
John Frere of Rypon, Adam Russell, William de Swygn-
inges, Adam de Wynkeslay, Richard Sammesone, William
Creuker, Richard son of Adam of Thorpe, Richard *le Schethe*,
William son of John of Cloutherum, and Reginald de
Asmunderby, who say upon their oath that Walter *le
Botiller* holds in the town of Stodlay Roger two tofts one
bovate and four acres of land with appurtenances, of
William de Aldefelde by homage and knight's service,
yielding scutage, that is to say, $7\frac{1}{4}d.$ when current at 40s.
(*quando scutum currit ad xls.*), when more, more, and less,
less. The said William holds the said tenements of the
Sir Roger de Munbray and he of the King in chief, and
so it is to the damage and prejudice of the said William

---

[a] Item dicunt quod patria preter illam donacionem et assignacionem predictas
magis solito non oneretur seu gravetur, quia ille Ricardus est infra sacros ordines.

[b] The writ and inquisition to be returned in time for the next Parliament
after Michaelmas next, and the parties to be warned to appear before the King.

that they be given in frank almoign by reason of losing the said services; to the damage and prejudice of Roger de Mumbray because he might have custody of the custody when it falls (*eo quod posset habere custodiam de custodia cum accidit*), and so to the damage of the King for the reason aforesaid.

The same Walter holds by divers feoffments of Jollan de Aldefelde one bovate and two acres of land with appurtenances in the same town by the service of a penny, a clove (*clavi gariofili*), a rose, and a peppercorn yearly for all service, and Jollan holds the same bovate and two acres, viz. 6 acres of John de Stodlay Roger, and 5 acres of William de Aldefelde by knight's service; John and William of the Sir Roger de Munbray by the same service, and he of the King in chief by the services aforesaid. All the aforesaid tenements are worth by the year in all issues (except the services) 36s.

The said Walter has no tenements remaining to him beyond the gift and assignment aforesaid to do the customs and services of that fee, or to sustain other charges. William de Aldefelde and Jollan are put in assizes, etc., for the said tenements, together with others which they hold in the said town and the country by that gift, will not be charged more than usual by default of Walter, because William and Jollan do to the King all the services due and accustomed.

XVI. THE MASTER AND BRETHREN OF THE HOSPITAL OF ST. NICHOLAS, YORK. *Inq. ad q. d.*

[23 EDW. I. No. 111.]

Writ directed to the Sheriff, and dated at Westminster, 1 Sept., 23rd year (1295).

INQUISITION taken at York before the Sheriff of Yorkshire and John de Lythegraynes on Monday the feast of St. Lucy the Virgin, 24 Edw. (19 Sept., 1295), whether or not it be to the damage or annoyance of the King, or of others, if the Master and Brethren of St. Nicholas Hospital, York, block up and enclose a certain way leading through the middle of the Hospital Court from the King's highway on the north side up to another way on the south side, and if they hold it blocked up and enclosed to them and their successors for ever, so nevertheless that they make another way of the same length and width in their own soil on the west side of the hospital, by William Sleght,

William de Carleton, Thomas de Benigburgh, Thomas de Whiteby, Richard de Skurueton, Stephen de Morton, Thomas *le Waider*, Adam *le Waider*, Thomas de Pikeringe, Gaudin Goldsmith (*aurifabrum*), John de Setrington, and Thomas Grunt (*sic*), who say upon their oath that it is not to the damage or annoyance of the King, or of any other, so long as the said Master and Brethren of the hospital make another way of the same length and width and as good in their own soil on the west side of the hospital.

XVII. HENRY SON OF MILISENT DE LA GRENE, *a felon.*
Year and day.

[23 EDW. I. No. 83.]

Writ directed to the Sheriff of Yorkshire, and dated at Canterbury, 18 Sept., 23 Edward (1295). Whether 3½ acres of land in Drax, held by Henry son of Milisent *de la Grene*, who was hanged for felony done by him, have been in the King's hand for a year and a day.

INQUISITION taken before the Sheriff at York on Wednesday before the feast of the Apostles Simon and Jude, 23 Edw. (26 Oct., 1295), by Adam son of Sewall of Ayremyn, Richard de Carleton, clerk, William Huberd of Newland (*nova terra*), Henry son of Silvester of Drax, Geoffrey *del Sturthe*, clerk, Thomas Clerk (*clericum*) of the same, Roger Knot of Newland (*nova terra*), William *le Tayllur* of the same, Adam son of William *le Clerke*, John son of Simon of Newhay (*nova haya*), John son of Gervase of the same, and Robert Copin of Langerake, who say that the 3½ acres of land with appurtenances in Drax came into the King's hand on Wednesday before the feast of St. Oswald the King in the year abovesaid (3 Aug., 1295), so that the year and day are not yet completed. The said Henry son of Milisent held the tenements aforesaid of William Smith (*fabro*), and the town of Drax which now holds them ought to answer to the King for the same.

Another writ of the same date and tenor, but mentioning three acres of land in Drax.

INQUISITION taken before the Sheriff at York, on the same day (26 Oct., 1295) by Adam son of Sewall, etc. (*as above*), who say that the three acres of land with appurtenances in Drax, etc. (*as in the foregoing inquisition*). The land was held of Adam de Breredyke by the said Henry.

XVIII. WILLIAM DE LASCELES OF OTTRINGHAM. *Inq. p. m.*

[23 EDW. I. No. 37.]

Writ directed to John de Lydegreynes, Escheator beyond Trent, and dated at Westminster, 18 Oct., 23rd year (1295).

INQUISITION made before John de Lythegreyns on Wednesday the morrow of St. Nicholas, 24 Edw. (7 Dec., 1295), by Richard Gunny, William Suthiby, Peter Ulbrythe, Peter Arnalde, William Franke, Thomas at the Meadows (*ad prata*), William Langedyke, William Smith (*fab'*), Robert Tuny, Geoffrey Hundeplace, William Broke, and Thomas son of Peter, who say on their oath that William de Lasceles of Oteringham on the day of his death held no lands or tenements of the King in chief, but he held in demesne 6*d.* annual rent and two cloves a year in Oteringham, of which John de Oteringham yielded a penny for 6 bovates of land with appurtenances; Simon Constable (*Constabular'*), a penny for one bovate; Peter de Gousil, a penny for a toft; Peter Sleye, twopence for a toft; Thomas Lambyn, a penny for a bovate of land; Ivo Baker (*pistor*), a clove (*j clavum gariofili*) for a toft; Peter Moys, a clove for a toft.

The said William held the said rent of 6*d.* and two cloves of the King in chief by foreign service, and nothing of others. John, his son, is his next heir, aged thirty-one years and more.[a]

XIX. GILBERT DE BLYTH, CHAPLAIN, *for* MASTER WILLIAM DE BLYTH, PARSON OF THE CHURCH OF PRESTON IN HOLDERNESS. *Inq. ad q. d.*

[23 EDW. I. No. 94.]

Writ directed to the Sheriff, and dated at Westminster, 18 Oct., 23rd year (1295).[b]

INQUISITION at Hedon before the Sheriff of Yorkshire on Saturday after the feast of All Saints, 23 Edw. (5 Nov., 1295), concerning a messuage with appurtenances in Hedon

[a] Feckenham, 21 March, 1289-90. Orders to the Escheator to seize the lands of which William de Lascelles of Holderness died seised in chief (*Rot. Fin.*, 18 Edw. I., m. 16). Westminster, 9 Aug., 1295. Orders to seize the lands of William de Lascelles of Otringham, deceased. York, 22 Feb., 1295-6. Notice to John de Lythegreyns, the Escheator, that the King had taken the homage of John, son and heir of William de Lasceles of Otryngham (*Ibid.*, 23 Edw. I., m. 10, and 24 Edw. I., m. 24).

[b] The writ and inquisition were to be returned in time for the next Parliament, and both Gilbert and William were to be there.

in Holdernesse, whether or not it be to the damage or prejudice of the King, or of others, if it be granted to Gilbert de Blyth (*Blyda*), chaplain, that he may give and assign the said messuage with appurtenances to Master William de Blyth (*Blyda*), Parson of the church of Preston in Holdernes', to have and to hold to him and to his successors, parsons of the said church, for ever, etc., made by William de Blaungy, William Grete, John de Burton, Rolland Dest, Hugh the Tanur, Richard Ernis, William de Frismareys, William *le Pestur*, Richard *le Taverner*, Henry Kembaud, Simon *le Tayllur*, and Stephen de Humbelton, who say that it is to the King's damage if the said Gilbert give and assign to Master William de Blyth and his successors for ever the said tenement in this, because then the King is excluded from escheat thereof; and in prejudice to the burgesses in this, because if Master William be enfeoffed to him and his successors for ever, he is not taxable in common tallages, or in watches, or in other charges (*misis*) of the town.

The tenement is held of the heir of Avelina Dest by a clove (*unum clavum gariophili*) yearly, and a rent to the King of 12*d.* a year. It is worth in all issues yearly 2*s.* No land or other tenements remain to the said Gilbert beyond the gift and assignment aforesaid, whereby he might be put in assizes, etc., nor was he so put before, because he is a chaplain; and the country is not charged or aggrieved in anything more than customary.

XX. WALTER DE WHIXLE *or* QUIXELEY OF NORTH GIVENDALE. *Inq. p. m.*

[24 EDW. I. No. 17.]

Writ[a] directed to John de Lythegraynes, Escheator beyond Trent, and dated at Westminster, 30 Nov., 24th year (1295).

INQUISITION taken at Pokelington on Saturday after the octave of Purification of the B.V.M.[b] (11 Feb., 1295-6), by Hugh de Lynton, Adam de Esthorpe, Martin Mauleverer, Elyas Clerk (*clericum*) of Japum, John *le Archer* of the same, Philip son of Ralph of Meltonby, Roger (?) son of John the Alblaster of Geveldale, John Duddeman of the same, Ralph *de Fraxynis* of Pokelington, John de Thorpe of the

---

[a] Note on the dorse that the writ was received on Saturday after the feast of the Conversion of St. Paul (28 Jan., 1295-6).

[b] The regnal year is not stated.

same, Henry de Holme of the same, and William Dolman of Milington. Walter de Quixeley held of the King in chief a messuage in Northgeveldale worth by the year 2s., nine bovates of land (at 40d.), and the third part of a watermill worth 20d. a year; and in Estgeveldale a bovate of land worth 3s. and a third part of a bovate worth 12d. Sum of the whole, 37s. 8d. He held the said tenements of the King by homage and service of the sixth part of an arblaster (or crossbowman), to be found at his own charges at York Castle for forty days in time of war; and at the end of that time at the King's cost, if then he wish to retain him longer.

The said Walter died in the quinzaine of Easter, 23rd year (17 April, 1299), and John de Quixeley, his son and next heir, is aged thirty-three years and more.[a]

XXI. SIMON DE PATESHULLE.[b] *Inq. p. m.*

[24 EDW. I. No. 66.]

Writ[c] directed to John de Lythegreynes, Escheator beyond Trent, and dated at Westminster, 12 Dec., 24th year (1295).

INQUISITION made on Sunday after the Epiphany, 24 Edw. (8 Jan., 1295-6), by Ranulf de Waldo, Gordan at the church (*ad ecclesiam*), William *le Fraunkeleyn*, Thomas de Fostone, Walter de Schouseby, William de Holethorp, Hugh Broun, and William le Wayt. Simon de Pateshulle held nothing of the King in chief in the county of York, but he held in Stangreve five carucates of land, each worth four marcs; of which he held 2½ carucates of the Paynel fee by knight's service, of Sir Roger de Moubray one carucate by service of 2s., and of the Prior of Hexhylsam 1½ carucates by service of one marc. He held in Nonyton 7½ carucates, each worth four marcs; of the Paynel fee six by knight's service; of Sir William de Roys (Ros) half a carucate by service of a pound of pepper; and of the Abbot of St. Mary's, York, one carucate by service of 5s. He held also in Waterholme of the Paynel fee by knight's service one carucate, worth by the year 100s.; in Schouseby of Matthew de Loveyn by knight's service one carucate, worth 40s.; in

---

[a] March 3, 1295-6. The homage of John, son and heir of Walter de Quixeley, taken at Newcastle-on-Tyne (*Rot. Fin.*, 24 Edw. I., m. 15).

[b] See No. VII.

[c] Received (by endorsement) on Thursday the feast of St. Thomas the Martyr (29 Dec., 1295).

Schottone of the Abbot of St. Mary's, York, one carucate, worth £4; in Kelkefelde of Arnold de Percy by knight's service half a carucate, worth 20s.; and in Neuhawe of the Paynel fee by knight's service two bovates of land, worth by the year 10s. All the aforesaid tenements he held of the inheritance of Isabel de Stangrewe, who was wife of the said Simon[a]; and John de Pateshulle son of Simon and Isabel is the next heir, and aged four years.[b]

XXII.   JOAN WIDOW OF ROBERT DE HILDEYERD.   *Inq. p. m.*

[24 EDW. I.   No. 23.]

Writ[c] dated at Saint Albans, 25 Dec., 24th year (1295).

INQUISITION made before John de Lythegrains, Escheator, at Hedon on Thursday after the feast of St. Hilary, 24 Edw. (18 Jan., 1295-6), by Peter *de la Twyere*, Robert de Boby, Walter de Flinton, William de Hoton, Ralph de Saint Martin, Thomas de Glouc[estre], William de Saint Quintin, William *de Camera*, Peter de Hildeyerd, Simon de Sprottele, Richard de Grymestone, and Nicholas de Thorne. Joan, who was wife of Robert de Hildeyerd, held of the King in chief as of the barony of the Earl of Albemarle in Holderness, a capital messuage in Reston,[d] worth by the year 20s.; a dove-house, 3s.; fifteen tofts held at will of the lord, each worth 3s.; and a small toft, 2s.; and a close, worth 3s. a year. She held also of the same 12½ bovates of land (at 13s. 4d.)

---

[a] There was first written that the said Isabel de Stangrewe is next heir, and aged twenty-three years.

[b] There are inquisitions taken in cos. Essex, Lincoln, Hertford, Bedford, and Northampton. The writ of *diem clausit extremum* directed to Malculm de Harleye, Escheator *citra Trentam*, is dated at Westminster, 2nd Dec., 24th year (1295). By the first (Essex) it is found that Simon de Pateshulle held no lands of his own inheritance in Essex, but of the inheritance of Isabel his wife, who was daughter and heir of John de Stengreve. By the second (Lincoln) the jurors find that Simon held certain lands and tenements in Lincolnshire of Richard Folyot, as those which Jordan de Folyot, father of Richard, gave to Simon de Steyngreve, grandfather of Isabel, in frank marriage with Beatrice his daughter. Here the jurors add that of the heir of Simon de Pateshulle, or of his age, they know nothing, because he was born in distant parts (*in partibus longinquis*). Attached to these inquisitions is a writ, directed to the Treasurer and Barons of the Exchequer, and dated at York, 22 Feb., 24th year (1295-6). It refers to an inquisition taken by Malculm de Harley, by which it is found that Simon held lands of the inheritance of Isabel his wife. The King desires to be certified whether he held other lands as of the Crown. The rolls to be searched and the result to be returned.

[c] Note on the dorse that the writ was received on Thursday after the feast of the Epiphany (11 Jan., 1295-6).

[d] Riston.

with certain *forland* there, worth 10*s.*; and a plot, called Brakenholme, 10*s.* a year. There are also two windmills, worth 20*s.* All the aforesaid tenements she held of the King in chief by knight's service, but not as of fee. The said Joan held also in the same town eight acres of land of the liberty of St. John of Beverley, by the yearly service of a penny; and they are worth 4*s.* a year. She held in Sutton in Holderness six score acres of meadow, and pasture for 1,000 sheep, of John de Sutton by the yearly service of a penny. Each acre is worth 6*d.*, and the pasture 50*s.* a year; and in Norton of the same John by the service of 8*d.* half a bovate, worth 10*s.* a year.

One Robert de Hildeyerd purchased all the aforesaid tenements, to hold of the chief lords of the fee to himself and the said Joan his wife and the heirs of Robert; and she held them for the term of her life by form of the feoffment, wherefore Robert de Hildeyerd, son of Robert and Joan, is her next heir, and aged twenty-three years.[a]

XXIII. CONCERNING LAND ENCLOSED WITHIN TOTTELAY PARK.

[24 EDW. I. No. 64.]

Writ directed to Thomas de Weston, the King's Bailiff of Holdernesse. Understanding that Thomas de Normanville, late Escheator beyond Trent, enclosed certain lands of divers men within the park of Tottele, which the King commanded to be made, inquiry is to be made what lands were so enclosed, and whose they were, with their quantity and value. Dated at St. Albans, 30 Dec., 24th year (1295).

INQUISITION[b] made before Thomas de Weston on Monday after the quinzaine of Holy Trinity, 24 Edw. (4 June, 1296), by Walter de Flynton, John de Fittelinge, William de Fassham, Ralph de Gloucestre, Henry de Wyueton, Ralph de Wellewyke, Richard Gunny, Nicholas *le Warde* of Burton, John de Ryhille, William *de Furno*, Alan *le Oyseleur*, and William *de Camera* of Holme, who say upon their oath that Thomas de Normanville enclosed within

[a] His homage was taken at Peterborough on 9 Feb., 1295-6 (*Rot. Fin.*, 24 Edw. I., m. 16.)

[b] On 6 June, 1297, the King, at Canterbury, appointed John de Lythegreynes and Thomas de Weston to cause due compensation to be made out of the King's demesne lands to the men and commonalty for the lands, which, as appears by the above inquisition, were included in Tottele Park by Thos. de Normanville (*Calendar of Patent Rolls*, 1292-1301, p. 251). On 15 July, 1300, the King, at Caerlaverock, near Dumfries, appointed John de Lythegreyns and Richard Oysel, bailiff of Holdernesse, for the purpose of carrying out this object, which had been delayed by the death of Thomas de Normanville (*Ibid.*, p. 527). The differences between the Patent Roll and the Inquisition are noted.

Totteley park:—Seventeen acres (at 9*d.* the acre) and 11 perches (in all worth ½*d.* a year) of arable land from the land of Lucy, daughter and heir of John Bernard; also one acre (18*d.*) and 8 perches (in all worth ⅜*d.* a year) of meadow; 4½ acres (at 9*d.*), one stang and a half,[a] and 2 perches of arable land from the land of William son of Nicholas, Stephen Gilbert,[b] and Robert Abby[c]; and from the same one stang of meadow (*unum stagnum prati*), worth 4½*d.* a year; 5 acres (at 9*d.*) and half a stang of arable land from the land of Michael *le Aumoner*, and from the same one stang of meadow, worth 4½*d.* a year; 2½ acres (at 9*d.*) and 15 perches (in all worth ⅜*d.*) of arable land from William Smith (*fabro*),[d] and from the same half a stang of meadow, worth 2¾*d.* a year; 2 acres (at 9*d.*), a stang and half, and 11 perches (in all worth ½*d.*) of arable land from Adam Gilbert,[e] and from the same half a stang of meadow, worth 2¼*d.* a year; 4½ acres (at 9*d.*), a stang and half, and 2 perches of arable land from Henry of the Park (*de parco*), and from the same a stang of meadow, worth 4½*d.* a year; also 5½ acres (at 9*d.*) of arable land from Peter Moys,[f] and from the same one stang of meadow, worth 4½*d.* a year; also 2½ acres (at 18*d.*), a stang, and a perch of meadow appertaining to the commonalty of the town[g]; also 3 stangs of arable land appertaining to the same commonalty, worth 6¾*d.* a year.

Sum of acres of arable land of free tenants... ...	43 a. 1st. 1 per.
Sum of annual value of the same	32s. 5¼d.
Sum of acres of meadow ...	4 ac. 1⅛ st. 9 perches
Sum of annual value of the same	6s. 7¾d.

They say also that Thomas de Normanville enclosed within the said park from the King's demesnes of Ruge-munde . . . . . . township of Burton Pydese eleven acres of pasture, the acre worth 14*d.* a year.

Sum of acres —11.	
Sum of money—12s. 10d.	

[a] Four acres 3½ roods. In the amount of meadow instead of a stang it is called a rood, and so elsewhere.

[b] Gilberd.

[c] White (*albi*).

[d] *Le Fevre.*

[e] Gilberd.

[f] Meys.

[g] Bondebrustwyk.

A writ, the purport of which cannot be made out. It appears to be the petition of Robert fitz Payne, to whom the King had given the manor of Idenn.

[On another membrane without heading the following particulars appear]:—

THE said jurors say also that the said Thomas de Normanville enclosed within the park of Tottelay:— From the land of Henry Ryra[a], which he holds of the King in bondage, 5½ acres (at 9d. the acre) of arable land, and one stang of meadow, worth 4½d. a year; from the land of William Abby[b] 2½ acres (at 9d.), half a stang of arable land, and half a stang of meadow, worth 2¼d. a year; from the land of Ralph Hotte 2 acres (at 9d.), a stang and half, and 11 perches of arable land (worth ½d. a year), and half a stang of meadow, worth 2½d. a year; also from the land of Laurence Smith[c] (*fabr'*) 4½ acres (at 9d.), one stang and half of arable land, and a stang of meadow, worth 4½d. a year; from the land of William Baldwyn[d] 2½ acres (at 9d.), half a stang, and 12 perches (worth ½d.) of arable land, and half a stang of meadow, worth 2½d.; from the land of Ralph Bernard 3 acres (at 9d.), 1 stang, and 16 perches of arable land (worth ¾d.), and half a stang of meadow, worth 2¼d. a year; from the land of Robert *le Turnour*[e] 3 acres (at 9d.), 1 stang, and 18 perches (worth 1d.) of arable land; from the land of Robert son of Roger 5 acres (at 9d.) and 18 perches of arable land (worth 1d.), and one stang of meadow, worth ½d. a year; and from the meadow of Robert *le Turnur* half a stang, worth 2¼d. a year.

Sum of acres of arable land of bondmen (*bondorum*) of Brustwyke	29½ ac. 1½ st. 15 per.
Sum of annual value of the same	22s. 5¾d.
Sum of acres of meadow of the same	1 ac. 1 st.
Sum of value	. . . .

[a] This man and the following are called *bondi* in the Patent Roll.

[b] White (*albi*) on the Patent Roll. Following every name are the words "*quam tenet de domino Rege in bondagio*" (which he holds of the lord King in bondage).

[c] *Le Fevre.*

[d] Baldewyne.

[e] Turner.

XXIV. EDMUND FYTON *or* FYTOUN. *Inq. p. m.*

[24 EDW. I. No. 9.]

Writ[a] directed to John de Lythegreynes, Escheator beyond Trent, and dated
at Ketene, 10 Feb., 24th year (1295-6).

INQUISITION made on Monday the morrow of the Close
of Easter, 24 Edw. (2 April, 1296), by Henry son of
Hugh of North Couton, Hugh de Couton, Robert de
Sadberge, Walter of the Bridge (*de ponte*), John son of
Alan, Robert de Boyvile, John son of Geoffrey, Alan his
brother, Robert Franckelain, Thomas Justise, William son
of Alexander, and John *le Taylour.* Edmund Fytoun held
of the Honour of Rychemond Castle by knight's service
the land and tenements underwritten, viz. a capital
messuage in Couton,[b] worth by the year with herbage and
fruit of the garden half a marc; two carucates of land in
demesne worth four marcs, and 40 acres of meadow (at
2s. 6d.), 100s. a year; also a marsh and a pasture which
contain about 10 acres and are worth half a marc; in
bondage 11 tofts and 14 bovates of land, worth £9 8s. 6d.
He had also 15 cottages worth by the year 50s. 6d., and
from farm of free tenants 3s. 6d. yearly; and did suit at the
Court of Rychemond every three weeks, paying yearly for
castle-guard 14d. in March for the aforesaid tenements, and
for fines of Gillinge Wapentake 5s. 4d. at Michaelmas.

John Fyton, son of the said Edmund, is his next heir,
who on St. Botulph's day next (17 June, 1296), will be 22
years old.[c]

XXV. WILLIAM DE NEWAL (NEUHALE). *Inq. p. m.*

[24 EDW. I. No. 4.]

Writ[d] directed to John de Lythegreynes, Escheator, and dated at York,
22 Feb., 24th year (1295-6).

INQUISITION made at Harewode before William de
Thorneton, clerk of J. de Lythegreyns, Escheator beyond
Trent, appointed to act in his absence, on Wednesday after
the close of Easter, 24 Edw. (4 April, 1296), by William

---

[a] Note on the dorse that the writ was received on Friday after the feast of
St. Gregory (16 March, 1295-6).

[b] East or Long Cowton (Vol. I., p. 227).

[c] Berewyke on Twede, 23 April, 1295. Fealty taken of John, son and heir of
Edmund Fytun, for lands and tenements holden of the Honour of the Castle of
Richmond, then in the King's hand (*Rot. Fin.*, 24 Edw. I., m. 13).

[d] On back a memorandum that this writ was received on Wednesday before
the feast of St. Gregory (7 March, 1295-6).

atte Becke, Nicholas *le Botiller,* John de Middelton, Robert *atte Becke,* Henry son of Jordan, Robert Petipas, Hugh Wygan, Robert de Lofthuse, Robert de Dyghton, Robert *atte Toune Ende,* Richard Schappeman, and Alexander Moyses,[a] who say upon their oath that William de Neuhale held no lands or tenements of the King, or of any other, because three years (*triennium*) before his death he enfeoffed Roger de Alwodely of a messuage and 27 acres of land with appurtenances in Neuhale,[b] to hold to him (Roger) and his heirs for ever. The said tenements are now in the seisin of the King by the death of Roger, who held them of the King by the services contained in the inquisition made of lands and tenements of the said Roger by reason of his daughters and heirs, Joan, Margaret, Alice and Anabil, being under age and in ward to the King. William de Neuhale was seised in fee of the said tenements on the day on which he married his wife, Anabil, who sues this inquisition, so that he could endow her[c]; wherefore they say that the said William had no other lands or tenements on the day of his death, or long before.

XXVI.   ROGER DE ALEWOLDELEYE (ALEWODELEYE).

Inq. p. m.

[24 EDW. I. No. 50.]

Writ[d] dated at York, 22 Feb., 24th year (1295-6).

INQUISITION made at Harewode before William de Thorneton, clerk of J. de Lythegreyns, the King's Escheator beyond Trent, and appointed in his absence, on Wednesday after the close of Easter, 24 Edw. (4 April, 1296), by William *Attebecke,* Nicholas *le Botiller,* John de Middelton, Robert *atte Becke,* Henry son of Jordan, Robert Petipas, Hugh Wygan, Robert de Lofthuse, Robert de Dighton, Robert *atte Tune end,* Richard Schappeman, and Alexander Moyses. Roger de Alewodeley held in fee in Alwoldeley,[e] a messuage valued at 12d. by the year, 12 tofts and 2½ carucates of land 50s., and a watermill 8s., of the

[a] These same jurors occur in the next inquisition.

[b] Newhall, par. Rothwell.

[c] Que istam inquisitionem sequitur, ita quod ipsam inde dotare potuit.

[d] By endorsement received on Wednesday before the feast of St. Gregory (7 March, 1295-6).

[e] Alwoodley, Harewood parish.

King in chief by the service of paying yearly 18s 8d. at
the manor of Harewode, doing suit to the Court there every
three weeks and paying to the King's scutage, when it is at
40s., 6s. 3d.; and when more, more; and when less, less; and by
service yearly of 13½d. for fine of the wapentake.   He yields
to the Prior of Boulton 5s. a year for the said mill.   The
same Roger held in fee in Neuhale a messuage valued at
5s. by the year, three bovates and seven acres of land,
valued at 12s. 4d., also 18d. rent by the yearly service of
3s. 2⅜d. at the manor of Harewode; finding for one day
three times a year one plough, and beside this, a plough
once in the year, or 2d. each time at the will of the lord,
and finding yearly six sickles or 6d. in autumn; and rendering to the King's scutage, when the fee (scutum) is at 40s.,
11¼d., and when more, more; and when less, less; also by
service of yielding to the King 1¼d. yearly for fine of the
Wapentake.

The said Roger and Alice his wife, who is yet alive,
jointly held in Neuhale half a carucate of land, which was
given to Roger with Alice in frank marriage, and is valued
by the year at 15s.   They held that half carucate of the
King in form aforesaid by the service of paying 5s. 1¼d.
yearly at the manor of Harewode, and finding a plough
one day three times a year, and also a plough for one day
twice in the year; or, each time, 2d. at the will of the lord,
and nine sickles or 9d. in autumn, rendering to the King's
scutage, when it is at 40s., 15d.; when more, more; and when
less, less; and by service of paying to the King yearly 2d. for
fine of the Wapentake.   While the manor (now in the King's
hand) was in seisin of the Countess of Albemarle, he held
all the aforesaid tenements of her by the said services, and
at the time of his death in like manner of the King by
the same services in form aforesaid.

Joan, Margaret, Alice, and Anabil, daughters of Roger,
are his next heirs.   Joan was aged eight years at the feast
of the Purification of the B.M. last (2 Feb., 1295-6);
Margaret, six years at the feast of the Nativity of St. John
last (24 June, 1295); Alice, three years at the feast of the
Annunciation of the B.M. last (25 March, 1296); and
Anabil, one year old at the feast of St. Peter *ad vincula*
last (1 Aug., 1295).

XXVII. ROBERT DE MARISCO. *Inq. p. m.*

[24 EDW. I. No. 1.]

[*Writ and inquisition wanting.*]

NOV. 28, 1295, Westminster. Whereas Roberto de Marisco, who held of the King in chief, has died (*diem clausit extremum*), as the King has learnt, John de Lithegrenes, the King's Escheator beyond Trent, is ordered to seize, etc. (*Rot. Fin.*, 24 Edw. 1., m. 20).

March 7, 1296-7. New Sarum. The King took the fealty of Robert de Marisco, son and heir of Robert de Marisco, of the county of York, deceased, for all the lands and tenements which the same Robert, his father, held in chief the day he died (*Ibid.*, 25 Edw. I., m. 16).[a]

XXVIII. WILLIAM DE CARTHORPE. *Inq. p. m.*

[24 EDW. I. No. 10.]

Writ[b] directed to John de Lythegreyns, Escheator, and dated at Berewyke upon Tweed, 23 April, 24th year [1296].

INQUISITION made at Beverley within the Liberty at the Cross outside the town before Sir John de Lythgreins, Escheator, on Wednesday after the feast of St. Augustine, 24 Edw. (30 May, 1296), by John *du Gard*, Stephen de Redenesse, John Goman, Hugh *le Cartewrihte*, Geoffrey Pakoke, Simon Hode, Robert de Osgotby, Richard · de Wetewange, Geoffrey de Norhwode, William de Scoresburg', Simon Catepayne, and Thomas *de Castello*. William de Carthorpe held of the archbishopric of York in the town of Beverley 12*d.* annual rent by attending twice at the archbishop's court, that is to say, at the feast of St. Hilary (13 Jan.) and the Nativity of St. John the Baptist (24 June), doing no other service. He held also 25*d.* rent within the provostry of Beverley in free burgage, and did no suit or other service.

John, son of William, is his next heir, and he was 22 years old at Easter last past (25 March, 1296).

---

[a] The Escheator accounted for 12*s.* 2*d.* of the rents of Robert de Marisco, who held in chief of the barony of Holdernesse, from 28 Nov. (1296) to 8 March, when he delivered the lands to Robert, the son and heir. Sureties for relief, William de Walecotes and William Boburth (*Ex. Q. R. Escheators' Accounts*, ¾).

[b] Note on the back that the writ was received on Monday after Ascension Day (7 May, 1296).

I NQUISITION taken at Roston on Tuesday before the feast
of St. William the Archbishop of York[a] (5 June, 1296),
by William Vestiby of Gemelling, Richard de Duddington
of the same, Richard Clerk (*clericum*), Thomas Brun, Henry
(*Heric'*) son of Robert Kelk, Geoffrey Raytel of the same,
John at Appelgard of the same, Robert son of Walter of
Poethorp, Walter (*Valter'*) Martin of Louthorp, John Vestiby
of the same, Simon Spinis of Naferton, and Robert Snyttiby
of Roston.   William de Carthorp held in Roston an annual
rent of a penny to be received by the hand of William
Dringe of Roston[b] for six bovates of land and three tofts;
also an annual rent of 8s. in South Dalton by the hand of
John Hernis for two bovates of land which he held of him
(William).   He also held 25s. annual rent in Bilton to be
received by the hand of the heir of John de Belton for 12
bovates of land which the said heir held of him.   The said
William held all the tenements aforesaid of the provostry
of Beverley by homage and suit at the Provost's court at
Beverley every three weeks.

John, son of William, is his next heir, aged 22 years and
more.

I NQUISITION taken at Caretorp[c] on Wednesday before the
feast of St. William the Archbishop of York, 24 Edw.
(6 June, 1296), by Thomas de Plumpstoft, Thomas de
Poynton, Andrew *le Mercer* of Caretorp, Robert Franceys
of the same, William de Besingby, Ralph Helard, Anselm
Drynge, Walter Martin, Hervey de Wyndosom, Thomas son
of Godfrey, Robert Bridde, and Ralph Yrefet.   The said
William held nothing of the archbishopric of York in the
wapentake of Dykering, but he held of the Abbot of St.
Mary's, York, a poor (*debile*) messuage worth nothing a year
beyond keeping it up, and four carucates of land in Carethorpe, worth £11 4s. a year, by the service of two marcs
yearly to the Abbot.   He held also there of the Chapter
of St. Peter's, York, 10 tofts and 19 bovates of land, worth
together £9 10s. and an annual rent of 3s. 7d., to be yielded
to the Chapter for the said 10 tofts and 19 bovates of land
which they hold in demesne; and for 13 bovates of land
which are held of him by free service of 3s. 4d., 40s. a year

[a] The regnal year is omitted.

[b] Ruston, near Driffield.

[c] Caythorpe, near Bridlington.

for all services. He held also of the Abbot of St. Mary's, York, a watermill and a windmill by the said services, and they are worth 20s. a year.

John, son of William, is his next heir, and he was aged 21 years and more at the feast of Easter last past.

INQUISITION taken at the Cross near Beverle on the north side, called Grith kross, on Wednesday after the feast of St. Augustine, 24 Edw. (30 May, 1296), by William de Burton, Robert Roland, Peter de Hay (?), William *en le Dale*, Hugh de Colvyle, John *le Esquier*, Davyd de Cawode, Geoffrey Frankelayn, William Hardy, William . . . . te, Thomas de Wimpthorpe, and Richard Clerk (*clericum*) of Burton. William de Carethorpe held of the archbishopric of York in Swth Burton[a] a capital messuage, worth nothing beyond keeping it up; four tofts worth 18s.; 20 bovates of land, worth £10 a year; and 10s. rent from a bovate of land which Ralph de Cycestre (*Cycestria*) holds, and 2s. rent from the Prior of Wartre, and thereof he yields yearly to Alexander de Cave 2s. and a pound of pepper, and to Osbert de Torneton 2s. He holds all the lands and tenements aforesaid of the Archbishop of York for the time being by homage and service of a penny and a pound of cumin yearly, and doing as much foreign service when it falls as appertains to land whereof twelve carucates make a knight's fee.

John, son of William, is his next heir, and he was aged 22 years at Easter last past in the 24th year of the king's reign.[b]

XXIX. MARGERY WIDOW OF WILLIAM DE CARTHORPE.

Inq. p. m.

[24 EDW. I. No. 99.]

Writ directed to John de Lythegraynes, Escheator, and dated at Jeddeworth, 1st June, 24th year (1296). On behalf of Margery, who was wife of William de Carthorpe, deceased, who held certain lands and tenements of the Archbishopric of York (vacant and in the King's hand) by knight's service, it is shown that whereas her husband and herself acquired two messuages and one carucate of land with appurtenances in South Burton, and were jointly enfeoffed thereof, and continued their

---

[a] Bishop Burton.

[b] Forfar, 5 July, 1296. Fealty taken of John, son and heir of William de Carthorpe. His lands to be restored, except a messuage and seven bovates of land in Suthburton, of which William, the father, and Margery, his wife, were jointly seised (*Rot. Fin.*, 24 Edw. I., m. 7).

seisin from the time of that feoffment for the life of the said William, nevertheless after his death they had been taken into the King's hand and unjustly detained, to the no mean injury and grievance of the said Margery. Inquiry to be made in presence of the heir, if he wish to· be present, as to the nature of the feoffment, and concerning the tenure and value of the messuages and land.

INQUISITION taken before John de Lithegraines at Sut Burton on the eve of the Nativity of St. John the Baptist, 24 Edw. (23 June, 1296), by Laurence de Etton, Ralph de Douway, William son of Peter of Cave, Adam *le Stabeler* of Skyren, Robert Stiward of the same, Alan de Pokethorpe, Robert Roland, William de Raventhorpe, Hugh de Colevile, Master William de Burton, William *in the Dale*, and Thomas son of Sesul of Midelton. To this inquisition and at the place and day above written, John son and heir of William de Carthorpe was warned by John de Roston, bailiff of Dikering, sworn, and by Laurence Loring of Pokethorpe and Thomas de Ridale, two freemen, to be here on Thursday before the feast of St. Botulph (14 June, 1296), and the said heir solemnly called came not. The jurors say by their oath that William de Carthorpe and Margery his wife were jointly enfeoffed of a messuage and seven bovates of land in Soutburton by John Daniel (to whom the said William first gave the tenements afore-said by his charter), to them, their heirs or assigns, and they continued their joint seisin from the feast of St. Hilary in the 23rd year of the reign (20 Jan., 1294–5) until the death of William, husband of Margery, viz. for a year and more. They were enfeoffed by the said John to them and their heirs lawfully issuing, with reversion, in default of such issue, to the heirs of William de Carthorpe, and to hold the tenements of the Archbishop of York, chief lord of the fee, by knight's service. The messuage is worth 3s., and the seven bovates of land are worth 70s. by the year in all issues.

XXX. STEPHEN DE OUSTWYKE *or* HOSTWYKE *for* JOHN UHTRIDE. *Inq. ad q. d.*

[24 EDW. I. No. 101.]

Writ directed to the Sheriff of Yorkshire, and dated at Rokesburgh, 4 June, 24th year (1296).

INQUISITION[a] made at Oustwyke[b] on Wednesday after the feast of the Nativity of St. John the Baptist, 24 Edw. (27 June, 1296), by Robert de Boby, Alexander de Holme,

---

[a] The writ is set out at length at the head of each inquisition.
[b] Oustwick.

John de Fittelinge, Henry de Wyuetone, Ralph de Gloucestre, Hugh Gilt, John de Ryhill, William *de Camera* of Holme, Nicholas de Thorne, Nicholas Warde of Burton, William *de Furno*, and William Arnald, who say upon their oath that it is not to the damage or prejudice of the King, or of others, if the King grant to Stephen de Oustwyke that he may give and assign a messuage and nine bovates of land with appurtenances to John Uthtride (*in writ* Ughtrethe), to have and to hold to him and his heirs for ever of the King and his heirs by the services therefor due and accustomed. The messuage is worth 40*s*., and each bovate 10*s*., by the year. Stephen holds the same of the King in chief, as of the Honour of Albemarle, by homage and knight's service; and he does suit every three weeks at the Wapentake Court of the King in Holderness, and renders to the King yearly at the feast of St. Michael, for castle-guard of Skipse, 12*d*.

Another writ directed to the same Sheriff, and dated at York, 20 Oct., 24th year (1296).

INQUISITION made at Hedon before the Sheriff on Friday the feast of [All] Souls, 24 Edw. (2 Nov., 1296), by Peter *de la Twyer*, Alexander de Holme, Robert de Boby, John de Fytlinge, John de Ryhill, William de Cameryngton, Simon *del Lund*, Peter Hildeyerde, Simon de Sprotle, Hugh Gylt, John *del Esthalle*, and Stephen de Percy, who say upon their oath that it is not to the damage or prejudice of the King, or of others, if the King grant to Stephen de Oustwyke, that he may give and assign a messuage and nine bovates of land with appurtenances in Oustwyke, to John Utherede, to have and to hold to him and to his heirs for ever of the King and his heirs by the services therefor due and accustomed. The messuage is worth 40*s*., and each bovate, 10*s*., by the year. Stephen holds the messuage and land of the King in chief, as of the Honour of Albemarle, by homage and knight's service; he does suit every three weeks at the Wapentake Court of the King in Holdernesse, and renders to the King yearly at the feast of St. Michael, for castle-guard of Skipse, 12*d*. There remains in the hand of Stephen a close in Oustwyke in Holdernesse, which is called Maldecroft, and worth 7*s*. a year; and is held of the King in chief, as of the Honour of Albemarle; and he does suit every three weeks at the Wapentake Court of the King in Holdernesse.[a]

[a] The license consequent on this inquisition was granted by the King at Bury St. Edmunds on 24 Jan., 1297 (*Calendar of Patent Rolls*, 1292-1301, p. 230).

XXXI.   Dean and Chapter of York.   *Custody of the manor of Bishopthorpe during vacancy of the see.*

[24 Edw. I.   No. 104.]

Writ directed to the keeper (*Custodi*) of the Archbishopric of York, the see being vacant,[a] and dated at Edinburgh, 7 June, 24th year (1296). On behalf of the Dean and Chapter of York it has been shown that whereas they granted their manor of Thorpe St. Andrew, near York,[b] and their hay of Langwathe with appurtenances, to John, Archbishop of York, deceased, to have and to hold to him for life, yielding yearly to the Treasurer of York for the time being for the manor twenty marcs, and to the Dean and Chapter for the hay a buck *tempore pinguedinis* and a doe *tempore fermesone ;* so that after his death both manor and hay should entirely revert to the Dean and Chapter. Nevertheless, after the Archbishop's death the manor and hay had been taken into the King's hand and unjustly detained from the Dean and Chapter. Inquiry to be made whether the alleged grant was made for life, or if in other, in what manner ; and the reason for seizure, and the estate of the Dean and Chapter in the manor and hay at the time of the grant, to be returned without delay.

INQUISITION made before John de Lythegreynes, keeper of the Archbishopric of York, at York on Tuesday after the feast of the Apostles Peter and Paul, 24 Edw. (3 July, 1296), by Walter de Hemelesey, William de Morby, Henry of the Cross (*de Cruce*), Matthew de Knapton, Robert Fox of Angrom, Richard son of Thurstan of Hoton, William Russell of Naburne, Henry de Thorpe clerk, John Hard of Elvyngeton, Walter de Heulay, William *le Turnur* of Wyhghale, and John de Menthorpe, upon the articles contained in the King's writ. They say upon their oath that Walter de Gray, formerly Archbishop of York, purchased from divers feoffees the manor of Thorpe St. Andrew, near York, to him, his heirs or assigns for ever ; and afterwards, in process of time, the archbishop, by ordinance made between himself and the Dean and Chapter of St. Peter, York, gave and granted the said manor with appurtenances to the Dean and Chapter under this form, that is to say, that they should pay once every year, so long as they held the manor, to the treasure of that church twenty marcs for his own obit to be observed every year there for ever, once a year on the day of his burial (*die sue deposicionis*) ; and for the support of a chaplain to celebrate for ever in the chapel of the manor of Thorpe for the soul of the lord John, formerly King of England, for his own soul, and for the souls of all the faithful. So that the Dean and Chapter after his decease should deliver and let the manor to farm to every Archbishop of York succeeding himself, for the

[a] By the death of John Romanus.
[b] Bishopthorpe.

amount aforesaid to be yielded every year, to hold for the term of his life only. And that, in every vacancy after the death of any archbishop, the manor should revert to the Dean and Chapter, and remain in their seisin for such time as the see should be void, for the yearly farm aforesaid. Afterwards lord Henry, father of the now King, by his charter confirmed the said grant, gift and ordinance, and the manor is worth by the year 20 marcs. And they say that the Dean and Chapter purchased the hay of Langwathe with appurtenances of the Prior and Convent of Wartre and afterwards demised it to William Wyckewan,[a] formerly Archbishop of York, for term of his life, rendering yearly a buck in the summer season and a doe in the winter season, so that after his death the hay with appurtenances should entirely revert to them. The Dean and Chapter after the consecration of lord John,[b] late Archbishop of York, demised to him for life the manor of Thorpe with the said hay, by yielding and doing the said services, with reversion to themselves after his death; and the now King by his charter confirmed to the Dean and Chapter the grant of the hay made to them by the Prior and Convent. The Dean and Chapter have always from the time of the grant up to now been in seisin, having custody alike of the manor and of the hay with their appurtenances for the said 20 marcs yearly to be paid to the treasurer of York. The hay is worth by the year 100s., and the manor and hay are held immediately of the Dean and Chapter by the services aforesaid.

Walter de Gray purchased the manor of Thorpe now sixty years past and more, and the Dean and Chapter purchased the hay with its appurtenances twenty years ago. John de Lythegreynes, the King's Escheator, seized the manor and hay into the King's hand because the last Archbishop of York died seised thereof, and because Malcolm de Harlay, sometime keeper of the Archbishopric of York, after the death of William Wyckewan, formerly archbishop, seised the manor until it was delivered by writ to the Dean and Chapter.[c]

[a] Archbishop 1279-1285.

[b] John Romanus, 1286-1296.

[c] A writ of the same date (7 June, 1296), was directed to the Treasurer and Barons of the Exchequer upon the complaint of the Dean and Chapter of York that Malculm de Harley, the King's Escheator, had seized into the King's hand the church of Kynewaldestowe, co. Nottingham. This is followed by the answer of the Treasurer and Barons to the effect that, during vacancies of the see, the church had not been taken into the King's hand, or its issues answered at the Exchequer. A later writ, of the King, given under the Privy Seal at Invirkeyragh,

XXXII.   SIR HUGH DE BABINGTON.   *Inq. p. m.*

[24 EDW. I.   No. 115.]

Writ[a] dated at Edeneburgh, 12 June, 24th year (1296), and directed to John
de Lythegreyns, Escheator.

INQUISITION made of the manor of Burgley,[b] formerly of
Sir Hugh de Babington, deceased, on Tuesday after the
Nativity of St. John the Baptist, 24 Edw. (26 June, 1296),
before Maurice de Brafferton by command of Sir J. de
Lithegreyns, the King's Escheator this side Trent, by
Alexander de Menstone, William *Attebeke* of the same,
John son of Lucoke, Michael Keller, Robert *de Curia*, John
de Bayldon, Walter Russell, Robert son of William, Ralph
son of Michael, William *del Stede*, Adam son of Thomas,
and Hugh Poydeseringe.   There are in demesne seven-
score 13 acres of arable land (at 4*d.*), 51*s.*, a culture called
Joanryddynge, worth 2*s.* a year; also 14 acres of meadow
(at 15*d.*), 17*s.* 6*d.*   The site of the manor with garden is
worth by the year half a marc, and pasture in the park
with other pastures is worth 1*s.* a year.   In rent of assize
at the terms of Pentecost and Saint Martin, £8 16*s.* 2*d.*; at
Pentecost only, 3*s.* 6*d.*; also at St. Peter's term, 18*s.* 5½*d.*;
of pepper, 3lbs., and of cumin (*de cimino*), 2½lbs.   A mill is
worth 106*s.* 8*d.* a year.   Works of 13 ploughs and 37
reapers in autumn are worth yearly 4*s.* 2*d.*

Sum of the value, £19 8*s.* 1½*d.*

The manor of Burgley with appurtenances is held of
the Archbishop of York in chief, and will answer for half
a knight's fee.

Richard de Babington is next heir of the said Hugh,
and aged 28 years.[c]

31 July, 24th year (1296), is addressed to his Chancellor, John de Langeton.
Whereas by inquisition taken before the keeper of the Archbishopric of York, and
by certificate returned by the Treasurer and Barons of the Exchequer, it is
apparent that the issues of the manor of Thorpe St. Andrew, of the hay of
Langwathe, or of the church of Kynewaldestowe, have not, during vacancies of the
see of York, been answered to the King, the Chancellor is commanded to deliver
the manor, hay and church, in due form without delay.

[a] Note on the back that the writ was received on Wednesday before the feast
of St. John the Baptist (20 June, 1296).

[b] Burley in Wharfedale.   Sir Hugh de Babington, nephew and heir of Godfrey
Giffard, Bishop of Worcester, and of Walter Giffard, Archbishop of York, did
homage to Archbishop Romanus in 1287 for the manor of Burley (*Kirkby's
Inquest*, p. 37*n*).

[c] 4 July, 1296.   Forfare.   The King took the fealty of Richard de Babynton,
son and heir of Hugh de Babynton, of the county of York, for the lands held by
Hugh of the Archbishopric of York, which was vacant and in the King's hands
(*Rot. Fin.*, 24 Edw. I., m. 8).

XXXIII. GERARD SON OF GERARD SALVAYN. *Inq. p. m.*

[24 EDW. I. No. 27.]

Writ[a] dated at Cluny, 26 June, 24th year (1296).

INQUISITION taken at York on the morrow of St. Luke the Evangelist, 24 Edw. (19 Oct., 1296), before John de Lithegraynes, Escheator, by William de Wetewange, Walter de Dalton, Martin *Attemar*, William de Thurkelby, Ralph son of Richard of Est Lutton, Richard Mohaute of Kyrkeby, Thomas son of Stephen of Lutton, Thomas West of the same, William Slexte of Warrom, John Putrel of Ledemer, Robert son of Geoffrey of the same, Jollan de Brydale, Ralph Wernoun of Boggethorpe, William de Torraldby, Richard de Thurkenthorpe, Clement de Cetryngton, Thomas de Lewenynge, Nicholas de Brunneby, and Elias (*Heliam*) de Yapom. Gerard son of Gerard Salvayn held no lands or tenements of the King in chief, or of others, in his demesne as of fee; but he held certain lands and tenements in Crohum and Sledemer of Gerard son of Robert Salvayn by homage and knight's service, which are worth by the year £10 15s. 4d.; of which lands he (Gerard) enfeoffed Gerard son of Robert Salvayn on 3 March, 23 Edw. (1294-5), namely, a year and more before his death. Gerard son of Robert from the day named was in peaceful seisin of the same. Joan and Nicholaa, sisters of Gerard son of Gerard, are his next heirs; Joan, aged 30, and Nicholaa, aged 25 years. Joan is the elder, and married to Adam de Thorpe, but she has no issue; Nicholaa is married to John Orme of Dunstapel, and has two sons and two daughters, of whom the elder son is aged 14 years.

Gerard son of Gerard Salvayn held all the lands and tenements which he had in Yorkshire of Gerard son of Robert Salvayn by homage and service. He died on the morrow of St. Botulph, 24 Edw. (18 June, 1296).

He had at some time two bovates of land in Little Thorpe, of which he enfeoffed Gerard son of Robert Salvayn, to hold to him and to his heirs as above, and they are worth 10s. a year.[b]

---

[a] Note of receipt on Thursday the morrow of the Assumption of the B. V. M. (16 Aug.. 1296).

[b] There are two other inquisitions for the counties of Bedford and Buckingham. By the second of these, taken on Sunday after the feast of St. James the Apostle, 24th year (29 July, 1296), it is found that Joan and "Nicole," sisters of Gerard, now deceased, are his heirs; Joan, aged 30 years at the feast of St. John the Baptist last (24 June), and Nicole, 25, at the feast of St. Mary Magdalen last (22 July). By the inquisition for Bedfordshire, taken at Flettewyke on Saturday after the Assumption of the B. V. M., 24th year (18th Aug., 1296), it is found that Gerard

XXXIV.   GILBERT FITZ WILLIAM.[a]   *Inq. p. m.*

[24 EDW. I. No. 15.]

Writb dated at Cluny, 2 July, 24th year (1296).

I NQUISITION taken at Brunnom[c] before John de Lythegreynes on Tuesday before the feast of St. Margaret,
24 Edw. (17 July, 1296), by Thomas Darayns, Hugh de
Lynton, Simon de Dreuton, Elias Clerk (*clericum*) of Yapum,
Robert Rouland, Richard son of John of Geveldale, Hugh
de Colevile, Thomas de Tansterne, Godfrey Fraunkelayn,
William de Heshill, Henry de Holme, and Roger at the
Hall of Clif (*ad aulam de Clif*). Gilbert fitz William held
of the King the manor of Brunnum, worth by the year
£20, by doing homage to the King, with suit at all the
county courts for the year, once in the year at the Triding
court of Crayhou, and once at the Wapentake court of
Herthill, beside yielding to the King for fines of the
Wapentake 3s. He held also a messuage in Hothom, worth
2s.; 8 bovates of land, 2 marcs; 8 acres of meadow, half a
marc; and 4 cottages, 8s. a year. He held these tenements
of Sir Ralph fitz William by homage and yielding yearly 6s.

Ralph fitz William is his next heir, aged 40 years and
more.

XXXV.   JOHN DE WALKINGHAM.[d]   *Inq. p. m.*

[24 EDW. I. No. 32.]

Writ dated at Berwick upon Tweed, 1st Sept., 24th year (1296). By
endorsement lands in the Liberties of Rypon and Knaresburgh, and in
the Wapentakes of Herthill and Langebergh.

I NQUISITION made before John de Lythegreynes, Escheator,
at Knaresburgh, on Wednesday after the feast of the
Exaltation of Holy Cross, 24 Edw. (19 Sept., 1296), by

and Maud his wife were jointly enfeoffed of certain lands in the Hyde near Luton
(held of Geoffrey de Luci); and that his sisters, Joan de Skeurus, aged 30, and
Nicolaa de Donesstapel, aged 24, are his next heirs. On 27 Oct., 1296, the King
took the fealty at Bentleye of Adam de Thorpe, husband of Joan, one of the
sisters and coheirs of Gerard son and heir of Gerard Salveyn (*Rot. Fin.,*
24 Edw. I., m. 4); and on 25 Nov., 1296, at St. Edmund's the homage of John
Eme, of Dunstaple, husband of Nicholaa, another of the sisters and coheirs of
Gerard son of Gerard Salveyn, of the county of Bedford (*Ibid.,* 25 Edw. I., m. 23).

[a] On 6 Aug., 1296, the King took the homage of Ralph fitz William, brother
and heir of Gilbert fitz William, at Aberbroth' (*Rot. Fin.,* 24 Edw. I., m. 6).

[b] The writ was received on Friday after the feast of the Translation of St.
Thomas the Martyr (13 July, 1296).

[c] Nunburnholme.

[d] Aged nearly eighteen in 1251, at the date of his father's, John de Walkingham,
death (Vol. I., p. 22). 24 Oct., 1296. Brotherton. Homage taken of Thomas de
Walkyngham, son and heir of John de Walkyngham (*Rot. Fin.,* 24 Edw. I., m. 4).

Thomas de Sallay, Ralph Ward of Scotton, Adam de Screvyn, Thomas son of Walter of Lofthuses, Thomas Turpin, John Tullehuse, Adam le Keu of Stavelay, William Tailor (*cissorem*) of Scotton, Richard Warde, William *del Gren* of Knaresburgh, John Pavely of the same, and William *Attekelde*. John de Walkyngham on the day of his death held in fee a messuage, two carucates and two bovates of land with appurtenances in Walkyngham of the lord Edmund, Earl of Cornwall, by homage and fealty, and by service of 8s. yearly, a moiety at Michaelmas, and the other moiety at Palm Sunday (*ad Pascha floridum*); also yielding yearly 12d. for boonworks (*precariis*), and doing suit at the Earl's court of Knaresburgh every three weeks. The said tenements are worth by the year 50s. Also the said John held in fee of Adam de Walkingham by the yearly service of a rose, a toft, and an acre of land in Farneham, worth 2s. a year.

Thomas, eldest (*antenatus*) son of John, is his next heir, and aged thirty years and more. [*By endorsement* "Knaresburgh."]

INQUISITION taken before the same Escheator at Pokelington on Wednesday after the feast of St. Michael, 24 Edw. (3 Oct., 1296), by Ralph Doway, Adam de Estthorpe, Thomas son of Joseph, Hugh de Coleville, Richard de Weley of Scipton,[a] John Fanecurt, Nicholas son of Elias (*filium Elye*), Richard de Herlethorpe, Henry de Hohn', John de Thorpe, Richard son of James (*filium Jacoby*) of Pokelington, and William Stra of Geveldale. John de Walkyngham held of the King a messuage in Northgeveldale,[b] worth by the year, 40d., 32 acres of arable land (at 5d.), 4 acres of meadow (at 18d.), a watermill, worth 10s. a year; also 5 tofts and 3 carucates of land, each carucate worth with the tofts, 20s., and two waste places, worth 2d. a year. He held also in Est Geveldale half a carucate of land, worth 10s. a year.

Sum in all issues by the year, 102s. 10d.

He held nothing of others in the Estthridinge. All the aforesaid tenements he held of the King by homage and service of finding, at his own charges for forty days in time of war, half a crossbowman, or arblaster (*balistarii*) in York castle.

Thomas son of John is his next heir, and aged 30 years and more. [*By endorsement* "Estridd(ingge)."]

[a] *Supton.*

[b] North or Great Givendale, near Pocklington, wrongly identified in Vol. I. (p. 22n) with the Givendale near Ripon.

INQUISITION made before the same Escheator at Stokesle
on Saturday after the feast of St. Michael, 24 Edw.
(6 Oct., 1296), by Stephen Guer, Richard de Fenton, John
de Fintres, Robert *del Houw*, William *del Houw*, William
Hestinge, John de Levynton, William Boy, William *le clerck*
of Hoton, Walter Lane, Richard in the Wylyes, and
William de Fulthorpe. John de Walkingham held of Robert
de Pothouw two tofts and two bovates of land in the town
of Caldingelby[a] by knight's service, viz. by homage and by
12*d.*, to scutage of 40*s.*; and to more, more; and to less, less.
They are worth, by the year, 8*s.*

Thomas son of John is his next heir, and aged 30 years
and more. [*By endorsement,* "Northridd(inge)."][b]

INQUISITION made before the same Escheator at Rypon
on Sunday after the Octave of St. Michael, 24 Edw.
(7 Oct., 1296), by John Frere, Nicholas Huberd, William de
Screvin, Robert *del Ledhus*, Robert de Shakilthorp, Walter
Stikebuc, William de Stayveley, William de Schirewode,
William *le Vavasur*, John Scot, Alan de Corbryge, and Adam
Marshal (*mariscall*') of Rypon. John de Walkyngham held
no land of the King in chief in the Liberty of Rypon, but
he held of one William Mesur and his heirs in the town of
Rypon, by the yearly service of 4*d.*, a toft with appurte-
nances, worth 8*d.* a year.

Thomas son of John is his next heir, and aged 30 years
and more. [*By endorsement,* "Westridd(inge)."].

XXXVI. JOHN HAYWARD. *Profits subtracted from his
bailiwick of the forest of Galtres.*

[24 EDW. I. No. 105.]

Writ directed to the officer (*tenenti locum*) acting as Justice of the King's
forest on this side Trent (*citra Trentam*),[c] and dated at Kirkeham,
14 Oct., 24th year (1296). Upon the complaint of John Hayward it
appears that many profits which appertain to him by reason of the
bailiwick of the forest of Galtres, lately granted to him for life, and
which other keepers of the bailiwick have been wont to receive, have
been newly withdrawn, so that he cannot have them as he ought
according to the grant made to him thereof. Inquiry is to be had as
to the profits received by former keepers; and what, if any, have been
withdrawn, by whom, and how, &c.

---

[a] Cold Ingleby, par. Stainton.

[b] Also endorsed:—Domino Johanni de Lythegrayns per Johannem de Redmersll'.

[c] In the inquisition called "*ultra* Trentam."

I NQUISITION taken at York on Thursday the feast of St.
Luke the Evangelist, 24 Edw. (18 Oct., 1296), in presence
of John de Langeton, the King's Chancellor, William de
Brameby, attorney of the Justice of the King's forest beyond
Trent, and John de Lytthegraynnes, Escheator beyond Trent,
by the oath of foresters and verderers of the forest of
Gautrys, as well as other honest and lawful men of the
bailiwick, that is to say: Robert*....... Ivo de Etton and
Richard Malbys, knights; Robert Haget, John Maunsel,
Robert de Supton, William Oissellur   of Gunnays,
verderers; Roger de Thornton, agistor; Walter *le Graunt*,
Nicholas de Bossale, Theobald de Tollerton, Walter de
Scotheby, Thomas Blaumfrount, Walter Ysacke, Simon de
Roucclife, John *le Stabler*, John Fre   , Walter son of
Peter and Thomas de Aldewerke, regarders; John de Hoby,
Hugh Gryvel, foresters; Thomas Maunsel, Thomas de
........., Robert Oliver, David de Roucclife, Stephen de
Strensale, Henry de Kyle, William Belle of Routclife,
Thomas de Brouddesforth, Richard Bisseman, Adam son of
Edmund, John son of Robert of Esingwolde, Richard de
Cramboune and Walter son of Alan of Hoby. They say
by their oath that one John de Ebor was forester, to whom
King Henry, father of the now King, granted that bailiwick
of the forest of Gautris which John Hayward now holds of
the King's gift, whereby he had the custody of the launds
of Ingolftwayt and Allewartoftes, for which he yielded to the
King 100s. For keeping them he had two grooms (*garciones*)
at his own cost, carrying spears in their hands; and he was
forester, with a horse and groom following him with bow
and arrows through the middle of the forest, and this by
grace of the Justice, going round the forest to attach
trespassers of vert and venison. Of other profits he had
none by reason of his bailiwick, but the Justice of the forest
answered to the King for such fines and attachments. One
William de Ryton and another named Roger, associated
with him, had the same bailiwick by charter of King Henry,
in which it is contained that they ought to appoint (*ponere*)
and remove all foresters, and answer for all issues of the
forest at the Exchequer; but they had nothing from the said
profits, because they were impeded by Geoffrey de Nevyle,
Justice of the forest, so that they had no estate therein.
After the decease of John de Ebor, the lord Edward, now
King, gave the bailiwick to William Gryvel for his whole
life, who was to answer to the King 100s. for custody of the

* Many of these jurors occur in No. XI, which is another inquisition on the same subject.

said launds, as John de Ebor heretofore had them; and the said William received nothing else from the bailiwick. Asked, if any other forester had the bailiwick before the King gave it to John de Ebor, they say that they can recollect no other having it before him.

XXXVII. JOHN RAYNER *for* THE MASTER AND BRETHREN OF ST. LEONARD'S HOSPITAL, YORK. *Inq. ad q. d.*

[24 EDW. I. No. 85.]

Writ directed to the Sheriff of Yorkshire, and dated at York, 20 Oct., 24th year (1296).

INQUISITION taken before the Warden (*Custode*) of the city of York on Monday after the feast of St. Luke the Evangelist, 24 Edw. (22 Oct., 1296), by John *Lespecer*, John de Warthyll, Adam de Bolingbroke, Nicholas de Clervaus, Robert de Neulande, John de Appelby, Robert Blaunchecote, Adam *le Wayder*, William de Carleton, William Lyngetayl, Gilbert de Arnale, and Robert de Grymestone, who say on their oath that John Rayner may for himself and his heirs grant, remise and quitclaim to the Master and Brethren of the Hospital of St. Leonard, York, and their successors for ever, 28*d.* annual rent which the said Master and Brethren have been used to yield for lands and tenements held of him by them in Blaykestrete, in the said city. And for this grant, remise and quitclaim the said Master and Brethren will for them and their successors grant, remise and quit-claim to the Friars Minors of the said city for ever 26*d.* annual rent paid to them yearly by the Friars Minors in the Bayle against (*versus*) York castle. They say that such is not to the damage of anyone, or to the prejudice of the King, or of others; and likewise that that rent is forthcoming from the garden of the Master and Brethren of the Hospital in Blaykestrete near their gate. The rent is held of the King by payment of a penny towards housegabel (*husgab' lum*) for all service. Dated at York the day and year abovesaid.

XXXVIII. ABBOT AND CONVENT OF THORNTON.

[24 EDW. I. No. 103.]

Writ directed to Thomas de Weston, the King's Bailiff of Holdernesse, and dated at York, 20 Oct., 24th year (1296). On behalf of the Abbot and Convent of Thorneton it is shown that whereas, by the charter of William, formerly Earl of Albemarle, they ought to receive every year the retithing of all cheeses of the Earl and his successors,[a] wheresoever made in England, and they and their predecessors used peacefully to enjoy such retithing from the time the said charter was made up to the day of the death of Isabel de Fortibus, formerly Countess of Albemarle, when those lands and tenements held by her, and which were the late Earl's, came into the King's hands as his escheat, such retithing had not been permitted by him (the Bailiff). Inquiry therefore to be made into the truth of the matter.

INQUISITION made at Hedon before Thomas de Weston, Bailiff of Holderness, on Sunday after the feast of All Saints, 24 Edw. (4 Nov., 1296), by Peter *de la Twyer*, Alexander de Holme, Robert de Boby, John de Fytlinge, Simon de Lunde, Stephen de Percy, Peter Hyldeyerde, Hugh Gylt of Sprotle, Simon de Sprotle, John de Ryhill, John *del Esthalle* of Aldeburgh, and William de Cameryngton, who say by their oath that William, Earl of Albemarle, by his charter, gave and granted for himself and his heirs to the Abbot and Convent of Thorneton the retithing of all his cheeses wheresoever they should be made in England; and made this gift for the health of his own soul and of the souls of his ancestors and successors. They say also that the Abbot and Convent and their predecessors always from the time of the gift and grant so made by charter, without any interruption and impediment up to the day of the death of Isabel de Fortibus, Countess of Albemarle, have received and had in the said Earl's dairies in Holdernesse, viz. Brustwyke, Cayngham, and Little Humber only, after the tithe of cheeses paid to parish churches, the retithing from the nine parts remaining; and have peacefully continued their seisin thereof. The retithing of cheeses in the said dairies cannot be valued, because it is uncertain, as the farms are stocked on the King's behalf, sometimes more, sometimes less.[b]

XXXIX. WILLIAM DE GEREMOUTHE THE ELDER. *Inq. p. m.*
[24 EDW. I. No. 29.]

Writ of *certiorari* directed to John de Totenhou, bailiff of the King's manor of Skipton in Craven, and dated at Brotherton, 24 Oct., 24th year (1296), upon the complaint of William de Geremouthe, son and heir of

---

[a] King Richard I. in 1190 confirmed to Thornton Abbey the gift of William, Earl of Albemarle, of the tithe of all his mills in England, and the retithing (*redecimationem*) of all his cheeses wheresoever they might be made in England (Dugdale's *Monasticon Anglicanum*, vi., 326).

[b] On the dorse a direction :—Let it be done to them as the inquisition witnesseth in the places of which the inquisition makes mention. [*On another membrane.*] Petition of the Abbot and Convent that, upon the inquisition made by Thomas de Weston who yet refuses to pay the retithing (*predictus tamen Thomas dictam redecimacionem eisdem Abbati et Conventui solvere contradicet*), the King will deign to provide a remedy.

William de Geremouthe the elder, deceased, that the lands and tenements of which his father was seised in fee had been detained from
him contrary to the custom of the manor. The cause of the detention
to be stated, and in what manner the father held of the King, and
whether the son is the heir, and of full age or not.

INQUISITION made on Saturday the morrow of St. Edmund,
the Archbishop of Canterbury, 24 Edw. (17 Nov., 1296),
before John de Thoternou, Bailiff of the manor and honour
of Skypton, by John Gylliot, Richard Tempest, William de
Marton and others, suitors of the Court of Skypton, and by
four townships, Apeltrewycke, Wodehous, Hertlington, and
Brinsale,[a] concerning the lands and tenements which were
formerly of William de Giruemout the elder, who say upon
their oath that the said William held on the day of his
death a toft and half a bovate of land in Wodehous in chief
of the King's manor of Skypton, and did suit every three
weeks at the knights' court (*ad curiam militum*) of Skypton,
and yielded to the manor 9*d*. yearly rent.

William de Giruemout the younger is next heir of the
said William; and, on the day of the Exaltation of the Holy
Cross in the year abovesaid (14 Sept., 1296), he was aged
twenty-one years.

XL.   WILLIAM GAMELSTEPSON.   *Year and day.*

[25 EDW. I. No. 95.]

Writ directed to the Sheriff, and dated at Bures St. Mary, 10 Dec., 25th
year (1296).

INQUISITION taken at Donecastre on Thursday after the
Epiphany of the Lord, 25 Edw. (10 Jan., 1296-7), before
John de Birun, Sheriff of Yorkshire, by William de Darnall,
Adam de Cresseville, Thomas Frende, Thomas *le Rous*,
Roger Ancelin, Adam Ancelin, Thomas *le Serjaunt*, Richard
del Bernes, Adam son of Robert of Atterclive, Roger son of
Roger of the same, Lambert de Scheffeud, and Henry son
of Roger of Bramton, by virtue of the King's writ, to inquire
whether or not two messuages, two tofts, five acres of land,
and 9*d*. rent with appurtenances in Scheffeud, held by
William Gamelstepson, who was outlawed for felony (as it
is said), have been in the King's hand for a year and a day.
They say on their oath that William Gamelstepson, who
was outlawed for the death of Adam son of Hugh *le Pelter*
of Scheffeud, held two messuages, two tofts, five acres of
land, and 4½*d*. rent in Scheffeud' of Thomas de Furnivale,
knight; and those tofts with land and rent have been in the

---

[a] Appletreewick, Woodhouse, Hartlington, and Burnsall.

King's hand for a year and a day. The township (*villata*) of Scheffeud has held them for that time and ought to answer for them. They are worth by the year 1*s.* 5½*d.* As to the remainder of the rent, viz. 4½*d.*, nothing has been had.

XLI. LANDS OF PETER DE GOUSHULL AND OF RALPH HIS SON.

[25 EDW. I. No. 120.]

Writ directed to John de Lythegraynes, Escheator beyond Trent, and dated at Ely, 12 Feb., 25th year (1296-7), requiring him to certify as to the manner and reason of taking and detaining certain lands and tenements which belonged to Ralph de Goushull, deceased.

THE lands and tenements were first taken into the King's hand after the death of Peter de Goushull, father of Ralph, in the time of Thomas de Normanville, formerly Escheator, because the said Peter held certain lands of the King in chief of his Barony of Holdernesse. Afterwards I received the King's writ that I should restore the custody of his (Peter's) lands and tenements in Little Coldon to Eustace de Hacche, to whom the King had committed that custody up to the lawful age of Ralph, Peter's son and heir, who died before he arrived at lawful age: which mandate I executed in due form. Afterwards I received another writ, that an inquisition made by Thomas de Normanville was insufficient, because it made no mention as to what lands Ralph held of the King as of his Crown, or of an Honour, or Barony. Therefore I was commanded to inquire and certify the Court, which I did, and returned the inquisition with the writ to Chancery. Afterwards I received a further writ that, whereas Hauwise, late wife of Ralph, had taken an oath not to marry without the King's licence, I was to assign to her reasonable dower out of lands and tenements formerly her late husband's in fee; which assignment I made, and in like manner returned it to Chancery. Then I received a writ that, whereas Ralph who held of the King in chief had died, I was to take into the King's hand all lands and tenements in my bailiwick, of which he was seised in fee on the day of his death, and to inquire concerning the value of the same. I took the inquisition, and returned it with the writ to Chancery. For these reasons I took these lands assigned to Hauwise for her dower, as well as other lands which were of the said Ralph in my bailiwick

on the day of his death, and I shall hold them until I shall
have it otherwise in command from you.[a]

XLII. WILLIAM HERON AND WALTER HIS SON. *Inq. p. m.*

[25 Edw. I. No. 25.]

Writ after the death of William Heyron directed to John de Lythegraynes,
Escheator beyond Trent, and dated at Ipswich, 25 Dec., 25th year
(1296). By an inquisition taken at Newcastle upon Tyne on the day
of St. Hilary, 25 Edw. I. [Jan., 1296-7], it is found that Emellina,
daughter of Walter Heyron, is next heir of William Heyron, and aged
as the jurors believe six years: and that at this date she was with
the Lady Emellina de Hastings at her manor in Norfolk. By a later
inquisition at Morpeth, on Wednesday in Whitsun Week, 25th year
[5 June, 1297], it is shown that Walter Heron, the son of William
Heron, had a daughter named Emeline, aged seven years and a half,
who is his Walter's heir of blood and likewise next heir of William
Heron. Walter died long before his father, who deceased at Newcastle
upon Tyne on Sunday before the feast of St. Thomas the Apostle last
past (16 Dec. 1296). Mary, late wife of William, is here said to have
been dowered with a third part of the manor of Haddestone in
Northumberland. No inquisition for Yorkshire, taken under the above-
mentioned writ, is to be found in the file of documents. There
remains, however, a writ tested by Philip de Wylugby, which requires
the Escheator (John de Lithegreyns) to certify the Treasurer and Barons
of the Exchequer what lands and tenements were held by Walter
Heron, deceased, and whether he had more heirs than Emeline his
daughter. Dated at Westminster, 23 April, 25th year (1297), and
received (as appears by endorsement).

INQUISITION made at York on Wednesday before the feast
of Pentecost, 25 Edw. (29 May, 1297), before John de
Lithegreyns, by William de Notton, Hugh Bayard of Cothe-
worde, Richard of the Hall (*de Aula*) of the same, Robert
son of William of Caldhindeley, Richard *de Mora* of
Wolvelay, Henry *de Mora* of the same, Richard de Chyvet,
Ralph *de la Roche* of Bergh, John Gotte of Notton, Robert
de Swaluhille, John *filius Decani* of Morestone, and Robert
de Gillinge, concerning the lands and tenements which were
of Walter Heyron in the county of York on the day of his

[a] Jan. 20, 1297. Harwich. Grant to William son of Gley of the custody,
during the minority of the heirs of the heir of Peter de Goushull, of the manor
of Goushull, late of the said Peter, tenant in chief. On 16 June, 15 Edw. I.
(1287), the King granted him land to the value of £20 a year for seven years,
out of the wardships in the King's hands, and Mr. Henry de Bray, then Escheator
this side Trent, assigned him the said manor during the minority of the heir of
the said Peter, on condition that he should satisfy Cecily de Cleware, touching the
King's grant to her of land to the value of £10 a year for three years in that
manor. The heir died three years before his majority, whereby the manor was
resumed into the King's hands, and in recompense of his loss the manor was
recommitted to the said William for three years from 15 Oct., 22 Edw. I. (1294),
and that grant is now extended to the present term (*Calendar of Patent Rolls*,
101, p. 220).

death. The said Walter and Alice his wife held the manor of Silkestone with appurtenances by the gift and feoffment of Sir William Heyron, father of Walter, to have and to hold to them and the heirs of Walter, namely, the capital messuage and wood, and a moiety of the town of Silkestone of John de Nevyle, and the other moiety of Sir John de Heton by knight's service: which said manor is worth by the year in all issues, 20 marcs.

The said Walter held in Derton,[a] by feoffment of William his father, lands and rents worth by the year 18s. 4½d.; and of Margaret de Nevyle, by homage and service, other lands and tenements in Brereley, worth yearly 15s. He held nothing of the King in the said county.

Walter had a daughter and heir, named Emelina, who is aged seven years and a half, and no other heir.

William Heyron at the time of his death held of the Earl of Lincoln by knight's service the manor of Notton, which he had of the inheritance of the said Emelina by the law of England, and which is worth £20 a year in all issues; within which extent is a watermill that used to yield yearly 18s., but is now of no value.

The marriage of Emelina is worth £40. William Heiron, who held by the law of England the manor of Notton, died on the morrow of St. Nicholas the Bishop, 25th year (7 Dec., 1296).

[Coram Rege Roll. No. 152, m. 36ᵈ.]

MICHAELMAS TERM, 25 and 26 Edw. I. (1297). The King to the Sheriff of Yorkshire. After reciting a petition of Alice, widow of Walter Heyrun, who with the assent and wish of William Heyrun his father, deceased, a tenant in chief, had assigned to Alice in dower at the church door (*ad ostium ecclesie*) at Alverstain,[b] where he married her, a third part of the lands and tenements of the said William his father, which by William's death, and by reason of the minority of his heir, are in the King's hand; the King, wishing to know the particulars and to do Alice justice, orders the Sheriff to summon to appear before him, on the octave of St. Michael then next, wherever he might be in England, Walter de Tylneye, John de Hastynges, Nicholas de Hastinges, Walter d'Engletere and Simon de Bedingfeld, who were present at the celebration of the marriage

---

[a] Darton.
[b] Alleiston.

(*celebracioni sponsalium*) of the said Walter and Alice at the said church door, as Alice asserts, and to summon a jury, and to inform William de Felton,[a] the guardian of the lands.

On the day named the guardian, who was with the King in Flanders, being warned by William son of Hugh of Notton and Thomas Haliday of the same, appeared by his attorney, William de Houton. The witnesses of the marriage, except John de Hastinges, who was dead, appeared.

The jury find that immediately after the death of Alice's father, a certain knight, John de Roseles by name, came to Emelina, Alice's mother, for the purpose of making a marriage (*pro matrimonio contrahendo*) between Alice and Walter son of William Hayrun, in the name of the said William, so that Emelina should give William, for the marriage, 230 marcs. Afterwards John came to William Hayrun, who, being informed by him about the previous conversation, came to Emelina for the purpose of confirming such conversation (*pro predicta prelocucione confirmanda*). The said Emelina and William were satisfied about that conversation, namely, that Emelina should forthwith give him 20*li.* of the same money to pay part of his debts due to the King and others, which Emelina then did, when William departed without taking any further security about the said contract. Afterwards, on the eve of the Apostles Simon and Jude next coming, thirteen years ago (27 Oct., 1284), William returned, together with John de Roseles, Nicholas de Wrtele, William Hayrun, and Walter his son, afterwards Alice's husband, to Alverstan in Pikerynglyth, to the same Emelyna, for the final confirmation of the contract. And Emelina, having called her counsel to her, said she would in no way agree to give so much money for making that marriage, unless William would agree that his son Walter should dower Alice with a third part of all his (William's) lands in the realm, so that at length, after a great deal of talking and bargaining between them (*post magnum colloquium et contractum inter eos habitum*), the said William entirely agreed, whereupon they went on the same day to the chapel of the Blessed Mary in the same manor of Alverstan, to

---

[a] 1298, Dec. 20. York. Grant to William de Felton, constable of the castle of Beaumaris, in satisfaction of 128*li.* 10*s.* 7½*d.* due to him for his wages from 6. May, 24 Edw. I. (1296), until Michaelmas of that year, and for money spent by him in works of the castle in that year, of the custody of all the land late of William Heyron, tenant in chief, in co. Northumberland, and of Walter Heyron, son of the said William, in co. York, during the minority of Emelina, kinswoman and heir of the said William, and daughter and heir of the said Walter, with the marriage of the said Emelina. The lands and marriage being extended at 200 marcs he is charged with seven marcs 2*s.* 8½*d.* at the Exchequer (*Calendar of Patent Rolls*, 1292-1301, p. 390).

celebrate the said marriage. And after that the said Walter de Tylneye, the chaplain, began to celebrate that solemnity, and when he was come to these words, "With this ring I thee wed, and with my body I thee worship, and with a third part of all the lands of William, my father, I thee endow," William, the father, being present, agreed to this by these words, "And I give assent to the said endowing," and he commanded it to be done.[a] And afterwards he came to the altar, and swore on the altar that in nothing would he ever go against the said endowing. And thus they finished the said solempnity. And the jurors say that this was the manner, this the cause, and this what was done. And since it has been sufficiently proved and ascertained by the said witnesses and jurors, that Walter, Alice's late husband, by the assent and wish of the said William, his father, endowed her of all the lands and tenements of the same William at the church door when he married her, it is adjudged that the said Alice should recover her dower in the way she was endowed. And the Sheriffs of Northumberland and Yorkshire, in whose counties, etc., were ordered to cause the said Alice to have her seisin of a third part of the lands and tenements which were the said William's, according to the form of the said endowing and assignment.[b]

XLIII.   HAMO DE GRUSCY *for* THE FRIARS PREACHERS OF YORK. *Inq. ad* $_q.$ *d.*

[25 EDW. I.   No. 94.]

Writ directed to the Sheriff of Yorkshire, and dated at Plimpton (Plympton, Devon), 3 May, 25th year (1297).

INQUISITION taken before the Mayor and Bailiffs of the city of York on Monday after the feast of St. Dunstan the Bishop, 25 Edw. (20 May, 1297), by John *le Especer*, Reyner Spry, Clement de Pontefrayth, William Sleght, Adam Fox, Bartholomew of Newcastle (*de Novo Castro*), Adam *le Wayder*, William de Brummeby, Robert de Hedon, Richard Playndamurs, William *le Barber*, and Alan Sampson,

---

[a] "Et predictus Walterus de Tylneye capellanus predictam solempnitatem celebrare incepit, et cum perventum fuit ad illa verba, De anulo isto te disponso, et de corpore meo te honoro, et de tercia parte omnium terrarum Willelmi patris mei te doto, idem Willelmus pater presens ad hoc assensit per hec verba, Et ego predicte donacioni assensum prebeo, et hoc fieri fecit."

[b] 4 May, 27 Edw. (1299). Alice, widow of Walter Heroun, who died seized in chief, married without the royal license Thomas le Rous (*Ex. L. T. R. Memoranda Roll*, 26 and 27 Edw. I., m. 71).

whether or not it be to the damage or prejudice of the King, or of others, if the King grant to Hamo de Gruscy that he may give and assign three tofts with appurtenances in the City of York to the Prior and Brethren of the Order of Preachers for the enlargement of their place in the said city, to have and to hold to them and to their successors for ever. They say that it is not to the damage or prejudice of the King, or of others, if the grant be made. Those three tofts are held of the King by the service of 2d. for house-gabel, and they were also wont to yield to the Hospital of St. Leonard, York, 2s. yearly for all services, as in suits, views of frankpledge, &c.; and they are worth by the year 12d., because they are void and have been so for a long time. Hamo de Gruscy has lands and tenements in the said city beyond the gift and assignment aforesaid, which are sufficient to do all the services above mentioned.

XLIV. WILLIAM HAWYS *for* THE MASTER AND BRETHREN OF ST. LEONARD'S HOSPITAL, YORK. *Inq. ad q. d.*

[25 EDW. I. No. 94.]

Writ directed to the Sheriff, and dated at Westminster, 5 July, 25th year (1297).

INQUISITION taken before the Sheriff on Thursday after the feast of St. Everilda the Virgin, 25 Edw. (11 July, 1297), by William Sleht, Walter de Thorneton, Gaudin *le Orfeuer*, Roger de Schirburne, Adam de Hoperton, Robert *le Surrays*, Thomas Grunt, Richard de Bilburg', Roger de Bichehill, Walter *le Nayler*, Thomas de Rikehale, and Thomas de Tollerton, whether or not it be to the damage or prejudice of the King, or of others, if the King grant to William Hawys of York that he may give and assign to the Master and Brethren of St. Leonard's Hospital, York, 2s. 6d. annual rent in York, viz. in the street of Mikelgate near Use bridge, to have and to hold to them and to their successors for ever, so that they may give and assign to the Prior and Brethren of the Order of Preachers, York, 2s. 2d. rent in North stret, which they have been wont to receive from lands and tenements which were formerly of Henry de Sarazyn, to have and to hold to the Prior and Brethren of the said Order and their successors dwelling there for ever. They say on their oath that it is not to the damage or prejudice of the King if such grant be made. Those rents are not charged with any services, because the tenements out of which they issue are held of the King by the service of 2*d.* yearly for housegabel. William Hawys has sufficient lands and tenements remaining beyond the gift and assignment aforesaid to do all services.

XLV. WALTER LE BUTILLER (BOTELER). *Of a corrody held by him.*

[25 EDW. I. No. 63.]

Writ directed to the Sheriff of Yorkshire, requiring him to certify what rent or portion in the church of St. John, Beverley, Walter *le Butiller* had on the day of his death, what was its value, and whether he had such rent or portion by gift of John, late Archbishop of York, or his predecessors, or of Peter of Chester, late Provost of Beverley. Dated at Plympton, 6 May, 25th year (1297).

INQUISITION upon the corrody which Walter *le Boteler* had in the Bedern of Beverley, made by Laurence de Nafferton, Richard Lourance, Robert de Seton, Robert de Fosteton, Alan Mannynge, William de Barton, Stephen de Skyren, William son of Simon, John Aylewarde, John de Thoren, and Simon de Appelby, who say by their oath that the said Walter had the corrody by gift of John, late Archbishop for his (the Archbishop's) life, and not by gift of Peter of Chester, sometime Provost. He had that corrody as Canon of the church of Beverley, and the said portion is worth by the year ten marcs. Dated at Beverley on Friday after the feast of Holy Trinity, 25th year (14 June, 1297).

XLVI. DIONISIA WIDOW OF REMIGIUS DE POKELINGTON. *Inq. p. m.*

[25 EDW. I. No. 24.]

Writ[a] directed to John de Lythegreyns, Escheator beyond Trent, and dated at Clyst Episcopi, 12 May, 25th year (1297).

INQUISITION taken before John de Lydegraynes at Uluisthorp[b] near Pokelington on Friday before Whit-Sunday, 25 Edw. (31 May, 1297), by Nicholas de Clyf, Nicholas de Hothum, Hugh de Linton, James de Millington, Ralph Doway, Adam de Esthorp, Hugh de Colevyle, Henry de Herlethorp, Martin Mauleverer, Elias de Japum, John son of Dionisia, Robert Rouland, Ralph de Frenes, and Robert Dolman. Dionisia, who was wife of Remigius de Poke-

[a] Received 20 May, by a note on the dorse of writ. By another also there W. de Shireburne is named as "sub-escheator."

[b] Owsthorpe, Pocklington parish.

lington, on the day of her death held nothing of the King in chief, but she held of the heir of Isabel de Fortibus, formerly Countess of Albemarle, having been enfeoffed together with her husband by charters of the Countess granted to them and the heirs of Remigius. So she held 20 bovates of land in Pokelington, each bovate with meadow and appurtenances, worth by the year 10s.; a watermill, worth 40s. a year; the services of tenants of 21 bovates of land there (the service of each bovate worth 2s. 6d.); and rents of two cottars, yearly 2s.; and free courts every three weeks, worth by the year half a marc. She held also by the beforesaid charters in Meltonby four bovates of land, at half a marc each. And so the sum is £16 7s. 10d. in all issues by the year.

The said Dionisia held all the said tenements of the heir of the before named Countess by the yearly service of 3s. 6d. Roger, her son, is next heir of Remigius and of her, aged forty years and more [a]

XLVII.   ROBERT LUTEREL, *or* LUTERELL.   *Inq. p. m.*

[25 Edw. I.   No. 35.]

Writ[b] directed to John de Lythegreyns, Escheator beyond Trent, and dated at Westminster, 18 June, 25th year (1297).

INQUISITION taken at Hotunpaynul[c] on Saturday after the feast of the Translation of St. Thomas the Martyr, 25 Edw. (13 July, 1297), by Sir Peter de Rothyrfelde, knight, John Haringel, Michael de Bilham, Thomas Doyly, Jolan de Neuton, Peter *de Rodis*, Roger de Watton, Thomas de Barevile, William Paynel, John de Treton, ... de Hoton, and Adam Acharde, who say on their oath that Sir Robert

---

[a] On 4 Aug., 1294, the Sheriff of Yorkshire was ordered to restore to Roger, son and heir of Remigius de Pokelington, until the next Parliament, sixteen bovates of land, one mill, and fourteen marcs rent with appurtenances in Pokelington, which Remigius de Pokelington and Dionisia his wife held of the gift and grant of Isabella de Fortibus, late Countess of Albemarle, and which by the precept of Hugh de Cressingham and his fellows, Justices Itinerant in the said county, he took into the King's hand, and ejected the said Roger therefrom, as they belonged to the King as his escheat, together with the issues taken therefrom, from the time of taking the same into the King's hand, so as he shall answer to the King for the said issues, if he shall wish to have them (*Rot. Fin.*, 22 Edw. I., m. 7). May 12, 1297. Clyst St. Mary. Escheator ordered to seize the lands of Dionisia, widow of Remigius de Pokelington, and on 17 June following the fealty of Roger, her son and heir, was taken at Westminster (*Ibid.*, 25 Edw. I., mm. 10, 14).

[b] Note on the back that the writ was received 26 June.

[c] Hooton Paynel.

Luterell held his manor of Hotunpaynell of the King, and nothing of others, doing to the King homage and service for four knights' fees[a] for forty days at his own costs, or by four men with horses and arms. The manor [*for* capital messuage] with garden is worth by the year half a marc. There are in demesne 200 acres of land (at 4*d.*), £4; 10 acres of meadow (at 2*s.* 6*d.*), 25*s.*; and 20 acres of pasture (at 6*d.*), 10*s.*; a windmill, two marcs; rents of free tenants yearly, £8 3*s.* 8*d.*; rent of assize from bondmen, £4 16*s.*; rent of assize from cottars, 18*s.*; perquisites of Courts, 6*s.* 8*d.*

Geoffrey Luterell is son and heir of the said Sir Robert Luterell, and he was aged twenty-one years on the eve of Whit-Sunday, in the 25th year of the King's reign (2 June, 1297).[b]

XLVIII.   GEOFFREY SON AND HEIR OF ROBERT LUTEREL.
Proof of age.
[Curia Regis.   No. 152, m. 12.][c]

LINCOLNSHIRE. Reciting that inasmuch as Geoffrey, son and heir of Robert Luterel, deceased, who held of the King in chief, said that he was of full age, and prayed to have restored to him by the King the lands and tenements which are of his inheritance and in the King's custody up to the lawful age of the same Geoffrey, wherefore the King granted a day to the same Geoffrey, who was born at Irneham in the same county, and baptized in the church of the same vill, as it is said, for proving his age before the King on this day, namely from St. Michael's day (29 Sept., 1297) for one month, wherever, etc.; the Sheriff was ordered to cause so many and such lawful men, etc., to come before the King on the said day, by whom the said proof can be taken and the truth of the age of the said Geoffrey better known and inquired, and to make known to the King's clerk, Malculm de Harleye, Escheator this side Trent, that

---

[a] Here follow the words (as it seems, for they are indistinct) "in Wallia" or "in Gallia."

[b] A writ directed to Malculm de Harleye, Escheator *citra Trentam*, and of the same date (18 June, 1297). Two inquisitions follow, taken in cos. Lincoln and Nottingham. The latter makes the heir 21 years of age at the feast of Whit-Sunday instead of the eve, as found by the former.

[c] The roll for Michaelmas Term, 25 and 26 Edw. I. (1297). Geoffrey, son and heir of Robert Luterel, was 21 years old on the eve of Whit-Sunday, 25 Edw. I. (1 June, 1297), so he was born on the eve of the same feast, 4 Edw. I. (23 May, 1276). He was born at Irnham, near Grantham, in Lincolnshire, and baptized the day after his birth in the parish church there by a Canon. Only one godfather is mentioned, Geoffrey de Burton of Stallingburgh.

he should be before the King on the said day to show if
he had anything on the King's behalf, or knew anything
to say, why the King ought not to restore his inheritance
to the said Geoffrey, as to him who is of full age, if he
should be of full age.

The said Malculm did not come, and the Sheriff returned
that he had made him know by Roger de Ingoldeby and
Simon *le Clerk* of Ingoldeby.   And the said Geoffrey comes,
and likewise the jurors.   And the said Geoffrey says he is
full age, and prays that they proceed to take the proof of
his age.   And as the said Malculm[a] was sufficiently warned
and does not come, as appears by the return of the said
writ, and there is no hindrance to safely proceeding to take
the proof of age, therefore let the said proof be taken.

William de Coleville of Swynestede, 50, distant from
Irenham a league and a half, sworn and carefully examined
about the age, place of baptism and birth of Geoffrey son
of Robert Luterel, says on his oath that the same Geoffrey
was of the age of twenty-one years on the eve of Whit-
Sunday last past (1 June, 1297).   Asked how he knows this,
says he has a son, John by name, who was born three days
before the said heir, and was twenty-one years old four days
before Whit-Sunday last past.   Asked where he was born
and in what church baptized, says that he was born at
Irenham, and baptized in the church of the same vill,
namely on Whit-Sunday, and one godfather was Geoffrey
de Burton.   Of the other godfather and of the godmother
he knows nothing.   Of the other circumstances he is sure
by the talk of the country (*per dictum patrie*).

Roger Arnalde of Swafelde, 30, distant from Irenham
two leagues, sworn, &c., agrees with the one sworn before.
Asked how he knows this, says that one Simon de Corby,
his relative, had a son, John by name, who was born on
Wednesday in Whit-week last past (*sic*), and was twenty-
one years of age on Wednesday after Whit-Sunday last past
(5 June), and who after his father's death was in the custody
of Sir Gilbert Peche, his lord, by reason of his minority,
up to the quinzaine of St. Michael last past (13 Oct.), when
it was proved by inquisition in the great court of Corby,
that the same John was of full age, and in consequence of
this inquisition his lands and tenements were delivered up
to him.   Of the other circumstances he is sure by the talk
of the country.

Nicholas de Burton of Stanforde, 40, distant from Irenham
nine leagues, sworn, etc.   Asked how he knows this, says

---

[a] *Geoffrey.*

that he at that time was in the service of Master Robert Luterel (*stetit cum magistro Roberto Luterel*), who was then and is still rector of the church of Irenham. And he says that a certain Canon baptized the said boy. And he says that one Geoffrey, brother of the same Nicholas, gave him his baptismal name (*imposuit ei nomen baptismatis*), and that he was then present. And he says that he was in the said parson's service for twenty-two years, and that the said heir was born in the second year after he was in that service. Of the other circumstances he is sure by the talk of the country.

Geoffrey de Burton of Brassingburgh, 40, distant two leagues from Irenham, sworn, etc. Asked how he knows this, says that he was his godfather and gave him his name (*inposuit ei nomen*), and that at that time he was in the service of the father of the lady who was mother of the said heir. He says also that at the feast of the Purification of the Blessed Mary (2 Feb., 1276-7) next after the birth of the said heir he married, and that from the time of his marriage twenty-one years will have elapsed at the feast of the Purification of the Blessed Mary next coming. Of the other circumstances he is sure by report of the country (*per relatum patrie*).

Thomas Russelle of Hellewelle, 50, distant from Irenham three leagues, sworn, &c. Asked how he knows this, says he has a son, Roger by name, born on Friday, that is Good Friday[a] (3 April, 1276), before the birth of the said heir, and he says that Roger his son was twenty-one on Good Friday last past (12 April, 1297). He says also that he himself was present with the said heir's father on Whit-Sunday, when the same heir was born on the eve of Whit-Sunday. Of the other circumstances he is sure by the report of the country.

Ranulph Walshe of Careby, 40, distant from Irenham five leagues, sworn, etc. Asked how he knows this, says that at that time he was with Ralph St. Lo (*de Sancto Laudo*), and that this Ralph's wife came on Whit-Sunday, the morrow of the birth of the said heir, to talk with the said heir's mother whilst lying in childbed (*puerperio*), and that he himself was the esquire of the said lady, and then saw the said heir baptized in the church of Irenham the same day. Of the other circumstances he is sure by report of the country.

Hugh Dyne of Swafelde, 37, distant from Irenham one league, sworn, etc. Asked how he knows this, says that he

---

[a] Die Veneris, scilicet Parascevis.

has a sister, Isabella by name, who was born on the day of St. Mark the Evangelist (25 April) next before the said heir, and who was twenty-one years on the day of St. Mark the Evangelist last past. He says also that his mother went to the mother of the said heir when she was lying in child-bed, and when she returned she at once informed him about the birth of the said heir. Of the other circumstances he is sure by the talk of the country.

Peter at the church (*ad ecclesiam*) of Suafeld, 50 and more, distant from Irenham one league, sworn, etc. Asked how he knows this, says that at that time he had been in the service of the said heir's father for a long time before, and was his mower (*messor*), and says that he married at the feast of St. Michael (29 Sept.) next after the birth of the said heir, and that from that time twenty-one years have elapsed at the feast of St. Michael last past. Of the other circumstances he is sure by the talk of the country.

Robert on the hill (*super montem*) of Langeton, 40 and more, distant from Irenham a league and a half, sworn, etc. Asked how he knows this, says that he married at Christmas next after the birth of the said heir, and he says that from that time will be twenty-one years at Christmas next. He says, moreover, that he has a son, John by name, born two years after he married his wife, which John will be nineteen at Christmas next. Of the other circumstances, etc.

John Nichard of Eston, 36, distant from Irenham three leagues, sworn, etc. Asked how he knows this, says that his father gave him some land in Eston at Easter (5 April, 1276) next before the birth of the said heir, and that he then went to the father of the said heir, to satisfy him for having entry on the said land since it was held of him; and he says that from that time twenty-two years will have elapsed at Easter next. He says also that he has an after-born brother, Thomas by name, fourteen years younger than himself, and he is sixteen, and was born five years after the birth of the said heir. Of the other circumstances, etc.

Roger Westiby, 50, distant from Irenham two leagues, sworn, etc. Asked how he knows this, says that he was at one time clerk of Thomas *le Taillur*, the bailiff of that district (*patrie*), whose daughter he married, and he says that that bailiff went to the house of the said heir's father one time in winter, and he with him, and he then saw the said heir lying in a cradle, and that twenty-one years have elapsed since that time. Of the other circumstances he is sure by report of the country.

Henry de Blida of Bitham Castle (Chastel Bitham), 50, distant from Irenham three leagues, sworn, etc. Asked how he knows this, says that at the feast of Whit-Sunday, on the morrow of the birth of the same heir, he came to Irenham, to the bailiff of the said heir's father, to receive a certain sum of money by the father's order, for a bovate of land he had demised to the father for a term of eighteen years, and he says that that term was past (*transiit*) on Whit-Sunday three years ago, in consequence of which that land came into his hands. And he says that on the same day he saw the mother lying in childbed and the said heir at the church to be baptized. Of the other circumstances he is sure by report of the country.

And as the said heir has sufficiently proved his age before the lord King, and it is also clear by the appearance of the body of the same Geoffrey that he is of full age, namely twenty-one years, therefore let the said Geoffrey have seisin of the lands and tenements falling to him from his inheritance; and this record is sent to the Chancellor.

XLVIII*a*.   ROBERT DE BOULTON.   *Extent of lands.*

[Escheator's Inquisitions ultra Trentam.   Ex. Q. R.   Series I.   File 49.]
[m. 1]
    Writ of *certiorari*, dated at Westminster, 10 July, 25th year (1297), and directed to John de Litegreyns.[a]
[m. 2]

EXTENT of lands and tenements in the vill of Hoton Colswayn, held in chief by Robert de Boulton, and alienated by him to Thomas de Boulton, made before John de Lythergraynes, the Escheator, at Malton, on Sunday after the feast of St. James the Apostle, 25 Edward (21 July, 1297), by Walter Russell, William Russell, Walter Isaak, Elyas son of Ralph of Scowesby, Robert son of Nicholas of Hoton, Thomas de Barneby of Flaxton, Richard Freman of Barton, Richard Upiby of Malton, Geoffrey Wiggeman of Malton, John de Ebor of the same, Geoffrey de How of the same, and Geoffrey of the Brewhouse (*de bracyna*) of the same, who say that the chief messuage with a toft called Gaytescowe is worth 10*s.* a year. There are thirteen bovates of land at 40*d.* a bovate; free tenants, of whom Thomas *le Latimer* renders 20*s.* a year, Alan de Kirkam half a marc, the Prior of Malton one marc, Walter Russell 40*s.*; five

---

[a] *Dorso.*   Writ received 22 July.

cottars, each paying 20*d.* a year; an acre of meadow, worth
. . . . . . Sum of the extent, £5 6s. 6d.[a]

XLIX.   THE WARDEN AND FRIARS MINORS OF
SCARBOROUGH.   *Inq. ad q. d.*

[25 EDW. I.   No. 87.]

Writ directed to the Sheriff of Yorkshire, and dated at Westminster,
13 July, 25th year (1297).

INQUISITION, whether it be to the damage or prejudice of
the King, or of others, if he grant to the Warden and
Brethren of the Order of the Friars Minors of Scardeburch'
one hundred and seventeen feet of land in length and
fourscore feet in width in Scardebur', for the enlargement
of their church, made on Monday after the feast of St. James
the Apostle, 25 Edw. (29 July, 1297), at Scardebur', by Robert
Hamund, Robert at the Cross (*ad crucem*), Robert de
Norfolke, Ralph Gege, Henry de Brumpton, John Hamund,
Ralph Tailor (*cissorem*), John Husset, Robert son of Nel,
Simon Sage, John Halden, and Robert Coroner (*coronator'*),
who say by their oath that it is to the damage of the
King if he give to the said Warden and Brethren this
land, for it is worth 10s. a year.   If it be to the damage
of others, they know not.   As to how and for what cause
the land was taken, they say that one Adam Gumer,[b] to
whom the land belonged, having been pursued with hue and
cry from the town of Danby to York, was beheaded at
Danby, with two other malefactors; and for this cause, and
no other, the Bailiffs of Scardeburge took the land into the
King's hand.[c]

[a] *Dorso.*   "Finem fecit in memorandis termini Trinitatis hoc anno." The
sum of extent is wrong.   Without the rent of the acre of meadow the items
amount to £7 1s. 8d.

[b] "Dicunt quod quidam Adam Gumer cui dicta terra erat decapitatus fuit apud
Danby cum aliis duobus iniquis et cum utasio levato prosecutus a villa de Danby
usque ad Ebor.   Et ea de causa Ballivi de Scardeburg' ceperunt dictam terram in
manum domini Regis et non alia."

[c] *On the dorse of the inquisition is a memorandum to this effect:*—That John
de Picheforde of Scardeburgh', for himself and the commonalty of the town, came
into the King's chancery before the Chancellor, and Simon Gumer for himself;
and they prayed that the petition of those friars should not be granted, because if
it were that grant would be in prejudice and disherison; that is to say, to the
prejudice of the burgesses because the King's highway (*regia strata*) lies between
their close and the said house; and Simon says that that house is his right and
inheritance, whereof he obtained the King's writ of *mort d'ancestre* through the
death of his brother.

L. HENRY ELECT OF YORK.[a] *Of malefactors breaking into his park at Sherburn.*

[25 EDW. I. No. 118.]

Writ directed to the Sheriff, and dated at Odymer (Udimore, co. Sussex), 13 Aug., 25th year (1297).

JOHN DE LASCY, Robert de Pavely, Warin de Fenton, Richard Derling, Robert *de Camera* of Fenton, William *de Camera* of Milforth, William beyond the acre (*ultra acram*) of the same, Thomas at the Hallgate (*ad portam aule*) of Schirburne, John Broun of Barkestone, Richard de Sutton in the same, Thomas de Moldcroft in Fenton, and William Norris in Cawude, before the Sheriff of Yorkshire at Schirburne, by the King's command charged and sworn to inquire concerning the names of malefactors who entered the park of the venerable father, lord Henry Elect of York, at Schirburne, against the King's peace, and there, without licence, chased and by force and arms took wild animals (*feras*) and carried them off, and other wrongs to the same Elect did to his grievous damage. They say that Thomas son of William of Alverton called Page, Richard brother of the said Thomas, and William *le Smale* in Thornore are guilty, and did these things, together with many others unknown. Dated at Schirburne on the morrow of the Beheading of St. John the Baptist, in the 25th year of the King's reign (30 Aug., 1297).

LI. PHILIP LE LOU AND MARGERY HIS WIFE.

[25 EDW. I. No. 97.]

Writ directed to John de Lythegreyns, Escheator beyond Trent, and tested by Edward, the King's son, at Tunebrugge, 29 Aug., 25th year (1297), requiring to be certified as to the manner and reason of his taking the lands and tenements of Philip *le Lou* and Margery, his wife, in Hundeburton.[b]

I SEIZED the lands and tenements of Philip *le Lou* and Margery his wife in Hundeburton, which are extended at £10 by the year, because Alan de Walkyngham formerly (*dudum*) held them by the King's gift (as I understood); and I knew not, and could not then know, how they came to the hands of the said Philip and Margery, or how they went out of the King's seisin. And afterwards, on Wednesday after the feast of St. Michael, in the 25th year of the reign (2 Oct., 1297), by my office, I inquired at Hundeburton,

---

[a] Archbishop Henry de Newark, elected 7 May, 1296, but not installed until 15 June, 1298. (Raines' *Fasti Ebor.*, i., 352.)

[b] Humberton, near Boroughbridge.

by the oath of Roger de Mildeby, Elias son of Robert of Melmorby, Elias son of Adam of the same, William son of Serlo of Mildeby, Thomas de Coleville of the same, John *le Jovene* of the same, Jerome de Langlingethorpe, Thomas Conynge of Hundeburton, Alan Casse of the same, Thomas de Knaresburgh in the same, Robert de Buskeby, and Nicholas son of Nicholas of Boroughbridge (*de Ponteburgi*), who say on their oath that one William de Arderne formerly held three carucates of land with appurtenances in Hundeburton, valued at £10 a year, of Roger de Moubray, by the service of doing suit at his Court of Treske every three weeks, and when scutage is at 40s., paying 10s.; when more, more; and when less, less. The said William died when Roger de Moubray, now living, was under age and in ward to the King and Roger Lestrange (*Extranei*), and after his death the King seized all the lands and tenements of which he was seised in fee within the realm of England by reason of Richard de Arderne, brother of William, being an idiot,[a] and he immediately committed them to the lady Eleanor (*Alianore*) his consort, to hold during his pleasure. The Queen speedily after this granted and committed these lands and tenements in Hundeburton to Alan de Walkyngham, to hold during her pleasure for £10 to be paid to her yearly. So he (Alan) held them during his life, and after his death the King again seized them. Hereupon Philip and Margery, together with John Pecche and John *le Lou* and Amice his wife, prayed the King for livery of the said lands and tenements, together with others which were the said William's, and also for livery of Richard the idiot, as next heirs of both William and Richard. The King and Queen commanded that seisin of the lands and tenements in Hundeburton should be delivered to the said Philip and Margery and the other parceners, and that other lands and tenements should be delivered into the bailiwick of the Escheatry beyond Trent towards the south by a composition made between the Queen and the said parceners, of which the jurors know nothing.

[a] See Vol. I., p. 172. 14 Feb., 1250-1. Grant of freewarren to Hugh de Arderne in his demesne lands of Hampton and la Cnolle in Warwickshire (*Charter Roll*, 35 Hen. III., m. 12). 16 June, 1285. Inspeximus and confirmation of a covenant made between the King and Eleanor, the Queen Consort, of the one part, and Sir John le Leu and Amicia, his wife, of the other part, dated at Overton, 27 Sept., 12 Edw. I. (1284), whereby the latter for £30 a year in land for their lives in the manor of Neuton Harecurtt, co. Leicester, quitclaim to the former the whole share which the said Amicia has or may have of the inheritance of Richard de Arderne in the manors of Hampton in Ardern, la Knolle, Wutton and Solihull, co. Warwick, and rents and other things in the said county, and in the manor of Bourton-upon-Swale (Humberton); and in all other things whatsoever of the said inheritance (*Calendar of Patent Rolls*, 1281-1292, p. 174).

Asked if William de Arderne held anything of the King in chief, they say that neither he nor his brother Richard held anything; but, whatever they had, they held of the beforesaid Roger de Moubray (as they understand).

Asked what age Richard de Arderne was when the King seized the lands, and when he died, they say that he was thirty years old when the seizure was made, and that he died long before the decease of Alan de Walkyngham.

Asked if the King seized the lands and tenements for any other reason, or by any competent right other than the said idiotcy, they say for no other reason but that, and because Roger de Moubray, of whom they were held, was then under age.

LII. JOHN DE LONGVILERS.[a] *Inq. p. m.*

[25 EDW. I. No. 52.]

Writ dated at . . . ., 6 Oct., 25th year (1297).

STAYNCLYF. Inquisition made before John de Lithegraynes, Escheator beyond Trent, at Skypton in Craven, on the morrow of St. Clement, [Martyr] and Pope,[b] namely on Sunday, 26 Edw. (24 Nov., 1297), by John de Kyghelay, Henry Hall (*de aula*), Henry Croc . . . ., Alexander de Estebourne, William de Chefeld, Robert Bouch, Robert son of Geoffrey, Richard de Bradelay, John Broun, Adam son of William of Brockton, Thomas Revel, Robert Forbrase of Gayrgrave, of the lands and tenements which were John de Lungvilers, who died lately. He held in chief on the day he died the manor of Tokesford in the county of Nottingham,[c] but the jurors were entirely ignorant of its value. The same John held the manor of Glosbourune (*sic*)[d] in the county of York of Sir Robert de Styveton by homage, ward and relief, and foreign service. Of which manor with its appurtenances the lady Margaret de Nevyle[e] is fully dowered of the third part. There is a capital messuage there worth 2s. a year. In demesne 8 acres of arable land, each worth

---

[a] Son of William de Longvilers, brother of John de Longvilers, whose *Inq. p. m.* is given in Vol. I., 40.

[b] The feast of St. Clement, the pope and martyr, was celebrated either on Nov. 17 or Nov. 23. The specification that the morrow of the feast in the year 1297 fell on a Sunday, proves that the latter is the day intended. The addition of the day of week perhaps shows that there was some uncertainty in the scribe's mind as to when the feast ought to be observed.

[c] Tuxford.

[d] Glusburn.

[e] His first cousin and widow of Geoffrey de Neville.

5

8*d*. a year. Besides these there are in demesne 2½ acres of arable land, each acre worth 9*d*. a year. Nine bovates and two parts of half a bovate of land, each bovate worth 3*s*. 6*d*. a year. Five cottages, each worth 18*d*. a year. A share in a watermill, worth 13*s*. 4*d*. Sum, 62*s*. 8½*d*. *Free tenants*. Sir John Dawtrey (*de Alta ripa*) held a piece of land, for which he paid yearly 7½*d*. for all services. Robert son of Davit (*sic*) held two parts of two bovates of land by homage, ward and relief, and foreign service, and paying 16*d*. a year. Walter son of Elyas held a toft with a croft, paying 8*d*. a year. Adam Pedefer held two parts of two bovates of land by homage, ward, relief and foreign service, and paying 3*d*. a year. Robert son of David and Robert son of Walter held two parts of two bovates of land by homage, relief, and foreign service, and paying 3*d*. a year. Sum, 3*s*. 1½*d*. Sum of sums of the whole extent which he had on the day of his death in his hand, 65*s*. 10*d*. Thomas, brother of the said John, is his nearest heir. On Thursday, on the feast of the Absolution,[a] 25 Edward, was the same Thomas de . . . .

[*Dorse*] Licence granted to the wife of John de Lungvilers that she marry for a fine of 16*li*., and let it be enrolled in Chancery.[b]

<hr />

LIII. ROBERT DE TATESHALE. *Inq. p. m.*

[26 EDW. I. No. 40.]

[m. 7]
Writ dated at Carlisle, 9 Sept., 25th year (1297).[c]

[m. 2]
INQUISITION taken before Sir John de Lythegrayns, Escheator, at Hundemanby, on Wednesday next after the octave of St. Michael, 26th year (8 Oct., 1298), by Roger Spenser (*dispensatorem*), Aco de Flixton, Ralph de Foxholt', Ralph Bekard, Richard Wylez, William Faucuner, Roger de Lascy, Robert son of Walter, Anselm Dreng', William .

---

[a] *Absolutionis Dies*, or *Dies Jovis absoluti*, or *Le Jeudi absolu*, corresponds to Maunday Thursday, that is the Thursday before Good Friday. From the Notts. inquisition, which was taken at Tuxford, on Monday after the feast of St. Luke the Evangelist, 25 Edw. I. (21 Oct., 1297), before the same Escheator, it appears that Thomas, the brother of John de Longevilers, would be nineteen years of age on the feast of St. Ambrose the Bishop then next, that is 4 April, 1298. This does not quite agree with the finding of the Yorkshire jury, as Maunday Thursday in 1297 would fall on April 11, and in the year following on April 3. April 11 is the correct date as shown by the proof of age of Thomas de Longvilers (see No. LXXXIIa).

[b] Notts. *No day*. Alesia, widow of John de Lungvilers, deceased, tenant-in-chief, paid a fine of 16*li*. for licence to marry (*Rot. Fin.*, 33 Edw. I., m. 12).

[c] Writ to the Escheator *ultra* same date (m. 1).

Clerk of Hundemanby, John son of Laurence, and Richard de Thirnom. Robert de Tatessale the elder held in chief the manor of Hundemanby in barony, by doing suit at all the county courts of Yorkshire (*ad omnes comitatus Ebor.*) during the year, and at the riding court (*thriyingiam*) of Kraychou once a year next after the nearest county court for Yorkshire, and at the wapentake court of Rudestan next after the said riding court once a year. Capital messuage, worth 8*s.* a year. Twenty bovates of land in the demesne cultures, at 7*s.* a bovate. Forty-six acres one rood of meadow, at 2*s.* an acre. Several (*separales*) pastures, . . . *s.* 6*d.* Agistment in the common pasture, 6*s.* 8*d.* A stew (*stangnum*), 6*s.* 8*d.* In bondage, 25 bovates of land, with 25 tofts, each bovate with toft, 7*s.* Eight bovates of land, let to farm at will, 7*s.* a bovate. Thirty-five cottages, 4*li.* 5*s.* Market toll, 6*li.* 13*s.* 4*d.* Toll at Fivele, 13*s.* 4*d.* Windmill, 40*s.* Pleas and perquisites of court, 60*s.*

FREE TENANTS (*libere tenentes*). Adam de Gant', 13 tofts and ⸱ 30½ bovates of land, 10*li.* Walter de Buketon, one bovate of land, 6*d.*, one toft, 3*s.* Robert de Bovincton, one carucate of land . . . . and homage and foreign service. John de Marton, two carucates of land, 5*s.* 4*d.*, homage and foreign service. Andrew de Grimston, two bovates, 2*s.* 6*d.* Thomas de Cottegrave, two bovates, 2*s.* 6*d.* William Faucuner, half a carucate, 5*s.* William son of Roger, a toft, 4*s.* John Huning, a toft and bovate of land, 20*d.* Robert Thirning, a bovate, 12*d.* Thomas Baker (*pistor*), a toft, 2*s.* Richard de Weston, a bovate, 12*d.* Hugo Thorald, four bovates, 2*s.* 6*d.* Adam Cobbler (*sutor*), a toft, 2*s.* 8*d.* John Cant, a toft, 2*s.* 6*d.* John Birle (?), a toft, 12*d.* William son of John, four tofts, 4*s.* Stephen Tailor (*cissor*), a toft, 2*s.* John de M . . . . ton, a toft, 3*d.* William Carpenter (*carpentarius*), a toft, 2*s.* 8*d.* William Proctor (*procurator*), ... acres of land, 1*d.* Thomas de Gemeling, ... ½*d.* Walter Tailor (*cissor*), a toft and two acres of land, 4*d.* William Her . . . . , a plot of land, 1*d.* The heir of Gilbert de . . . . , 2 acres of land, ½*d.* Simon . . . . god, a toft and bovate of land, 4*s.* Walter de Louthorp, a toft and . . . . bovates of land, 4*d.*

The value of the manor in all issues, 55*li.* 5*s.* 6*d.* He held no other lands in the East Riding (*Estthiyingtt'*).

Robert de Tatessalle, son of the said Robert, is his nearest heir, and is of the age of thirty years and upwards.[a]

---

[a] The finding of the Lincolnshire jury (m. 4) agrees as to age. This inquisition was taken at Tatteshale on 28 Sept. Robert de Tatteshale the elder held the castle of Tatteshale with the manor of Candelesby and Boston (*Sancti Botulphi*) in chief by barony.

[m. 3]

INQUISITION made before John de Lythegreyns, Escheator, at Welle, on Friday next after the feast of St. Michael, 26th year (3 Oct., 1298), of the lands of Robert de Tateshale in the manors of Welle and Crakehale, by Wimer de Crakehale, William de Sutton, (Hugh) de Stayneley, Richard de Crakehale, Peter de Tyndale, Roger Oysel, knights; Richard son of Geoffrey of Synigethwayt, Nigel son of Conan of the same, Thomas de Witton, clerk, and Thomas son of Hugelina of the same; and afterwards at Thoraldeby on Sunday next following, about the lands and tenements of the said Robert, deceased, in the manors of Welle, Witton and Thoraldeby, by the same jurors.

As to the manors of Welle, Crakehale and Thoraldeby, Robert held nothing in them except by reason of Joan, daughter of Ralph son of Ranulph,* his wife, who held them as her property of the inheritance, which descended to her by hereditary right after Ralph's death, and which were assigned to her as one of the daughters and heirs of the same Ralph. Robert and Joan his wife, who is still surviving, held the manors in the aforesaid form of John of Britany, as of the honour of his castle of Richemond, by service of 45s. a year, and by doing suit at the same John's court of Richemond every three weeks, and by paying to the scutage when it happens, 7li., when the fee (scutum) is 40s.; and when more, more, and when less, less, for all service.

Capital messuage in the manor of Welle extended at nothing, as there is in the said messuage no orchard, dovecote, herbage or any certain profit, which may be taken yearly, except only the easements of the houses. There are about 200 acres of arable land by the greater hundred (per majus centum) of the demesnes, at 6d. an acre; 43 acres of meadow of the demesnes, at 2s. an acre; about 200 acres of wood in severalty, called Chauncewith, the herbage of which, with the sheepfold (bercaria) in the same wood, 60s. Sum of demesne lands, meadows, and woods, 12li. 6s.

In the same manor 31 acres of land, held in bondage (in bondagio), worth by the year, with the customs of the bonders (bondorum), who now hold them, 9s. a bovate. Sum of the bondage land (bondagii), 13li. 19s.

Twenty-five cottages, for which the cottars (cottarii), who hold them, yield for the same cottages and other small holdings, 50s. Sum, 50s.

---

* Ralph's other daughter and heiress, Mary of Middleham, married Robert de Neville (Vol. I., 113).

Two watermills, 7*li.*; out of which they yield to the heirs of Gilbert de Clifton 6*li.* Sum of the mills clear, 20*s.*

Pannage of the woods of Welle, 20*s.* one year, and another a marc, and another less, and another nothing, as in the present year, when all the pannage has failed (*deficit*).

Advowson of the church, of which John de Metingham is now the parson, 50 marcs.

In Nosterfelde, which is member of the manor of Welle, are two carucates of land, worth 40*s.*

Fines and perquisites of the court of Welle, 20*s.*

Sum of the sums of the manor of Welle with Nosterfelde, 33*li.* 15*s.*

Manor of Crakehale.

A capital messuage, 40*d.* In demesne about six score acres of arable land, at 8*d.* an acre ; 24 acres of meadow, at 2*s.* Sum of the demesnes of land and meadow (*de dominicis terre et prati*), 6*li.* 8*s.* Eighteen bovates of land held in bondage, at 9*s.* Sum, 8*li.* 2*s.* Twelve cottages, 24*s.* Two watermills, one for grinding corn and one for fulling, 6*li.* Sum of sums, 21*li.* 17*s.* 4*d.*

Hugh de Swyllingeton holds in Thorpe Pirrow freely (*libere*) three carucates of land, and yields 4*s.* 6*d.*, and does suit at the lord's court. The heir of William de Lascels holds in Thexton and Arlaththorpe[a] freely five carucates, and yields 5*s.* 9*d.* . . . . hold in Yarnewyke three carucates of land, and yields with Roger de Ingoldeby, who holds a carucate of land in the same, 3*s.* 5*d.* Ralph de Richem(ond) holds freely in Gaytenby a carucate of land, and ·yields 21½*d.* Wymer de Crakehale holds freely in Crakehale a carucate of land of the lord, and yields 22*d.* John Tortmayn holds freely in Neuton[b] three and a half carucates of land, and yields 4*s.* 8*d.* Roger de Aske holds freely in Gaytenby a carucate of land, and yields 21½*d.* The heir of Stephen Maulovel holds freely in the same two carucates of land, and yields 20½*d.* . . . . de Clifton holds three carucates of land in Clifton, and yields 3*s.* 6*d.* Simon de Stutteville, for twelve carucates of land in Watlous and Haukeswell, yields one marc. Peter de Thoresby yields, for half a knight's fee, 7*s.* Sum of the rent of free tenants, 49*s.* 4*d.*, of which the lord yields to Sir John of Britany 45*s.*, and to Robert de Musters 4*s.*, and so clear sum from free tenants, 4*s.*[c]

[a] Theakston and Allerthorpe, both Burneston parish.

[b] Newton-le-Willows.

[c] This sum should be 4*d.*

Fines and perquisites of either manor (*i.e.* Welle and Crakehale), 30*s.* Sum, 30*s.*, out of which 20*s.* from Welle.

Sum of the sums of Crakehale, 22*li.* 11*s.* 4*d.*

Manor of Thoraldeby.

Capital messuage worth nothing beyond the support of the houses. About four score acres of arable land in demesne, at 6*d.* . . . . at 2*s.* an acre. Herbage of the Hyghnyng', half a marc. Sum of the demesnes of lands, meadow, and herbage, 62*s.* 8*d.*

Two vaccaries, 100*s.* Two sheepfolds, 40*s.* Sheepfold by Swynewatheco . . . . , 20*s.* Sum of the vaccaries and sheepfolds, 8*li.*

In the same manor, in the vill of Thoraldeby, ten bonders (*bondi*) hold twenty bovates of land, and in the vill of Neubygging seven bonders hold 13 bovates of land, each bovate with bonder's works, 5*s.* In the vill of Burton seven bonders yield for the land they hold 4*li.* 6*s.* 8*d.* Sum of the bondage holding (*bondagii*), 12*li.* 11*s.* 8*d.*

In Thoraldeby 15 cottars yield, for their cottages and holdings, 26*s.* 3*d.*; and in Neubigging 17 cottars yield, for their cottages and holdings, 52*s.*; and in Burton 19 cottars yield, for their cottages and holdings, 66*s.* Sum of cottars, 7*li.* 4*s.* 3*d.*

A watermill in the vill of Thoraldeby, a third part of which pays to the lords of Thoraldeby 40*s.*; also a fulling mill, paying 26*s.* 8*d.* At Neubiging a mill, worth 26*s.* 8*d.* The third of the mill of Aykescharth[a] yields 13*s.* 4*d.* A third part of the mill of Thorneton Rust yields to the lord 8*s.*, and is worth so much (*et tantum valet*). Sum of mills, 114*s.* 8*d.*

Agistment in Bischip'dale, 10*s.*

Roger Oyselle holds freely a messuage and three bovates of land by service of doing suit . . . . belonging to so great a holding, when scutage is due (*pertinens ad tantum tenementum quando scutagium currit*). The same Roger holds four bovates of land at farm at the lord's will, and yields 20*s.* a year . . . . . . free tenants, yielding 6*s.* 8*d.* Fines and perquisites of court, one marc. Sum, 10*s.* 10*d.*

Sum of the sums of the manor of Thoraldeby, with its members, 39*li.* 7*s.* 3*d.*

The manors of Thoraldeby, Welle, and Crakehale are the right and inheritance of the said Joan, as is aforesaid.

John de Tateshale, son of the same Joan, is the nearest heir of the said Robert and the same Joan, and is of the age of 34 years and upwards.

---

[a] Aysgarth.

[m. 6]

INQUISITION and extent made before J. de Lythegreynes, Escheator, at Thoraldeby, on Sunday next after the feast of St. Michael the Archangel, 26th year (5 Oct., 1298), of the manor of West Wytton, which belonged to Robert de Tatersale, lately deceased, by the oaths of Wymer de Crakehale, William de Sutton, Robert de Sutton, Hugh de Staynley, Richard de Crakehale, Peter de (Tyn)edale, Roger Oysel, knight, Stephen de Burelle, Richard son of Geoffrey of Swyningthwait, Nigel son of Conan of the same, Thomas de Witton, and Thomas son of Hugelina of the same.

A capital messuage, with curtilage, 2s. In demesne eight score acres of arable land, at 6d. an acre. Five acres of meadow, 10s. A parcel of meadow in the common field (campo), containing about six acres, 6s. 8d. Twenty bovates of land in bondage, each bovate with works, worth 6s. 8d. Ten cottars yielding, for their cottages, 7s. 6d. An assart, 14d. . . . . 4s. A sheepfold, 20s. A park of wood (parcus bosci), containing about 60 acres, with pasture and herbage, 20s. Two watermills, 4li. Richard Oysel holds a messuage and 40 acres of arable land freely, and yields 3s. 6d. and a pound of cumin, price 1d. Imanya de Chamera holds freely a messuage and 30 acres of land, and yields 12s. Thomas son of Alexander (Allex') holds freely a messuage, with 16 acres of land, and yields 12d., and does suit of court. Thomas son of John holds freely a messuage, with three acres of land, and yields 2s. Walter Halpeny holds freely a messuage, and yields a pound of cumin, price 1d. Thomas de Swiningthwayt holds freely a messuage with 60 acres of land, and yields 10s., and does suit of court. John de Hyspannia holds freely a messuage with 66 acres of land, and yields 9s.[a] Geoffrey de Eston holds freely a messuage with 14 acres of land, and yields 4s.[a] Nigel Clerk holds freely a messuage with 14 acres of land, and yields 10d.[a] Nigel Conayn holds freely a messuage with 20 acres of land, and yields 6s. 6d.[a] Agnes de Barton holds freely a messuage and 7 acres of land, and yields 5s.[a] Roger Pillok holds freely a messuage with 6 acres of land, and yields 2s.[a] Richard son of Geoffrey holds freely a messuage with 14 acres of land, and yields 4s. 6d.[a] Adam Stampe holds freely a messuage with 4 acres of land, and yields 16d. Fines and perquisites of court, 10s. Sum, 22li. 7s. 3d., out of which the same Robert paid John of Britanny 6s. 4d., so there remains clear 22li. 11d.

All the aforesaid rents and farms are yielded at the terms of Whitsuntide and Martinmas.

[a] All these do suit of court.

Robert de Tatersale held the said manor of Wytton of John of Britanny (*Britannya*) as of the honour of the castle of Rich(emund) by the service of 6s. 4d., and doing suit at the court of the same John at Richemund every three weeks. The said Robert died seised of the said manor of Wytton in his demesne as of fee.

Robert de Tatersale, son of the said Robert, is the heir of the same Robert, and is of the age of 24 years and upwards.[a]

LIV. EDMUND, EARL OF LANCASTER.[b] *Inq. p. m.*

[25 EDW. I. No. 51a.]

Writ[c] directed to John de Lythegr[eynes], Escheator beyond Trent, requiring him to return the true value of knights' fees and advowsons of churches, which were of Edmund, the King's brother, and which had been taken into the King's hand by reason of his death. Tested by Edward, the King's son, at Westminster, 20 Oct., 25th year (1297). A writ of similar tenor directed to Malcolm de Harleye, Escheator *citra Trentam*, but dated at Westminster, 18 Oct., 1297. Several of the Extents in this file were taken at dates from 21 July to 31 Aug., 1297, but the writs are not now to be found. By later writs of 25 April, 1298, sundry persons were assigned to inquire into the value of all lands, tenements, knights' fees and advowsons of churches, which were held by Edmund, the King's brother, at the time of his death.

[a] On 21 Oct., 1298, the homage was taken at Durham of Robert de Tateshale, son and heir of Robert de Tateshale of the county of Lincoln, for his father's lands. Joan, the widow, was to have reasonable dower (*Rot. Fin.*, 26 Edw. L, m. 2). Robert the son's *diem clausit extremum* is dated at Stratheghyn, 28 Oct., 31 Edw. I. (1303). (*Ibid.*, 31 Edw. I., m. 6). The Escheator was ordered to assign dower to Eva, Robert's widow, on 1 Oct. in the same year, by a writ tested at Loghendorm. Nothing in Yorkshire (*Ibid.*, m. 3). In 1302 Robert de Tateshale presented a petition to the King, claiming the *serjauntie de la butelerie*, as of the inheritance of the Earl of Arundel, and which after the death of Hugh Daubeny descended to his four sisters. The petitioner's grandfather, Robert de Tateshale, was son of the eldest sister (*issit de eynesce soer*). (*Rotuli Parliamentorum*, i., 154.)

[b] Edmund, second son of Henry III., surnamed Crouchback, from his having gone to the Crusades with his brother Edward, born 16 Jan., 1245; died during the wars in Gascony, 1296, buried in Westminster Abbey, having married first, April, 1269, Avelina, daughter and heiress of William de Fortibus, Earl of Albemarle, who died without issue the same year. He married secondly Blanche, Dowager Queen of Navarre, and Countess Palatine of Champagne and Brie, daughter of Robert, Count of Artois, (brother of St. Louis, King of France), and had three sons and two daughters, the eldest of whom, Thomas, Earl of Lancaster, was beheaded at Pontefract in 1322 (*Foster's Peerage* (1881), p. lxxvii). On 20 March, 1296-7, the homage of Henry de Lancastre, son of Edmund of happy memory (*bone memorie*), late our brother, was taken at Wymburne Minstre for the castle, vill and honour of Monemuwe, the castles of Grosmont (*de Grosso monte*), Skenefrith and Whitecastle (*de Albo castro*), and the manors of Radeleye and Menstrewrthe, with all the lands and tenements he had beyond the Severn, saving the dower of Blanche, Edmund's widow (*Rot. Fin.*, 25 Edw. I., m. 16). On 18 April, 1298, the King at Fulham ordered Malculm de Harleye, Escheator this side Trent, to restore the Earldom of Ferrars, which had been given to the King, to Blanche, Queen of Navarre, widow of the King's brother Edmund (*Ibid.*, 26 Edw. I., m. 13).

[c] Note on the back that the writ was received 12 Nov., and the counties to it applies are set down here—Yorks., Notts., Derby, Lancaster and ⁿberland.

EXTENT of lands and tenements which the lord Edmund, brother of King Edward, held of the King in chief on the day of his death in the Wapentake of Pikeringe, Esingwold, and Scalleby, that is to say, how much they were worth in all issues yearly, made by William Malkake, Thomas de Edbriston, Robert de Wyerne, Robert *del Clife*, Peter de Neville, Adam *le Brus*, John son of Hugh, William son of Thomas, Roger de Wrelton, William Thornefe, Hugh Broun, and William *de la Chimene*, who say on their oath that at Pikeringe there is a ruined castle (*castrum debile*), which is of no profit by the year. In demesne of arable land are nine score 17 acres (at 8*d.*); in a demesne meadow, which is called Kingeshenge, 30 acres (at 18*d.*), and beside this there are 10 acres of meadow reserved for the keep of the bailiff's horses, which if put to farm would be worth 12*d.* the acre. There are also 30 acres in a meadow called Constabilhenge, at 12*d.*, and in a meadow called the Frith are 7 acres, at 6*d.* Sum, £10 17*s.* 10*d.* In Daleby is a meadow worth 20*s.* a year, and the agistment of Daleby, with the adjoining dales (*cum vallibus adjacentibus*), is worth 60*s.* The turbary of Watmor is worth in common years 5*s.* There is a park of Blaundebi, the agistment of which is worth by the year 100*s.*, and pasture . . . . . . with a portion of meadow, worth 40*s.* Two watermills there are worth £20. Also toll and market are worth 60*s.* Annual rent from four score and 7 bovates held of ancient bondage (*que tenentur de antiquo bondagio*), £6 3*s.* 6*d.* Works of the said bovates are worth yearly, with repair of the millponds, £4 4*s.* 6*d.* Rent of 14 cottages, 10*s.* 6*d.*, and their works, with repair of the said ponds, 11*s.* 1*d.* There are works, called *Lovebones*, yearly worth 6*d.* Also John Tr Robert and Roger *le Lunge de advocacione*, 4*d.* Rent of free burgages, worth 15*s.* 8*d.*; of lands set to rent at will, except Gothelaund, 33*s.*; of certain meadows and pastures set to rent at will in Gothelaund and Alaintoftes. From a watermill, £18 15*s.* 7¼*d.* From lands set to rent in the forest, 21*s.* 2¾*d.* Rent of sokemen, £41 13*s.* 9½*d.* Works of Midelton, called *Waterbones*, 3*s.* 4*d.*; rent of Barony, 61*s.* 2*d.*; rent of serjeanty, with 2*s.* from a forge in Levisham, £4 11*s.* 4*d.*, beside (*preter*) 63*s.* 4*d.* which the Earl Marshal used to yield for his bailiwick of Scaleby, of which they speak below. Also from fines of Barony, yearly 3*s.* 8*d.*; fines of socage, 40*s.* 3*d.*; works of palisade (*operibus hurcinii*)[a] every third year, 44*s.* 10½*d.*, so they are worth every year 14*s.* 11½*d.* Pleas and perquisites of the Wapentake, with reliefs, are worth £10; pleas and

[a] See Vol. I., pp. 216, 298.

perquisites of the bailiwick of Pikering, with reliefs, 40s.; pleas of attachment of the forest, with agistment of parks in the fence month (*mense velito*), £4 a year. Lawing of dogs (*expeditacio canum*) every third year is worth 40s., of which, by division in three parts, the value every year is 13s. 4d. The farm of Scaleby yearly, at Michaelmas term, £35; from four bovates, which were of Thomas de Flixton by escheat, and from six bovates of land in Scaleby, which the King recovered by writ of *Quo warento*, £4 7s. 1d.; the agistment of the Hay of Scaleby, £4. Sum, £185 4s. 10½d.

Sum total, £195 12s. 8½d. Of which, in decay of 12 acres of land in Gothelande, which Robert *le Ridere* and William Launcelevedy held, 9s.; from a plot (*placea*) of land near the Weyte house (*juxta dom' le Weyte*) in Pikering, 4d.; from Gotheland mill, 5s.; from 3 bovates of land in Scaleby, 10s.; from works of ponds, from reprises of the mill (*de operibus stagnorum, de reprisis molendin'*), 6s. 3d.; from the marsh of Folketon, 5s., because no distress is found. Sum of decay and reprise, 35s. 7d.

Also in wages of a bailiff by the year, for custody of the Castle, Wapentake, and Forest, £12; in support of a chaplain celebrating in the castle for the souls of the King's predecessors, 60s.; to one Sapiencia, nurse of the late lord Edmund, by his gift for term of her life, 20s.; in keeping up the houses and walls in the Castle, yearly 20s. Sum of the whole reprise, £18 15s. 7d.[a]

And besides, the forest-attachments in the bailiwick of Scaleby are worth yearly 20s.; the agistment of herbage of Langedon in the same bailiwick, 40s.; the agistment of Aleintoftes, 16s.; chiminage in the hay of Scalleby, with millstones, heath, except coarse grass, together with dried breckons (*bruera, exᵃ herba grossa, cum feugera marcessente*), 20s., all which appertained to the bailiwick of the Earl Marshal, which bailiwick was taken into the King's hand before the Justices of the forest last in eyre at Pikering, and yet remains in the King's hand, for which bailiwick the Earl Marshal used to yield to the lord by the year 63s. 4d. Sum, £180 0s. 5½d.

Also the manor (*manerium*) of Esingwald and Hoby[b] is worth yearly of assized rent, £41 14s. 5½d.; pleas and perquisites there, with reliefs, 40s. Sum, £43 14s. 5½d.

---

[a] Here the remainder has been written £176 17s. 1½d., but struck through with the pen.

[b] Huby.

[By endorsement.]

Sum of the extent of Pykering, with ⎱ £223 14s. 10½d.ᵃ
ancient farm of the Earl Marshal ⎰

LV. JOHN DE MONCEAUS, SON AND HEIR OF INGELRAM DE MONCEAUS *or* MUNCEUS, *under age.*ᵇ

[25 EDW. I. No. 44.]

TWENTY-FIFTH year (20 Nov., 1296–20, Nov., 1297). And (John de Lythegreyns accounts) for £11 18s. of the issues of the lands which were Ingelram de Mounceaus, and which remained in the King's hand from Michaelmas (29 Sept., 1296) to 9 Sept. before he delivered those lands to Thomas, son and heir of the same Ingelram, by the King's writ. And the same Thomas found security for his relief, namely, Walter de Kelke, Alan de Roston, Roger de Grimeston, and Robert Lorimer of Seton, who are all of the county of York.ᶜ

LVI. ROGER DE MOUBRAY. *Inq. p. m.*ᵈ

[26 EDW. I. No. 36.]

[m. 1]

Writᵉ tested by Edward, the King's son (during his father's absence in Flanders), at Westminster, 21 Nov., 26th year (1297).

ᵃ By a subsequent membrane (25) extents are tabulated of lands and tenements *citra Trentam* which (except lands not yet valued) amount to £524 6s. 10d., whereof a third part is £174 15s. 7½d.; and so two parts (or thirds) are £349 11s. 2¾d.

Then the extent of lands and tenements *ultra Trentam*, except those in the county of Northumberland, £669 11s. 3d., whereof a third part is £223 3s. 9d.; and so two parts (or thirds) are £446 7s. 6d.

Sum total *citra* and *ultra Trentam*, £1,193 18s. 1d., whereof a third part is £397 19s. 4¾d.; and so two parts (or thirds) are £795 18s. 8¾d.

ᵇ See Vol. I., p. 139. As the inquisition is illegible I give an extract relating to the property from the account of John de Lithegreyns, Escheator beyond Trent, for the period between 17 Aug., 23rd year (1295), up to Michaelmas, 25th year (29 Sept., 1297), that is for two whole years and six weeks (*Escheators' Accounts ultra Trentam* ⅞). In the same place are accounts for the estates of the following persons connected with Yorkshire :—Elyas de Rillestone, Ralph son of Peter de Goushulle, John de Rodmer (*lege* Redmer), John de Tocotes, Thomas de Moleton in Thurgranby, Simon de Pateshulle, Dionisia, widow of Remigius de Pokelinton, William de Vesci, Robert Luterel, Richard de Eston, Gilbert de Clare, Earl of Gloucester, in Preston in Craven, and Edmund Fitoun in Couton.

ᶜ St. Paul's, London, 9 Sept., 1297. Fealty taken of Thomas, brother and heir of John de Munceus, for the lands of Ingelram de Munceus, John's father, who held of the inheritance of the Earl of Albemarle (*Rot. Fin.*, 25 Edw. I., m. 5). John de Mounceus was dead before 19 July previous, when orders were given to seize his land (*Ibid.*, m. 8).

ᵈ In an action entered on the De Banco Roll, 12 Edw. I. (no term), fo. 6 (*Coll. Top. et Gen.*, i., 142), in which Roger de Moubray recovered the church of

[m. 2]

INQUISITION taken at Hovingham, before John de Lythe-graynes, the King's Escheator, on Sunday after the Epiphany, 26 Edw. (12 Jan., 1297-8), by John de Besingby, Roger Raboc, Robert de Colton, John son of Absolom, Richard de Holthorpe, Henry de Holthorpe, Henry de Hale of Friton, Walter de Scouesby, Robert son of Ralph of Hovingham, Robert Forester, John Frere, and Hugh de Thorneton. Roger de Moubray held of the King in chief, in the Wapentake of Ridale, the manor of Hovingham, with appurtenances, by homage and suit at the County [court] of York every six weeks, and at the Trithing [court] of the Northtrithinge once a year, and at one Wapentake [court] of Ridale. The capital messuage, with gardens and dove-house, is worth by the year 15s. 4d. In demesne are ten score and one acres of arable land (at 6d.), 44 acres of arable *forland* (at 6d.), and 50 acres of meadow (at 18d.). Two watermills, worth 33s. 4d.; from rent of free tenants, 47s. 10d.; also from the Abbot of Rivaulx, 26s. 8d.; from the heirs of John de Stayngrif, 2s.; 3 lbs. of pepper, at 8d.; 2 lbs. of cumin, at 1d.; a pair of gilt spurs, 6d. a year. Eleven bovates of land, with tofts, are worth by the year £7 6s. 8d. There are cottages worth 55s. 6d., and agistment in the common pasture 2s. a year. There are twelve workings of ploughs for one day, each of which is worth 4d.; also four score workings with sickles (*faucillis*) in autumn for one day, worth 6s. 8d. There is a Hallemote court, worth yearly 6s. 8d.

Sum total of the manor, £27 6s. 10d.

Melton Moubray against the Prior of Lewes, this pedigree of the family is given:—

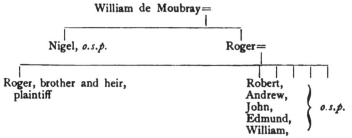

Roger the younger, whose inquisition is given above, was the son of Roger de Mowbray and Maude, daughter of Roger de Beauchamp. He married Roesia, sister of Gilbert de Clare, Earl of Gloucester, died at Ghent in Flanders, and was brought over to Fountains and there buried in 1299 (*Cottonian MSS.*, Cleop. D. iii., fo. 192). If this date be correct, his body must have remained unburied for nearly two years, as the writ (given above) is dated 21 Nov., 1297. There is no doubt that he was buried at Fountains, as his effigy is still preserved there. John de Creppingges and John de Blaby, of Yorkshire, knights, were the executors of his will (*Memoranda Roll*, L.T.R., 25 and 26 Edw. I., m. 93).

° Note on the back of the writ that it was received on 1 Jan. following.

John de Moubray, son of the said Roger, is his next heir; and on the day of the Beheading of St. John the Baptist, in the 25th year (29 Aug., 1297), he was aged eleven years.[a]

[m. 3]

INQUISITION taken before the same Escheator at Kyrkeby-malsarde on Wednesday after the feast of St. Hilary, 26 Edw. (15 Jan., 1297-8), by Sir John de Draycotes,[b] William de Aldefelde, Richard de Shupton, Adam Russell, William Russell, Thomas de Cressenay, Elias de Graintelay, William de Sunninges, Richard son of Sampson, Nicholas *le Venur*, William de Brathayt, and Thomas *le Colthirde*. Roger de Mubray held the manor of Kyrkebymalsarde of the King in chief of the Barony of Treske by doing suit at the County courts of York yearly, and homage to the King with foreign service, and finding five harnessed horses (*equos coopertos*) in the King's war for the barony and all other lands. The capital messuage, with gardens, is worth by the year 6s. 8d. There are seven score acres of arable land (at 6d. the acre), and 20 acres untilled (at 5d.), 29 acres of meadow (at 16d.). A several pasture, called Warren (*Varenna*), is worth 26s. 8d. a year; and a vaccary, 26s. 8d. The agistment in Scheldene and (Gran)telay[c] is worth 5s., and turbary 5s. Rents of free tenants by the year, 33s. 1d.; a pound of pepper, worth 12d., and a pair of gloves, a penny. There are 16 bovates of land in bondage, each worth by the year 7s. One bovate by itself is worth 6s. Twenty cottages are worth yearly 34s. 8d. A pasture called Staynemore is worth by the year 2s.; pannage, 12d.; fines and pleas of Court, 26s. 8d. So the manor is worth in all issues by the year, £20 3s. 7d.

John de Mubray, son of the said Roger, is his next heir, and aged twelve years and more.

[m. 4]

INQUISITION taken at Threske, before the same Escheator, on the day of St. Hilary, 26 Edw. (13 Jan., 1297-8), by Robert Oliver, Robert de Foxoles, William de Norton, Roger

---

[a] Westminster. Nov. 29, 1298. Grant to William de Brewosa, staying with the King in Flanders, of the marriage of John, son and heir of Roger de Moubray, tenant in chief, so that he cause the said John to be married to Alina, his daughter. Mandate to Roesia, late wife of the said Roger, to deliver the said John to be married as above (*Calendar of Patent Rolls*, 1292–1301, p. 323).

[b] *Traycotes.* See m. 7.

[c] Skelden and Grantley, near Ripon.

de Stapelton, William de Baxeby, William Clerkson (*filius clerici*), William de Sutton, William de Scheffeld, Robert Yoel, William Fayrhehe, William Cook (*cocum*), and William Talenaz. Roger de Moubray held the manor of Threske, with appurtenances, of the King in chief, in barony, by homage and foreign service, and doing suit at all county courts of York yearly, at the Thrythinge [court] of Yarlestre,[a] and at the Thrithinge [courts] of Craykehouhe and Wyndeiates once a year. The capital messuage is worth nothing beyond keeping it up, but there are fifteen score acres of arable land in demesne (at 5*d*. the acre); 42 acres of meadow in demesne (at 2*s*. 6*d*.). There are five bovates of land, with five tofts in bondage, each bovate with toft, worth yearly 11*s*., and 6 acres of *forland*, at 12*d*. the acre. Agistment in the park is worth yearly a marc, and pannage in the same park, 6*s*. 8*d*. Pannage of the borough, called Thystelthacke, is worth 12*d*.; agistment in the moor, 20*s*. Rents of free tenants yearly, 69*s*. 2*d*.; also 9 lbs. of pepper from free tenants at 12*d*., and 5 lbs. of cumin at 1*d*. a year. There are 8 cottages, worth yearly 22*s*. 4*d*., and a plot (*placia*), called Castelstede, 6*s*.; and 6 waste tofts, 6*s*. a year. There are two mills, an oven, with market tolls and pleas of the borough, which are worth by the year £44, of which these receive yearly: Robert de Creppinges and William de Brakenb[ergh], £6 13*s*. 4*d*. of old time (*a tempore antiquo*); Philip Bretoun, 20*s*. of old time; Thomas de Colevile, £13 6*s*. 8*d*. by gift of Roger de Moubray; and John de Blaby, £10, also by his gift. So there remained clear to Roger de Moubray on the day of his death £13. There are five score workings of sickles (*faucillarum*) in autumn for a day, which are worth yearly 8*s*. 4*d*. There is a free court every three weeks, which is worth by the year 40*s*. And so the manor of Threske is worth in all issues yearly £37 13*s*. 3*d*.

John de Moubray, son of the said Roger de Moubray, is his next heir, and aged twelve years and more.[b]

---

[a] Called in Domesday Gerlestre, now represented by the wapentake of Birdforth, of which Thirsk is the chief town. In Domesday times Crayke was included in the wapentake of Gerlestre, so it is possible the Craykehouhe mentioned above was in the vicinity of that place. Another Craikhou was the place for the meeting of the wapentake court of Harthill (*Monastic Notes* (Yorkshire Record Series), i., 59).

[b] M. 5, in a very illegible state. It relates to Burton in Lonesdale, which appears to be a member of the Barony of Threske. Heir 12 years and more on the feast of the B.M., 25th year (15 Aug., 1297).

[m. 6]

Writ[a] directed to John de Lythegraynes, and dated at Temple Lyston, 19 July, 26th year (1298). The Chase of Nydderdale and certain woods there have not yet been valued. This is now to be done without delay.

[m. 7]

INQUISITION made before the same John de Lythegreyns at Kirkeby Mallesard on Sunday after the feast of St. Peter *ad vincula*, 26 Edw. (3 Aug., 1298), concerning the chase of Niderdale and certain woods in the manor of Kirkeby Malesarde, which were Roger de Moubray's, and of which he died seised in fee, by the oath of John de Draycotes, William de Aldefeld, William Russel, Thomas *de la Cressener*, Elias de Granteley, William Sunnynge, Richard Sammesune, Nicholas *le Venur*, William de Brathwayt, Thomas *le Colte-hyrd*, Richard son of Ranulph, and Adam de Wynkesley. In the said manor there are three woods, the underwood of which was not extended before among the other lands and tenements of the said Roger, that is to say, Baggewythe wood, Glumesker wood, and Bowfalle wood. In these woods the underwood can be sold every year to the value of two marcs, without causing waste. There is also a lead mine, not included in the former extent, which is yearly worth 30s. In the free Chace of Niderdale, which was the said Roger's, and of which no mention was made in the former extent, there can be taken every year ten stags and six bucks in the summer season (*tempore pingwedinis*), ten hinds (*bisse*) and six does in the winter season (*tempore fermesone*), and ten roebucks (*cheverelli*) throughout the year. There are also three small aeries of sparrowhawks (*spervariorum*), which are valued at 3s. a year.

Sum, 59s. 8d., out of which the Chief Forester ought to take 20s. a year; and so there remains clear, 39s. 8d.

For the keeping of which Chase Roger de Moubray, who lately died, gave by charter to a certain Chief Forester a gown (*robam*), or 20s. a year.[b]

---

[a] Note on the back that the writ was received on 29 July.

[b] A writ [m. 8], tested by Edward, the King's son, at Westminster, 23 Nov., 26th year (1297), was directed to Malculm de Harleye, the King's Escheator on this side Trent, under which an extent [m. 9] of lands and tenements, which were of Roger de Moubray in the county of Lincoln, was taken at Eppeworthe on Saturday, the feast of St. Thomas the Apostle, 26th year (21 Dec., 1297). The total yearly value is here set down at £106 13s. 11½d., out of which was paid yearly for Sheriff's aid 8s. Then two foresters, who yearly receive livery and two gowns, valued together at 66s. 8d. So that there remained clear, £102 19s. 3¼d. The son and heir, John de Moubray, is found to have been eleven years old at the feast of St. Cuthbert last past (4 Sept.); but by an inquisition for Leicestershire (apparently taken at Melton Moubray) his age is said to be thirteen years at the feast of the Beheading of St. John the Baptist, in the 25th year (29 Aug., 1297); and by that for Burton in Lonesdale, co. York, twelve years and more at the feast of the Assumption of the B.M., 25th year (15 Aug., 1297). An entry in a calendar, printed in the *Coll. Top. & Gen.* (iv., 262), states that John, son of Sir Roger de Moubray, was born on the second of the Nones of Sept. (4 Sept.), 1286.

LVII.   GILBERT DE GAUNT.[a]   *Inq. p. m.*

[26 EDW. I. No. 38.]

Writ directed to John de Lythegraynes, Escheator beyond Trent, and dated at Canterbury, 17 March, 26th year (1297-8).

THE inquisition taken for Yorkshire is illegible, having been washed with an infusion of liquid, now turned a dark brown. No coherent sentence can be made out. The printed *Calendar of Inquisitions* (Vol. i., 147) shows the following : —

Helawe manor, in Gomerset,
Mosedale vaccary,
Smerbergh   „
Bladesey   „
Fyton
Kirton
Sconesdale   „
Scaldecotes   „   } Yorkshire.[b]
Ivelishe   „
Gomerset   „
Fremington town,
Helawe town,
Crakepote vaccary,
Rincroft   „
Baconrawe   „
Helawe, suit of court,

[a] Succeeded his father, Gilbert de Gaunt, in 1274 (Vol. I., p. 137). By an inquisition taken in Lincolnshire before the Sheriff, on Monday after the feast of the Ascension, 26 Edw. (19 May, 1298), the heirs of Gilbert de Gaunt are found to be Roger de Gertheston (Garriston, near Bedale), called in the Yorkshire inquisition Roger, son of William de Ger[theston], aged 24 years and more ; Peter, son of Peter de Mauley, 18 years and more since Christmasday last (25 Dec., 1297); and Julia or Juliana de Gaunt, sister of Gilbert, aged 40 years and more. His lands were ordered to be seised on 16 March, 1297-8 (*Rot. Fin.*, 26 Edw. I., m. 15). On 10 June, 1298, the King took the homage at Neuburgh of Roger, son of William de Kerdeston, cousin and one of the heirs of Gilbert de Gaunt, deceased, and of Juliana, sister and another of the heirs of the same, for the purparties falling to them of all the lands and tenements which the same Gilbert, the uncle (*avunculus*) of Roger and brother of Juliana, held in chief on the day of his death, except the manors of Barton-on-Humber, Folkingham, Hekinton and Edenham in Lincolnshire, which Gilbert long before his death had granted to the King, who had regranted them to him for life. The property was to be divided by the Sheriff of Lincolnshire between them and Peter, son of Peter de Mauley, the third heir of the said Gilbert, saving the dower of Lora, Gilbert's widow (*Ibid.*, 26 Edw. I., m. 8). From a suit entered on the *De Banco Roll*, Mich. term, 9 Edw. II., m. 4, 28*d*, it appears that Gilbert de Gaunt, senior, had four daughters, Helewisa, who died without issue ; Juliana ; Nicholaa, mother of Peter de Mauley ; and Margaret, mother of Roger de Kerdeston (*Reliquary*, N.S., ii., 140).

[b] Some of these places can still be identified. Helawe is Healaugh in Swaledale ; Gomerset, Gunnerside ; Mosedale, perhaps Mossdale, four miles N.N.W. of Hawes ; Smerbergh, Smarber ; Bladesey, Blades, near Feetham ; Fyton, Feetham ; Kirton, Kearton ; Sconesdale (*lege* Stonesdale), Stonesdale ; Ivelishe, Ivelet ; Fremington, the same ; Crakepote, Crackpot ; and Rincroft, Rawcroft. Scaldecotes and Baconrawe (? Ratonrawe) seem lost.

LVIII. PRIOR AND PREACHING FRIARS OF SCARBOROUGH.
Inq. ad q. d.
[26 EDW. I. No. 59.]

Writ dated at Westminster, 10 April, 26th year (1298), and directed to the Sheriff.

INQUISITION taken on Friday next after the feast of the Holy Trinity, 26 Edw. I. (6 June, 1298), and made by John Gerard, Adam son of Robert, Thomas *le Carecter*, Simon Gelle, Roger at the Cross (*ad crucem*), John son of Hugh, Ralph Gedge, Roger Clampe, William *le Knagg'*, Robert *le Coroner*, Robert Gedge, and John *le Chalcer*, who say on their oath that it is not to the hurt of the King or to the damage of the town of Scardeburg, or of anyone else, if the King grant leave to the Prior and Friars of the Order of Preachers of the same town to pave a street in the same town within the wall thereof towards the east, which street reaches from the house of John de Pickeford to the house of John *le Blake* towards the church of the same Friars, but rather for the easement and utility of the men of the said town and of others going to hear divine service at the said church; and also that the passage through the same street would be very much improved if it were paved. The street contains a width of twenty-seven feet between land formerly belonging to Symon Gomer and the corner of the earthen wall (*angulum muri terrei*) of the Friars Minors, of twenty-four feet between the church of the same Friars and the workshop (*fabricam*), of eighteen feet between the land formerly belonging to Roger de Gateshaued and the wall of the same Friars Minors, and of twenty feet between the waste (*vasta*) of the said town and the wall of the same Friars. From the house of John de Pyckeford to the house of John *le Blake* it contains in length thirty-nine perches.

LIX. SIR HENRY DE PERCY *for* THE ABBOT AND CONVENT OF WHITBY. *Inq. ad q. d.*
[26 EDW. I. No. 64.]

Writ dated at Wylton, 7 June, 26th year (1298), and directed to the Sheriff.

INQUISITION made at Wyteby on Wednesday next after the feast of St. Botolf, 26 Edw. (18 June, 1298), by Walter de Percy of Dunesley, Nicholas de Lythe, John Hersant, William Herman, Walter son of Robert of Haukesgarth, Stephen Belebarbe, Thomas de Neuby, William son of Osbert of Dunesley, John Daivel', Geoffrey de Everle, Geoffrey *de la*

6

Launde, and John son of William of Rysewarpe, who say
that it is not to the hurt or prejudice of the King or of any
others if the manor of Haukesgarth be granted to the Abbot
of Wyteby and his successors for ever by Sir Henry de
Percy, as they say the manor is held in chief of the Abbot
and Convent of Wyteby for homage, suits of court every
three weeks, and 12s. a year, and nothing is held of any
other lord (*et nichil tenetur alicui alio domino*), nor does it
do any service to anyone except only to the Abbot and
Convent; and so they say it is to the profit of the King,
because at the time of vacancy the King will have custody
of the manor where before he had not, as of the other lands
of the Abbey of Wyteby. The manor is worth by the year
in all issues 100s. Nothing is held of any other lord, but
of the Abbot only (*nichil tenetur alicui alio domino nisi
tantum Abbati*).

Dorso :—Let it be done for a fine of £20.[a]

LX.   WILLIAM DE BEAUCHAMP, EARL OF WARWICK.
Inq. p. m.

[26 EDW. I. No. 41.]

[m. 2]

Writ of *diem clausit extremum* directed to John de Lythegreyns, and dated
at Durham, 12 June, 26th year (1298).[b]

[m. 3]

INQUISITION taken at Dichall' before John de Lythegreynes,
the Escheator, on Sunday after the feast of St. Peter
and St. Paul, 26 Edw. (6 July, 1298), by Roger Hancelyn,
Richard de Bernes, John de Birley, Robert son of Juliana,
Peter de Crosseley, Thomas Frend', John de Huseley, Robert
de Brixherd', Robert de Osegerthorp', Adam *de Bosco*,
Thomas *le Serjeaunt*, Adam Roboc, who say on their oath,
the said William (de Bello campo) held a tenement in the
manor of Schefeld, called le Dichall', of the dower of Maud
(Matild') his wife, which fell to her of the lands and tenements there belonging to her first husband, Gerard de
Furnivall'. This tenement after Maud's death ought to
revert to Thomas de Furnivall', now lord of Hallumschire,
as to the relative and heir of the said Gerard.

Guydo de Warewyck, son of the said William, is his
next heir, and is of the age of 23 years and upwards.[c]

[a] See *Whitby Chartulary* (Surtees Society), ii., 499, 524.

[b] *Dorso.* xxix Junii fuit hoc breve receptum et execucio demandata.

[c] [m. 1].   Northalverton, 12 June (1298).   Writ of *diem clausit extremum* of
William de Bello campo, late Earl of Warwick, addressed to Walter de Gloucester,
Escheator *ultra*.

LXI.   ROBERT DE TYBETOT, KNIGHT.   *Inq. p. m.*

[26 EDW. I.   No. 39.]

Writ[a] directed to William de Gloucester, Escheator beyond Trent, and dated at Northalverton, 12 June, 26th year (1298) ; and another writ of the same date, directed to John de Lythegreyns, Escheator this side Trent.

INQUISITION made at York before John de Lithegreins, the King's Escheator beyond Trent,[b] on Wednesday after the feast of the Translation of St. Thomas the Martyr, 26 Edw. (9 July, 1298), by Sirs Robert de Berley, Robert de Ecclesale, knights ; John *le Vavasour*, Robert Tilley, Peter de Bosevile, Robert de Bosevile, John Haungel,[c] Robert de Reynebergh', Baldwin de Cateby, Adam Celer of Mekerburg', Laurence de Roderham, clerk, and Richard Tyes, who say by their oath that Robert de Tibtoft, knight, held of the King in chief, as of the Honour of Tikhill Castle (now in the King's hand), the manor of Benteley, with appurtenances, jointly with Eva his   , by the gift of . . . . . . Adam *de Novo mercato* made to them thereof for ever. The capital messuage of the same is worth by the year 6s. 8d. There are in

[m. 4]. Leicestershire. No date. Vill of Kybbeworthe Beauchaump held "ad ponend' unam mappam super mensam domini Regis die Natalis Domini." Gwydo, the son and heir, of full age.

[m. 5]. Oxfordshire. 26 June. Guydo, aged 27 and upwards.

[m. 6]. Middlesex. Morrow of the Apostles Peter and Paul (30 June). A messuage and eight acres of land in Westminster, 53s. 4d. a year. Gwydo de Warr', 24 and upwards.

[m. 7]. Gloucestershire. At Kenemerton, Saturday, the eve of St. Peter (28 June). William de Bello campo and Maud, his wife, held a quarter of the manor of Kenemerton of the Earl and Countess of Gloucester. Gwydo, the nearest heir of the said William de Bello campo and Maud, his wife, aged 27 and upwards.

[m. 8]. Gloucestershire. At Wynchecombe, on Thursday after the feast of the Apostles Peter and Paul (3 July). Heir 27.

[m. 9]. Worcester Castle. Monday after the same feast (30 June). He held the "salina de Wychio cum boiller' eidem pertinente."

[m. 10]. Worcestershire. Saturday, the eve of the same feast (28 June).

[m. 11] Bucks. At Hamslape, on Saturday after the Nativity of St. John the Baptist (28 June).

[m. 12]. Warwick. Thursday after the feast of the Apostles Peter and Paul (3 July). Held the castle of Warwick at 5s. a year. Heir 26.

[m. 13]. Cyrencestre. Monday after the feast of St. Peter (30 June). Heir 27 and upwards.

[m. 14]. Warwickshire. Thursday after the Nativity of St. John the Baptist (26 June). Sutton in Colefeld. Heir 26 and upwards.

[m. 15]. Cyrencestre. Monday after the feast of St. Peter (30 June). Heir 27 and upwards.

[m. 16]. Rutlandshire. Extent of lands. Thursday after the feast of the Apostles Peter and Paul (3 July).

[a] By endorsement received 14 June.

[b] The words, "coram Johanne de Lithegreins, Escaetore domini Regis ultra Trentam," are written over the line with a *caret*.

[c] A John Haringel, probably the same person as the abovenamed John Haungel, was living at Hooton Paynel in 1297 (*Yorkshire Lay Subsidy*, 25 Edw. I., p. 67).

demesne 358 acres (at 8*d.*), and 46 acres of meadow (at 2*s.* 6*d.*), 115*s.* Also £40 annual rent from free men, natives, and cottars, paid yearly at the feasts of St. Michael, Christmas, Easter, and the Nativity of St. John the Baptist. A pasture called North Wode is worth yearly £4 . . . . 10 marcs. The said Robert and Eva held the manor jointly, with its appurtenances, of the Honour of Tikehill Castle, by the service of 40*s.* yearly to the Castle-guard, viz. a moiety at the feast of St. Thomas the Apostle (21 Dec.), and the other moiety at the feast of the Nativity of St. John the Baptist (24 June), and 6*s.* 8*d.* for fine of the Wapentake, and 2*s.* for Waytemete and Schirrefstuthe.

They also jointly held the manor of Hagenthweyt,[a] with appurtenances, of Sir William fitz William of Sprotteburg', by homage and service of a penny to be yielded to him, and by the foreign service which appertains to it, by gift and feoffment of Peter of Chester (*de Cestria*). The capital messuage is worth yearly 2*s.* There are in the manor 134 acres and one rood of arable land (at 8*d.*), and in demesne 18 acres of meadow (at 2*s.*), 12 acres of pasture, worth yearly 6*s.* 8*d.* There are 8 marcs 13*s.* 1*d.* yearly rent received from freemen, natives, and cottars, at two terms, viz. at the feast of St. Martin in winter (11 Nov.) and Whitsuntide.

Payne (*Paganus*), son of the said Robert, is his next heir, and aged 17 years at the feast of the Nativity of St. John Baptist last past (24 June, 1298).[b]

The said Robert died at Nettelstede [in Suffolk], on Thursday after the feast of St. Dunstan last past (22 May, 1298).[c]

[a] Hamthwaite, par. Aldwick-le-Street. "This place has disappeared from the villare of this district. But the manor of Hamthwaite frequently occurs among the manors held of the honour of Tickhill, and it extended over lands in the vicinity of Hampole and Adwick. It formed part of the two knights' fees held of William fitz William of Sprotborough. But it was subsequently held by Windham, the lord of Bentley (Hunter's *South Yorkshire*, i., 356).

[b] In the inquisition for Lincolnshire (1 Aug., 1298) the jury find :—" Et quod quidam Payn filius predicti Roberti est propinquior ejus heres, et erit etatis xix annorum ad festum S. Martini proximo venturi." The Cambridgeshire inquisition concurs with this in stating that the heir was eighteen on the previous Martinmas (11 Nov., 1297).

[c] By an inquisition, taken at Bentley (here Benteleye) in Suffolk, on Thursday, the eve of the Assumption of the B.V.M. (14 Aug., 1298), in the same year, the age of the heir is said to be 17 on St. John the Baptist's day last (24 June); but the father is said to have died on Thursday after the feast of St. *Augustin* (29 May), which date is a week later than that stated in the foregoing inquisition for Yorkshire. Of the two records, that for Suffolk should be the more trustworthy, for the decease happened in that county ; but, supposing an error to have been made, and that it should have been written Thursday *before* (instead of after) the feast of St. Augustin, the two records would agree in making the date 22 May, 1298. Moreover, the Yorkshire jury must have procured the information specially for the

LXII. ALEXANDER DE AUNOU.[a] *Inq. p. m.*

[Escheator's Inquisitions ultra Trentam. Series I. File 49.]

WRIT and inquisition of possessions alienated in co. York by Alexander de Aunou. Writ (in bad state) directed to the Escheator beyond Trent, but apparently no mention of Yorkshire. The inquisition is to be returned to the Exchequer at York on the morrow of St. Michael (30 Sept.). Witness, P. de Wylughby, deputy (*tenente locum*) of our Treasurer at York, 20 June, 26th year (1298). The inquisition (in bad state) was taken at Aischeton (Ashton) near Bristol, 13 or 14 Aug., 26th year (1298).

purpose, as they could have had no personal knowledge of the matter. Beside the inquisitions for Yorkshire and Suffolk there are others for the cos. of Lincoln, Nottingham, Essex and Cambridge. Sir Robert de Tibotot, one of the most eminent persons of his age, married Eva, daughter and heiress of Payne de Chaworth (Hunter's *South Yorkshire*, i., 325). On 6 March, 1298-9, the King took at Certeseye the homage of Payne, son and heir of Robert de Tibotot, of the county of Notts., for the manor of Langar, in which the said Robert and Eva, his wife, and the said Payne were jointly enfeoffed and seised on the day of Robert's death, as by an inquisition made by Walter de Gloucester, Escheator this side Trent, and returned into Chancery, is manifest. The King retained half the manor in his hand in consequence of Payne's minority (*Rot. Fin.*, 27 Edw. I. m. 22). Besides Payne, Robert de Tibotot had a son, Robert. In 1295 (?) Ralph de Tony had licence from the King to assign to Robert, son of Robert Tibotot, and his daughter, as her marriage portion, and their heirs, land to the value of £100 a year in his manors of Neweton and Stratford, co. Wilts., held by him in chief; and if there should be less than that value of land in those manors, the deficiency to be made up in his manor of Saham (Saham Tony, co. Norfolk), likewise held in chief (*Calendar of Patent Rolls*, 1292-1301, p. 131). Before his death Robert Tibotot made arrangement for the marriage of his son Payne with Anneyse, daughter of William de Ros. This he did by a chirograph made at Bayonne on 1 March, 25 Edw. I. (1296-7), confirmed by the King at St. Albans on 25 April, 1298, whereby, after providing for the marriage, it was agreed that Ros should dower (*dourra*) Payne and Anneyse in land to the value of £100, to wit, the manor of Linton on Use, and if that manor should not be worth so much, he should provide the residue in the manor of Wythone (Market Weighton), to hold to them and their heirs with reversion to himself. Robert was to dower Anneyse with land to the value of 100 marcs a year, to wit, the manor of Harleston, co. Cambridge, to be supplemented if necessary out of his manor of Strethale, co. Essex. Sealed in the presence of Henry de Lacy, Earl of Lincoln, the King's Lieutenant in the Duchy of Guyenne. Witnesses, Philip de Kyme, Henry de Grey, John de Moun, John de Sutheleye, and John de la Mare (*Ibid.*, p. 346). On 21 Nov., 1299, the King, then at Market Weighton, granted to Eva, widow of Robert Tibotot, the marriage of Payne, Robert's son and heir, a minor in the King's custody, a treaty having been already made between the said Robert in his lifetime and William de Ros for a marriage between the said Payne and a daughter of the said William, before the King made his grant of custodies and marriages to Edmund, Earl of Cornwall, his kinsman, the marriage having remained uneffected through the death of the said Robert (*Ibid.*, p. 480).

[a] A Thomas de Auno, whose *Inq. p. m.* was taken in 1246, died seised of lands at Carthorpe, in the parish of Burneston, near Bedale (Vol. I., p. 3). No one of this name occurs in *Kirkby's Inquest*, or the documents published therewith.

LXIII.   RICHARD FITZ JOHN.   *Inq. p. m.*

[25 EDW. I. No. 30*b.*]

Writ directed to John de Lythegreyns, commanding him to certify the true value of knights' fees and advowsons of churches held by John fitz John. Dated at Stirling (Stryvelyn), 4 Aug., 26th year (1298).

INQUISITION made upon the value of lands and tenements which were held of Richard fitz John in Skelbroke, near le Gailes, in the county of York, on Thursday after the feast of the Purification of the B. M., 27 Edw. (5 Feb., 1298–9), by Thomas Hony, Richard de S   , William Hony, Richard at the Bridge (*ad pontem*), Richard *del Welhede*, Reginald Collan, Adam son of Peter, Richard Sp   , Robert son of Stephen, Thomas de Bathelai, Henry de Scaucebi, and [Roger] son of Alan, who say that Edmund *le Botiller*[a] holds of him his capital messuage in Skelbroke[b] and an alder-bed, which are worth by the year 20s.; also five score and two acres of land (at 8d. the acre), four bovates of land (the bovate containing 12 acres, at 8d. the acre), and a watermill, worth 6s. 8d. a year.

The said Edmund has tenants who hold of him in the same town, viz. Walter son of Oliver of Skelbroke, bovate and a half of land by homage, and a bovate by a needle yearly; Robert son of Stephen, a bovate of land and a mill by homage, and 4s. 6d. a year; William Hony, half a bovate by homage, suit of court, and 12d. a year; Peter son of Robert, half a bovate by the same service; Adam son of Peter, half a bovate by the same service, except suit of court; Adam *Attetouneshende*, a bovate by homage, suit of court, and 2s. a year; Walter Snoute, half a bovate by service of 6s. 8d. a year; Agnes *la Botillere*, a bovate by homage, and 1d. a year.

Richard Hunt, a cottage for 20d.; Richard at the Bridge, a cottage for 12d.; William Husband, a cottage for 12d. Constance Tailor (*sissor*), a cottage for [12d.]; Emma daughter of Husband, a toft with croft, for 3s. 6d. a year.

The said Edmund held all the said tenements of Richard fitz John by homage and a hawk (*nisum*) yearly; and the said Richard held of the Earl of Lincoln by homage and suit at the Earl's Court of Pontefract.

[a] Son of his sister Joan. Her inquisition for Southants was taken in 31 Edw. I., when it was found that Joan la Botelere died on Thursday before Easter in that year (4 April, 1303), her heir Edmund le Botelere being thirty and more. The Essex inquisition makes Edmund le Botiller, son of Joan la Botillere, twenty-four and more (*Cal. Gen.*, ii., 644).

[b] Skelbrook, par. South Kirkby.

A writ directed to Richard de Haveringe, Escheator beyond Trent, refers to the extent made by John de Lythegreyns, late Escheator, as being insufficient, because although it is stated that Edmund *le Butiller* held of Richard fitz John certain lands and tenements in Skelbroke by homage and service of a hawk (*nisi*) yearly, no mention is made whether or not he held them by knight's service. He is therefore commanded to inquire without delay into the truth of the matter. Dated at Westminster, 10 April, 27th year (1299).

INQUISITION made at York before Master Richard de Haveryngge, Escheator beyond Trent, on Wednesday after the quinzaine of Easter, 27 Edward (6 May, 1299), by Thomas de Raynevile, Matthew Mellynge, William de la , John Scot of Camesale, William de Preston, Richard de Fethirstan, William son of Elias of the same, John son of Roger of Wilmerlay, William de Tumbeholme, John *del Wodehalle*, Henry de Mayningham, and William son of Roger of Pudesay, who say upon their oath that Edmund *le Botyler* held in Skelbroke, in the county of York, half a knight's fee of Richard fitz John (who held of the King in chief) by service of a hawk yearly and doing to the King's scutage, when current, so much as appertains to half a knight's fee, and not by any other service.[a]

LXIV. HOSPITALS OF ST. NICHOLAS AND ST. THOMAS THE MARTYR, SCARBOROUGH.

[26 EDW. I. No. 65.]

[m. 1]

Writ dated at Brade, 20 Aug., 26th year (1298), and addressed to Mr. Ralph de Odiham, clerk.

[a] It appears that Richard fitz John was dead before the 26 Sept., 1297, the date of the writ, tested by Edward, the King's son (during his father's absence in Flanders), and directed to Malculm de Harlegh, Escheator *citra Trentam* (*Rot. Fin.*, 25 Edw. I., m. 5). Walter de la Haye, the Escheator in Ireland, was ordered to seize his lands on 4 Dec., 1296 (*Ibid.*, 26 Edw. I., m. 19). From inquisitions taken for the counties of Essex, Wilts., Devon, Surrey, Northampton, Buckingham and Lancaster, his heirs are found to be :—

(1) Maud, wife of William de Beauchamp, Earl of Warwick, his eldest sister ;
(2) Robert de Clifford, son of Isabel de Clifford, daughter of Isabel de Vipont (*Veteri ponte*), his second sister ; and Idonea de Leyburne (late wife of Roger de Leyburne), daughter of the same Isabel de Vipont ;
(3) Richard, Earl of Ulster, son of Avelina, his third sister ; and
(4) Joan la Botillere (late wife of Theobald le Botiller), his fourth sister.

On one membrane is an extent of lands held by him of the King in chief. The sum total is £451 12s. 3d., of which a third part is £150 10s. 9d.; but in the assignment of dower made to Emma, late wife of Richard, which follows the above-mentioned extent, amounts in yearly value to £150 1s. 2¼d. The total amount for partition is made (by another membrane) £307 15s. 11¾d.; to be divided into four equal parts, of which one fourth part, or £76 19s., is to be divided into two parts.

[m. 3]

INASMUCH as the King has been informed that certain men of the town of Scard' have destroyed and squandered certain goods and chattels of the Brethren and Sisters of the hospitals of St. Nicholas and St. Thomas the Martyr of the said town, and that the said hospitals were of the foundation of his progenitors, Kings of England, the King sent his beloved clerk, Master Ralph de Odyham, by his writ, to make inquiry by the oath of honest and lawful men of the county of York, etc. The inquisition was made at Scardeburgh on Thursday next after the feast of the Decollation of St. John the Baptist, 26 Edw. (5 Sept., 1298), by Henry Sampson, Henry de Brompton, Robert de North-folk, John Gerard, Robert Alwy, Robert son of Nelle of Scard', Aso de Flixton, William de Hundmanby, clerk, John Meadows (*de pratis*) of the same, Walter Elward of Folketon, Simon Stule of Flixton, and Thomas son of Matilda of Wallesgrave, who say on their oath that both the hospital of St. Nicholas and the hospital of St. Thomas the Martyr were founded of old by burgesses of Scard', and that the goods and chattels of the hospital of St. Nicholas are applied to the use (*cedunt in usus*) of the Brethren and Sisters of the same hospital, and that no one of the town of Scard' has consumed, squandered, or destroyed the said hospital, and that no one has appropriated to himself without warrant its lands or tenements, and that the goods and chattels, lands and tenements, are now in the hands of the Brethren and Sisters of the same hospital. They say, however, that the bailiffs of Scard' for the time being, together with four men of the same town, audit the accounts (*audiunt compotum*) of the said house each year. They say also that they have eight oxen, price eight marcs; seven cows, price of each 5*s*.; six horses (*jumenta*), price of each 2*s*.; 8 score sheep, price of each 12*d*.; 8 score fleeces, price £6; 4 carthorses (*afros*), price of each 5*s*. Five bovates of land, at 10*s*. the bovate.

The hospital of St. Thomas the Martyr was founded by burgesses of Scard', who had the custody of the houses, and appointed and deposed the master at their pleasure from the time of Hugh de Bulmer, who first gave his land for the foundation of the house, to the time of William *le Champeneys*, who was Master, and whom Roger Wasthose ejected with the Brethren and Sisters of the same. Concerning this he falsely informed the King (Henry III.) that H., his grand-father, had given a carucate and a half to the hospital in frankalmoign, in consequence of which false suggestion the King (seized) the custody of the hospital until the burgesses obtained from the Court an inquisition. By this inquisition, which was made by the country, Roger was removed from the custody of the hospital. Whilst the burgesses were obtaining the inquisition Roger Wasthouse destroyed the hospital and sold the goods and chattels, vessels, and other things belonging to it, and carried away all the money received for the goods. Afterwards the hospital lay waste and the lands uncultivated to the time of Roger Uctred, mayor of Scard', who obtained the custody of the land of the hospital for six years, and out of the issues of the same repaired the walls of St. Thomas's hall. After Roger's time the land lay uncultivated up to the time of Henry *le Mercer*, who had the custody of the same for seven years, and rendered an account to the commonalty of Scardeburgh, out of the issues of which he paid £12 to the said commonalty. After Henry's time the lands lay waste up to the time of Robert Ham', who had the custody of them for three years by the appointment of the same commonalty, and paid out of the issues £10 to the said commonalty, out of which Robert de Ruston had 40s., and there are still owing, after account rendered by the same Robert to the said commonalty, £8 out of the said £10. Simon de Folketon and William de Neuby received goods and corn to the value of £8 for one complete year of their wardship, and have paid to the commonalty of Scardeb' £4 10s. From that year the lands lay uncultivated up to the present year, till Robert *le Caretter*, John son of Hugh, and Thomas *in Solio*, and their Brethren, took from the commonalty twenty-six acres of land in Burtondale for 14s. 8d. a year . . . . of land belong to the said hospital, namely, Halgarthe, herbage 3s.; St. Thomas's meadow opposite the hall, 3s.; grange with garden, which Robert Ham' bought for the said hospital, 5s.; land of Henry Forne, 6s.; from a meadow belonging to St. Thomas's below Gildusclive, which Thomas de Lyndleigh held, 12d.; from a croft at Engrif . . . which Thomas . . . . . . holds, and which belongs to the said hospital, 2s.; from a toft which Almer held by the new ditch (*novum fossatum*), which belongs to the said hospital, 12d.; from . . . . which likewise belongs, 2s. 6d.; from land in Burtondale, the sum appears. Sum total . . . . . .

[m. 2]

Again, the ten burgesses of Scardeburg' pray the King and his Council, if it please them, that whereas there are two hospitals in the said town of Scardeburgh, the one of St. Nicholas and the other of St. Thomas the Martyr, founded by the ancestors of the said ten burgesses, which have been taken into the King's hand by Ralph de Hodyam, who found by inquest made in this matter, that these two hospitals were founded by the ancestors of the said Burgesses, and not by the King or his ancestors, which inquest was returned to the Chancellor, and remains in Chancery; wherefore they pray the King and his Council for a writ of livery of these hospitals. *Back.* Let the inquisition be seen.[a]

LXV. JOHN UGHTRED, *or* OUHTRED, *or* UCTREDE.[b]
Inq. p. m.
[26 EDW. I. No. 34.]
Writ dated at Steynwegges, 24 Sept., 26th year (1298).

[m. 2]

INQUISITION made before John de Lithegreynis, Escheator beyond Trent, on Monday after the feast of St. Wilfrid the Bishop, 26 Edw. (13 Oct., 1298), by John de Fittelinge, Thomas son of Simon of Humbelton, Thomas Kinge, Richard de Ettheredewyke, Richard de Grimmestone, Henry de Fittelinge, Adam *le Oysilhour*, John de Ristone, Stephen *del Hille* of Oustewyke, Stephen Bonde of the same, William Levenyt, and Nicholas Schertfrende, who say on their oath

---

[a] Uncore au Rey e a sun Counseyl prient les diz Burgeys de Scardeburg' si luy plest qe la ou ili ad ij hospitals en la dite vile de Scardeburgh' le un de Seynt Nicolas e l'autre de Seynt Thomas le Martyr foundous de les auncestres les diz Burgeys les quels sunt pris en la meyn le Rey par Rauf de Hodyam le quel Rauf trova par enquest sur ceste chose charge qe mesmes ceux deux hospitals sunt fundus de les auncestres les burgeys avauntdiz e ne mye du Rey ne de ses auncestres la quele enqueste fu returne au Chaunceler e demort en la Chauncelrye dount il prient au Rey e a sun Counseyl bref de deliveraunce de mesmes ceux hospitals. *Dorso.* Videatur inquisitio.

[b] March 28, 1307. Carlisle. The Escheator ordered to restore her lands to Joan, daughter and heiress of John Ughtred, who married John de Rue, she having proved her age (*Close Roll*, 35 Edw. I., m. 9). Feb. 2, 1301-2. Edeneburgh. "The King to Master Richard de Havering, his clerk, Escheator beyond Trent, health. Whereas among the lands and tenements which we have assigned in dower to Isabel, widow of John Ughtred, deceased, who held of us in chief, as of the Honour of Albemarle, of the lands and tenements of which the same John was seised in his demesne as of fee, we have assigned to the same Isabel a messuage with two crofts adjoining for pasture in the vill of Oustwyke; and whereas afterwards at the prayer (*ad prosecutionem*) of William de Hamelton, Dean of York, to whom we granted the custody of two parts of all the said lands and tenements to the full age of the said John's heir, who suggested that that assignment was made to the same Isabel contrary to the usual custom of our Chancery, since there was another messuage on the above-named lands and tenements, we commanded you to cause Brian Burdon, who married the said Isabel, and the said Isabel to be present in our Chancery on the Octaves of the Purification of the B.M. last past (9 Feb., 1300-01), and the Dean also; and whereas Brian and Isabel were warned by Richard Bond, of Oustwyke, and Amand Serjaunt, of the same place, to be present, but as they were neither present themselves nor sent their attornies, we now command you to seize the said messuage and crofts, and keep them till further order (*Rot. Fin.*, 30 Edw. I., m. 14).

that John Ouhtred held a messuage, with two crofts adjoining for pasture, in Oustewyke, and they are worth by the year 20s., save the repair of the houses. He held there nine bovates of land in demesne, each worth yearly 9s. There is a windmill, which yields nothing yearly.

These held of him:—John de Fittelinge, a toft and two bovates of land by foreign service; Stephen Bonde, a toft and a bovate for a penny rent, and 3 acres 1 rood of land by free service of 2d. yearly; Stephen Warde, a toft and half a bovate by foreign service, and yearly rent of 3d.; Stephen Addelstane, a toft by free service of 3d. yearly.

All these tenements the said John held of the King in chief, as of the Honour of Albemarle, by foreign service. He also held there of Amand *de Ruda* twelve acres of arable land, worth 12s. a year, by foreign service.

Joan, daughter of the said John, is his next heir, and aged five years and more.

[m. 3]

INQUISITION taken at Scardeburgh, before the same Escheator, on Monday after the feast of St. Luke the Evangelist, 26 Edw. (20 Oct., 1298), by the oath of Robert Hamonde of Scardeburgh, Roger *le Chareter* of the same, Simon Belle, Roger Clampe, Robert de Nortfolke, John Hamonde, Richard Cordewayner, Adam son of Robert, Roger at the Cross (*ad crucem*), Robert *le Mercer*, Simon de Folketon, and John Raynebalde. John Uctred held of the King in free burgage a capital messuage in Scardeburgh, worth by the year 40s.; also 67 acres of arable land, worth yearly 18d. the acre. He had there free tenants, who held of him by certain services, namely, Jollan de Wandesford, a house at 12d. a year rent; Henry Clerk (*clericus*), a house at 9s.; Thomas Cordewan, for a house, 7s.; Stephen Fyschwasser, for a house, 6s.; Robert Godewyn, for a house, 4s.; Simon Muriel, for a house, 3s.; Robert Whale, for a house, 3s. 6d.; Richard Cut, for a house, 17s.

There are also certain burgages which yielded to him 73s. 11d. yearly. These held of him, at yearly rents:— Robert Hamonde, for a house, 3s.; Henry de Brumpton, for a house, 2s. 6d.; Ralph de Steyntone, for a house, 12d.; the wife of *le Scirmissour*, for a house, 12d.; Robert *le Mercer*, for a house, 10s.; Alice Portelewe, for a house, 18d.; John *le Chareter*, for a house, 24s.; William Lepet, for a house, 2s.; Robert *le Tailliour*, for a house, 3s.; William de Harom, for a house, 9s.; Robert de Tireswell, for a house, 3s.; William de Harom, for a house, 3s.; the Hall of Pleas of

Scard', 15s.; Thomas Gauteron, for a house, 3s. 6d.; John de Roston, for a house, 2s. 6d.; Thomas *le Salter*, for a house, 2s., and for land at the Sandepittes, 12d.; Roger *le Tailliour*, for a house, 8s.; the dwellinghouse (*mansio*) which was Ralph de Crayke's, 24s.; the messuage which was Adam de Semer's, 20s.; Adam de Helperthorpe, for a house, 12d.; Alan *de Luda*, for a house, 8s ; Isabel Veter, for a house, 5s.; John de Gatesete, for a house, 8s., and for another house, 4s.; Margaret Hebbe, for a house, 7s.; the tenement formerly of the Mayor of York, 5s.; Walter Wiseman, for a house, 15s.; Henry White (*albus*), for a house, 14s.; land formerly of Thomas Haldan, for a house, 8s.; Thomas Folke, for a house, 10s. 6d.; land formerly of Emma Haldan, near the sea, 12s.; John Uppesecke, for land in the field of Scard', 5s.; William Moriz, for land in Scard', 20d.; Robert at the Cross (*ad Crucem*), for land there, 14s.; John *le Chareter*, for a house, 4s.; Walter Wyseman, for a house, 8s.; Elena Forge, for a house, 6s.; Richard *le Barber*, for two houses, 12s.; a stall (*selda*), with solar, 15s.; Geoffrey son of Ivo (*Yvonis*), for a house, 10s.; Alan de Hornese, for a house, 10s.; Robert Swan, for a house, 6s.; Maud (*Matild'*) Lygard, for a house, 2s.; Robert de Lindebergh, for a house, 2s.; Thomas de Whallesgrave, for one acre and one rood of land in Wallesgrave,[a] 2s. 8d. All these aforesaid tenants held of the aforesaid John, deceased, in Scard', in free burgage, by the services aforesaid.

There are also other tenants who held of him in Scard', at his will, at yearly rents, viz.:—John de Seleby, for a burgage, 9s.; William de Nessingwal, for a burgage, 18d.; John Hamonde, for a burgage, 2s.; Master John, clerk (*clericus*), for a burgage, 14s.; Roger Clamp, for a burgage, 13s. 4d.; William Goldsmith (*aurifaber*), for a burgage, 6s.; Adam Suthwalde, for a burgage, 8s.; John de Gatesheved, for a burgage, 16s.; William de Rudestane, for a burgage, 3s.; Richard de Cokermewe, for a burgage, 7s.; Maud (*Matild'*) Weddinge, for a burgage, 4s.; Alice Cant, for a burgage, 4s.; Margaret Cusser, for a burgage, 4s.; Hugh son of Martin, for a burgage, 2s. 6d.; John son of Adam of Malton, for a burgage, 2s. 6d.; Mariot under the Wall (*sub muro*), for a burgage, 6s.; William le Harremaker,[b] for a burgage, 3s. 6d.; Eliote, for a burgage, 3s. 6d.; Roger Girdler (*zonarius*), for a burgage, 4s.; Philip de Jernemewe, for a burgage, 3s.; Robert Pramp, for a messuage, 4s.; Martin Cobbler (*sutor*), for three burgages, 18s. 6d.; William Frende,

---

[a] Now Falsgrave.

[b] Or Hairemaker.

for a burgage, 6s.; Roger Linbuner, for 6 burgages, 8s.;
William Frend, for a burgage, 7s.; Geoffrey Wlispe, for a
burgage, 4s.; Geoffrey Mustard, for two burgages, 8s.; William
Kakenodil, for a burgage, 3s. 6d.; Roger Jubber, for a burgage,
4s.; Geoffrey Spiche, for a burgage, 13s.; Roger *le Cutelier*,
for a burgage, 5s.; Roger son of Ranulf, for a burgage,
3s. 6d. All the aforesaid tenements the said John Uctred
had by devise (*ex legacione*) of one Master Robert de
Scardeburgh his uncle (*avunculi*), which said tenements he
(John) devised on his dying bed (*legavit in lecto suo mortali*)
to Avice his mother for the term of her life, as is contained in
his testament, saving dower in the same to Isabel his wife.

And the jurors say that such is the custom of Scardeburgh, that every tenant there can *in extremis* devise his
tenements to whomsoever he will except to religious men,
and the said Avice by the said devise[a] [was seised thereof
after] the said John died.

Sum of all the sums aforesaid, £40 13d. Of which the
said John Uctrede yielded every year for the aforesaid
tenements to the burgesses of Scardeburgh', because they
have the town at fee farm from the King, 27s. in the name
of Gabelage (*gabulagii*), to make up £66 of silver which
they pay every year at the King's Exchequer for the farm
of the said town. He also yielded to the same burgesses
. . . . . . to make up £25 which they pay every year to the
King's Exchequer for the manor of Wa[lesgrave], which
manor they have, in like manner, at fee farm from the King.
He also yielded to them . . . . escheat, which Robert
Uctrede, grandfather of John, rented (*arentavit*), which said
9s. he paid by his own hand at the King's Exchequer every
year. He yielded also to certain . . . . . . by the year, 36s.
2d. Sum of the annual payment, £4 3s. 2d. [Remainder]
£35 17s. 11d.

Joan, daughter of the said John, is his next heir, and
aged five years.

INQUISITION taken at Bridlinton, before the same Escheator,
on the day of St. Luke the Evangelist, 26 Edw. (18 Oct.,
1298), by John de Marton, Norman de Kernetby, Ralph
Helard, Peter de Thornholm, William de Liesingby, John
Hiringe, Anselm (*Aunselmum*) Dreng, John de Burton,
Richard Astin, William son of Stephen, Henry de Wyndesen,
and Adam de Haye, who say on their oath that John

---

[a] The lower portion is (towards the end of several lines) worn and illegible.

Utreth held the grange of Oketon[a] by demise of the Abbot
of Meux for term of his life and that of Isabel his wife.
The capital messuage there is worth by the year 5s. There
are 30 bovates of land, each worth yearly 7s. The said John
held nothing of the King in the Wapentake of Dykeringe.
Total yearly value, £10 15s.

The said John held nothing of the King in the Wapentake of Dykeringe on the day of his death, and Joan, his
daughter, is his next heir, aged four years and a half.

INQUISITION taken before the same Escheator at York on
Wednesday after the feast of All Saints', 26 Edw.
(5 Nov., 1298), by Ralph de Doway,[b] Richard de Kyllyng-
wike, Elias de Yapum, Richard de Hawton, Richard de
Geveldale, Adam de Estorpe, Hugh de Colevile, William
Gerge, Martin Mawleverer, William de Geveldale, John
Fanecurte, and Thomas de Kardoyl, who say on their oath
that John Uctrede and Isabel his wife held the manor of
Gowthorpe[c] by the gift of John de Meux (*Melsa*), father of
Isabel, in frank marriage with her. The capital messuage
is worth by the year 3s. There are 12 bovates of land (at
10s. each) and 12 acres of meadow (at 2s.); a windmill, worth
8s.; and two cottages, 2s. a year. Sum, £7 17s. He held
the said manor of the Archbishop of York by knight's
service, and doing suit at his Court of Wylton every three
weeks. He also held in the town of Gowthorpe, by feoffment
of Alexander de Gowthorpe, to him and to his heirs, nine
acres of land (at 6d. the acre), and an acre of meadow, worth
18d. a year. Sum, 6s. He held these tenements of John de
Gray by knight's service. He held also to him and to his
heirs, by feoffment of Robert son of Alice, a waste plot
(*placeam*) and half an acre of land, worth 12d.; also 2 acres
of land (at 6d.) in the same town by feoffment of Thomas
son of Alice and of John Herewarde. Sum, 2s.; and he held
the said tenements of the Archbishop by knight's service.
Also he held in Yolthorpe[d] of William de Autri a bovate of
land, worth 6s. 8d. a year; of Robert Tailor, 40s. annual
rent, going out of 3 bovates of land which are of the fee of
· the Barony of Skerkenbeke [*sic*]; of the Archbishop of York

[a] Octon, par. Thwing.

[b] *Dway.*

[c] Gowthorpe, par. Blacktoft.

[d] Youlthorpe, par. Bishop Wilton.

in Bilton[a] two bovates, at 13s. 4d. each, and two cottages there, worth 2s. Sum, 28s. 8d. They are held by service of a penny. He held also of William de Autri, by knight's service, three acres of land in Ful Sutton,[b] at 6d. the acre, and two cottages, worth 2s. a year. Sum, 3s. 6d.

Sum total (except the manor of Gowthorpe), £4 6s. 10d., whereof a third part, 28s. 11½d.

LXVI. Two Inquisitions about Trespasses done against the King at Drypool in Holderness, and about the Port of Hull, Wreck, etc.

[26 Edw. I. No. 56.]

No writ.

[m. 1]

INQUISITION before Simon Constable on behalf of Sir Philip de Wilgeby, King's Escheator beyond Trent, by Stephen de Oustwyke, Michael de Chillam, Roger de Dole, John Bernard, William de Gemeling, Henry de Wiueton, Roger de Wiueton, William de Grimston, John Lubias of Dripol, Thomas Scholfin of the same, Peter de Rue in Sutton, Ralph Sturnel of the same, John *de la Wyke*, William *de la Wyke*, John Buk' of the Wyke, and Hugh Belle of the same, made on certain trespasses done to the King, made at Dripol in Holdernesse. They say that certain strangers from the east (*quidam extranei de partibus orientalibus*) came with a ship to Hulle, and that one of them fell ill, who on Sunday before Ascension Day (28 April) prayed for his ecclesiastical rights, and had them by the priest of Dripol. When this was done he went to Beverley in search of health, and when his doctors despaired of his health, on Saturday before St. Augustine's day he returned to his ship, and died as he was returning; and when he was dead his companions, as is the custom, watched him during the whole night on their ship, and on Sunday, the feast of St. Augustine (26 May),[c] 1297, carried his body to be buried. When they were come in the churchyard of Dripol to bury him, there came some on behalf of the Archbishop of York, that is, John Haget, John Mynot, Ralph *le Porter*, and William Clerk of Patrington, with a great crowd of the Archbishop's natives, as from

---

[a] Bilton, par. Swine.

[b] Full Sutton, a parish near Pocklington.

[c] St. Augustine's Day, May 26, fell on a Sunday in 1297, which shows that this inquisition was taken in that year.

Schiteby, Wodmanse, and Thoren,[a] and carried away the
corpse by force from the churchyard, and made a view of
his death by the said villans within the fee of Albemarle,
in prejudice of the same liberty and in contempt of the
King, and said by the oath of the bailiffs that he had died
by misadventure (*mortuum infortunio*), and therefore they
sequestrated into the Archbishop's hand the whole ship with
the chattels in it. They carried the sail ashore, and asked
£20 for the delivery of the ship with its gear (*atilia*) and
goods. All this they did unlawfully, because . . . . . . with
the port and water on both sides of the water, from the exit
of the Vielhulle right into the Humber, in all things which,
to . . . . ought of right to belong to the lordship of
Heudernesse.

[m. 2]

INQUISITION made by order of the King, before Sir Philip
de Wilgeby, the Escheator, by Adam de St. Martin,
John de Danethorp, Stephen de Oustwyke, William son of
Martin of Grimston, William de Frothingham, John de
Camerington, John Bernard of Brustwyke, William *de la
Chaumbre* in Holm, Henry de Preston, Walter de Flinton,
William de Sunderlandwyke, and Geoffrey de Sprotle, who
say that the whole tenement of the Vielhulle right into the
Humber is of the Earl of Albemarle's fee on the west side
of the Hull, and on the east side the whole tenement is
held of the said Earl in chief. And because the Earl's fee
extends on both side the water, they say that the whole
lordship of the port and water by right ought to belong to
the said Earl and his heirs, yet Sir Walter de Gray, late
Archbishop of York, in the time of King Henry, father of
the present King, appropriated the whole of the said lordship
of the water to himself and his successors, but by whose
consent, warrant, deed, or will they know not.[b] Interrogated
about wreck and wandering animals (*animalibus vagis*) and
other things which appertain to the King's crown, which
the Archbishop of York has appropriated to himself at
Patrington, whether he has appropriated them lawfully or
not, they say not lawfully, but unlawfully, and this lately
(*de novo*), after the death of the Earl of Albemarle last
deceased.[c]

[a] Skidby, Woodmansea and Thearne.

[b] At Whitsuntide, 1269, an agreement was entered into between Lady Joan de
Stuteville, and Archbishop Walter Gray and the chapter of York, about the free
passage of the water at Hull, which was then claimed by the Lady Joan, whose
rights descended to the Wakes (*Letters from Northern Registers*, Rolls Series, p. 20).

[c] William de Fortibus, the last Earl of Albemarle, who had seisin of the honour
of Holderness, died in 1260 (Vol. I., p. 73a).

LXVI*a*. ROBERT DE STOTEVILLE, *a foreigner. Extent of lands.*

[Escheator's Inquisitions ultra Trentam. Ex. Q. R. Series I. File 49.]
[m. 9]

Writ dated at York, 26 Oct., 26th year (1298), and directed to John de
Litegreenes, the Escheator, ordering him to make inquisitions about the
lands of Robert de Stoteville, a foreigner (*alienigena*), in Bowel in
Staunford, co. Northumberland, Ekinton, co. Derby, Kirkeby, co. Notts.,
and Boultone, co. York.

[m. 12]ᵃ

Extent of lands of Robert le (*sic*) Stotevile in Boulton,ᵇ
by William Lourd of Addewyck, Ralph son of Nicholas
of the same, William Kemp of Boulton, Gilbert Tanner of
the same, William son of Michael of the same, William son
of Walter of the same, Robert son of Thomas of the same,
Ralph son of Ranulph of Golthorp, Adam Forman of the
same, Robert Grimbald of Thirneschwo, Adam Swalwe of
the same, Ralph Scharp of Golthorp, who say that the same
Robert had a messuage in Boulton worth 2s. a year; a
meadow, 2s.; land, 4s. 2d. He owes to the chief lord of the
fee for the same, 6d. Lady Eda Bertram had her dower in
the same land in the time of Robert Stotevile, and still has.

LXVII. HENRY SON OF GILBERT LE CARPENTER.
Extent of lands. •

[24 EDW. I. No. 113.]

Writ tested by J. de Metingham at York, 14 Feb., 27th year (1298-9), and
directed to the Sheriff of Yorkshire. It has been shown by Henry, son
of Gilbert *le Carpenter* of Milford, that William *de Camera* of Milford,
in the King's Court before the Justices at Westminster, falsely and by
deception of the Court recovered his seisinᶜ against Henry of 30 acres of
land with appurtenances in Shireburne by default of Henry, although he
was never summoned to answer of that plea, nor was the land ever
taken into the King's hand by Henry's default, as customary. Therefore
he (the Sheriff) is to cause to come before the Justices at York in 15
days from Easter-day Walter Shepherd (*Bercarium*) of Milford, and John,
son of Roger of Barkestone, the first summoners, by whom he sent to
the Justices that Henry was summoned to be at Westminster in 15 days
from the feast-day of St. John the Baptist. Also to cause to come
before the same Justices at York Richard Derlinge of Fenton, John
Kawode, Thomas at the gate (*apud portam*) of Shirburne, and William
Belle of the same, by whose view that land was taken into the King's
hand, and Alexander de Sutton and William Malebraunche, the second
summoners, by whom it was sent to the said Justices in 15 days from

ᵃ The Northumberland inquisition [m. 10] was taken at Schipeley on Monday
after Martinmas (17 Nov., 1298). The Derbyshire inquisition [m. 11] was taken at
Ekinton on Monday, the morrow of All Souls (3 Nov.). Richard Chaplain paid
six *wode cosks* for his holding here. The Notts. inquisition [m. 13] is undated.

ᵇ Bolton-on-Dearne and Adwick-on-Dearne.

ᶜ From a note at the foot of the writ, it is shown that the case is entered on
the De Banco (Common Plea) Roll, Mich., 24 Edw. I., m. 204.

St. Martin's day, that Henry was to be there before them to answer to William as well as of the principal plea as of the said default. The Sheriff or his under-sheriff to be in person at York to certify thereof, together with the summoners and the viewers. William is also to be had there to answer as well to the King as to Henry of the said falsehood and deception.

[On a separate strip of parchment the following particulars appear] :—

Names of the first summoners.

Walter *Bercarius* of Milford is dead.

Manucaptors of John son of Roger of Barkestone, { William Malebraunke. John *le Carpenter*.

Names of those by whose view the land was taken into the King's hand.

Manucaptors :—

Of Richard Derlinge, { Thomas de Maldecrofte. John son of Gilbert.

Of John de Cawode, { John Sele. Richard son of Elias.

Of Thomas *ad portam*, { Peter *ad portam*. William *atte strete*.

William Belle of Shyreburne is dead.

Names of the second summoners.

Manucaptors :—

Of Alexander de Sutton, { Paulinus *le Hopper*. Robert de Sutton.

Of William Malebranke, { William de Staveleye. Robert *le Daye*.

Of William *de Camera*, { Adam Barne of Milford. William beyond the water of the same. Richard Barne of the same. William *le Provost* of the same.

EXTENT and appraisement made by virtue of the King's writ of thirty acres of land with appurtenances in Shyreburne by Peter at the Gate (*ad portam*) of Shyreburne, William *del Strete* of the same, John at the Spring (*fontem*) of the same, John Sele of the same, Peter Douke, and Thomas Grante of Shyreburne, sworn, who say upon their oath that the said 30 acres of land are worth by the year 12s. There are no issues, because the land lies untilled (*frisca et inculta*). It was taken into the King's hand, according to the tenor of the writ.

LXVIII. JOHN DE SETON.[a] *Inq. p. m.*

[27 EDW. I. No. 8.]

No writ.

[m. 2][b]

INQUISITION made by order of the King directed to the Escheator, before the Escheator at Driffelde, on the Nativity of the Blessed Mary, 27 Edw. (8 Sept., 1299), by Richard de Brunne, John de Crouncewyk, Adam *le Stabeler*, Alan de Pokethorp, Walter de Cotum, Thomas de Carliolo,[c] Thomas de Wymthorpe, William Fossarde, John Sommonur of Lokguton, William de Northorpe, Thomas Walran, and William Marshall (*marescallum*) of Ake, who say upon their oath that John de Seton held nothing of the King in chief in the Wapentake of Harthill (Herthylle) in the county of York, but he held in Suze Brune,[d] in the said Wapentake, seven and a half tofts, with fifteen bovates of land, of which each bovate, with[e] the said tofts, is worth by the year 13s. 4d. in all its issues, paid half yearly at Whitsuntide and Martinmas. Total, £10. There is no other approvement. [*Nec est ibi aliquid aliud appruamentum.*]

[a] On Oct. 24, 1299, the King took at Westminster the homage of Christopher, son and heir of John de Seton, deceased. Master Richard de Havering, the Escheator *ultra*, was ordered to restore his land (*Rot. Fin.*, 27 Edw. I., m. 4). On June 13, in the next year, the King ordered the same Escheator to partition the lands, which had been held in dower by Sarra, widow of Richard de Levyngton, between Richard de Kirkbride, Adam de Twynham, Gilbert de Sutheyke, and Walter de Corry, nephews and heirs of the said Richard, and Maude de Karrigg' and Emma de Karrigg', sisters, nieces and co-heirs, and Christopher de Seton The inheritance was to be divided into six parts, but the share of Maude and Emma, who were staying in Scotland with the Scots, enemies and rebels to the King, was to be retained in the King's hand (*Ibid.*, 28 Edw. I., m. 7). On Oct. 12, 1305, Richard Oysel, the Escheator *ultra*, was ordered to hand over to Christopher de Seton the vills of Gamelesby and Unthank in Cumberland, which his father, John de Seton, had granted in tail to Robert de Brus and Christiana, his wife, who had died without heirs (*Ibid.*, 33 Edw. I., m. 2). According to the inquisition relating to his Cumberland property, which was taken on Friday after the Nativity of the Blessed Mary, 27 Edw. I. (11 Sept., 1299), John Seton held one third of the manor of Skelton in chief by the service of cornage, and another third by a rent of 26s. and homage and fealty. Christopher Seton married a sister of King Robert Bruce, and was ancestor of the Setons, afterwards Earls of Winton and Eglinton. From his possessing the manor of Seaton, near Whitby, it would seem as if he derived his name from that place. There was a Durham family named Seton, whether the same or not is uncertain, who held land in S.E. Durham, in the neighbourhood of Seaton Carew, of the Scotch Bruces, who may have been the ancestor of the great Scotch house.

[b] The first membrane relates to property in Cumberland.

[c] Called Thomas de Cardoyl in 1295 (Vol. II., 171), when Thomas de Wymthorpe appears as Thomas de Wymundthorpe.

[d] Southburn, in the parish of Kirkburn.

[e] Query, "with its proportion of" understood.

John de Seton held the said land in Suze Brunne of William *le Latimer* son of William *le Latimer* by homage and foreign service, whence eight carucates make one knight's fee. His son Christopher is his next heir, who was 21 years of age at Lady day last.

[m. 3]

SIMILAR inquisition taken at Stokesley on Monday, the feast of the Exaltation of the Holy Cross, 27 Edw. I. (14 Sept., 1299), by Robert de Ackelom, John de Merske, John de Malteby, William Humette, William *del Hou*, Robert de Elredley, Walter *de la Chaumber'*, Hugh de Stunstale, Alan de Bolleby, John son of Thomas of Hylderwelle, Thomas de Boington, and John *du Vale*, who say that John de Seton held the manor of Seton[a] in his demesne as of fee of William *le Latimer* and Lucy his wife by the service of the fourth part of a knight's fee for all service, and he held nothing there of the King. There is there a chief messuage, and it is worth 3s. a year in herbage. There are 224 acres of land in demesne. Each acre 6d. a year. Total, £6 12s. (sic). Five acres of meadow, at 2s. an acre; total, 10s. A watermill, worth 13s. 4d. a year. There are also these firmars, namely, John de Dale,[b] who holds one toft, worth 16d. a year, and 24 acres, at 6d. an acre; total, 13s. 4d. John son of Thomas holds 2 bovates of land, at 3s. a bovate; total, 6s. Agnes daughter of Yvo holds one toft, worth 2s. Alan Glede holds one toft and one bovate of land, worth 3s. a year. Robert Foreman (*prepositus*) holds one toft, worth 12d. a year. Robert Warand holds one toft, worth 16d. a year. Marjory de Redding' holds an assart, worth 4s. a year. Henry Piper holds an assart, worth 4s. a year. John de Rome holds a toft, worth 8d. a year. These firmars pay their farms, to wit, the said sums by equal half-yearly payments at Whitsuntide and Martinmas. Total of the extent, £9 13s. 8d. Et non est ibi aliquid aliud appruamentum. (The finding as to Christopher repeated.)

LXIX. ROBERT DE SPROXTON. *Inq. p. m.*

[27 EDW. I. No. 30.]

[m. 1]

Writ of *diem clausit extremum* on the death of Robert de Sproxton, addressed to John de Lythegreyns, Escheator *ultra*, and dated Kyngeston, 23 Feb., 27th year (1297-8).

a Seaton, near Whitby.
b Called above John *du Vale*.

INQUISITION taken at Sproxton on Monday after the feast of St. Ambrose, 27 Edw. (April 7, 1298), by . . . . de Thornton, John son of Absolon, John de Etton, Richard de Waux, Robert Forester (*forestarii*) of Steyngreve, ... Geoffrey Wyche, John Chapeleyn, Nicholas de Schalton, Roger Sauwel, and Peter son of Margaret. Robert de Sproxton held in chief 11½ bovates of land, of which each contains nine acres of land, by the perch (*perticata*) of 18 feet, each bovate 5*s.*; 16 acres of meadow (2*s.*), a water-mill, 26*s.* 8*d.* A toft and two bovates of land were held of the said Robert in bondage, yielding 13*s.* 6½*d.*; and 4 hens at Christmas, worth 4*d.*; and 40 eggs at Easter, worth 1*d.* A bakehouse (*fornus*), from which he took yearly 4*s.* He had the following free tenants:—Robert son of Drogo, holding a toft and two bovates of land, 7*s.* 0½*d.*; Alice daughter of John, a toft and two bovates of land, 7½*d.*; Robert Clerk, two bovates of land, 7*d.*; Drogo *le Parker*, a toft and one bovate of land, 3*s.* 3½*d.*; Nicholas de Newton, a toft and 6 acres of land, 19*d.*; Peter de Sproxton, a toft and two bovates of land, 3½*d.*; Geoffrey son of Juliana, a toft and 8 acres of land, 9*d.*; Isabella de Neuton, a toft, two bovates of land, a piece of marsh containing three acres, 7¾*d.*; Adam Diuer, a toft and bovate of land, 9½*d.*; Mariota daughter of Isabel, a toft and 4 acres of land, ½*d.*; the heir of Adam son of Lyne, a toft and 2 bovates of land, 6¾*d.*; Nicholas de Themelby, a toft, 2*s.*; Hugh son of Thomas, three acres of land, 3*d.*; Richard *le Akhbrenner*, a toft and acre of land, 6*d.*

He also had the following cottars (*cotarios*):—Roger Sawel, holding a toft and croft, 2*s.* 1½*d.*, and 2 hens, worth 2*d.*, and 20 eggs, worth ½*d.*; Benet *le Tinkeler*, a toft, 3*s.* 2*d.*; John *le Mauwer*, a toft and croft, 3*s.* 1½*d.*, two hens, worth 2*d.*, and 20 eggs, worth ½*d.*; Emma Scot, one toft, 20*d.*; Richard Askbrenner, a toft and croft and acre of land, 3*s.* 1½*d.*, and 2 hens, worth 2*d.*, and 20 eggs, worth ½*d.*; Ralph son of Cidreda, a toft and acre of land, 3*s.* 1½*d.*, two hens, etc.;[a] William *le Mauwer*, a toft and croft and ½ acre of land, 2*s.* 5½*d.*, two hens, etc.;[a] Alice daughter of Robert, a toft and croft and acre of land, 3*s.* 1½*d.*, and 2 hens, etc.;[a] Robert Godehyne, a toft and croft, 3*s.* 3½*d.*, 2 hens, etc.;[a] Agnes Diuer, a toft, a croft, and half acre of land, 2*s.* 6*d.*, and 2 hens, etc.;[a] Geoffrey Miller, a toft, a croft, and half acre of land, 3*s.* 1½*d.*, 2 hens, etc.;[a] Stephen Bridkoc, a toft, a croft, and an acre of land, 3*s.* 1½*d.*, 2 hens, etc.;[a] Hugh son of Tille, a toft, a croft, and an acre of land, 3*s.* 1½*d.*, 2 hens, etc.;[a] William Godebarne, same, 4*s.* 1½*d.*, etc.[a]

[a] Price as before.

Also 7 tofts lying waste, worth 3s. 9d.; a turbary, worth 2s.; a piece of meadow in a place called le Walter Crok', worth . . . .

He held the above in chief by homage and the service of the fourth part of a knight's fee, and paying the King by the Sheriff of Yorkshire 13s. 4d., and for the fine of the Wapentake 2s.   Sum of the said lands and tenements, £9 17d.

He held of the abbot of St. Mary's, York, a chief messuage in Sproxton, 4s.; 8 bovates of land (5s.) ; 50 acres of wood, as it were waste, in which thorns grow, 2s.   He pays the abbot for these tenements 2s. 8d. a year.   Sum of the tenements held of the abbot, 43s. 4d.

He also held in Sproxton 7 bovates of land (5s.), 4 cottages, 13s. 4d., paying for the same to the abbot of Rievaulx 26s. 8d.   Maude, who was the wife of the said Robert, was enfeoffed of these by William de Sproxton, and had peaceable seisin thereof for thirteen weeks before the said Robert married her.

William son of the said Robert is his next heir, and was 21 at the feast of the Invention of the Holy Cross last past (May 3).   Robert had demised a moiety of all the said tenements to Sir Osbert de Spaldington for a term of 24 years, of which two had expired at Martinmas 26 Edw. (1298).

LXX.   RICHARD FOLIOT AND JORDAN FOLIOT.   *Inq. p. m.*

[27 EDW. I. No. 49.]

[m. 1]

Writ of *diem clausit extremum* on the death of Jordan Foliot, dated at Merton, 2 May, 27th year (1299).[a]

[m. 6]

Writ dated at Stepney (Stebeneth), 15 May (1299), and addressed to Richard de Haveringg.   Whereas the King had ordered him to seize the lands of Jordan Folyot, deceased, which were held in chief; and John de Warenne, Earl of Surrey, and Henry de Lacy, Earl of Lincoln, had asserted that the lands Jordan died seized of in his demesne as of fee, were held of them and not in chief, so that the custody thereof belonged to them ; the Escheator is to ascertain the truth.   "Per ipsum Regem ad instantiam predictorum comitum."

[a] Similar writ [m. 2] on the death of Richard Foliot, addressed to Walter de Gloucester, Escheator *ultra*.   Derbyshire inquisition [m. 3] taken at Wyunefeld on 1 July.   Richard held the castle and soke of Horeston for life, of the King's gift.   The Notts inquisition [m. 4], taken at Retford on 27 June.   Margery, Jordan's wife, who was still surviving, was jointly enfeoffed with her husband by Richard, Jordan's father, for the term of Margery's life, in the manors of Grymmeston and Wellawe and the hamlet of Besthorp with the soke of Grimmeston and its members.   Held of Henry de Lacy, Earl of Lincoln, and the Countess, his wife.   Both these inquisitions concur with the Yorkshire one as to the ages of Jordan and his son.

[m. 5]

INQUISITION concerning the lands and tenements of Richard Foliot and Jordan Foliot, made at York, 23 June, 27 Edward (1299), before Mr. Richard de Haveringg', Escheator, there being present Thomas de Fisschebourne, seneschal of the Earl of Lincoln, and Thomas de Schuffeld, seneschal of the Earl of Warrenne (*Warrennie*), who both had been forewarned for this purpose, by the oath of Simon de Kyme, Thomas Folejaumbe, knights, Richard Tyeys, John de Arches, Alan de Arches, Robert de Skelbroke, Thomas de Reynevyle, John de Flynthull, Peter de Bosevyle, Thomas de Sayvyle, Alan Alger, and Richard de Fetherstan. Richard Foliot held on the day of his death nothing in ˙chief of the King, nor of anyone else in his demeŝne as of fee, in the county of York. He had a rent of £10, to be received yearly from his son Jordan and Margery his wife, for the term of his life, from the manors of Northon and Fenewyke.[a] Jordan, son of the said Richard, was his nearest heir oñ the day of his death, and was of the age of fifty and upwards. Jordan died within five weeks after his father's death.

Jordan Folyot held nothing of the King in chief in his demesne as of fee, nor in demesne, nor in service, in the county of York. Jordan and Margery his wife, jointly enfeoffed by Richard his father in the manors of Northon and Fenewyke, held these manors on the day of Jordan's death of Henry de Lacy, Earl of Lincoln, by the service of three knights' fees. Margery is still surviving. The manor of Northon worth in all issues £29 a year, and the manor of Fenewyke £15 a year. Richard, son of the same Jordan, is his nearest heir, and was of the age of fifteen on Christmas last past.

LXXI. WILLIAM LE VAVASSUR *for* THE CHAPEL OF ST. LEONARD OF HAZELWOOD. *Inq. ad q. d.*

[27 EDW. I. No. 56.]

Writ dated at York, 13 July, 27th year (1299), and directed on behalf of the King by W.,[b] Bishop of Coventry and Lichfield, treasurer to John de Langeton, Chancellor of England, referring to the inquisition which is sent sealed in a box (*in quodam pixide consignatum*) to cause William *le Vavassour* to have the King's letters of license notwithstanding the Statute of Mortmain.[c]

[m. 2]

Writ *ad q. d.* dated at Stepney (Stebenhethe), 16 May, 1299.

[a] Norton and Fenwick, in the parish of Campsall, near Doncaster.

[b] Walter de Langton.

[c] *Patent Rolls*, 27 Edw. I., m. 12, for license dated Sept. 13 (p. 436).

[m. 3]

INQUISITION made before Sir John de Biron, Sheriff of Yorkshire, on Whit Tuesday, 27 Edw. I. (9 June, 1299), concerning land and rent in the vills of Heselwude and Cokesforthe,ᵃ by Thomas at Gate of Scirburne, William de Horingtone, David de Cawode, James de Berlay, Robert de Mikelfeud, Thomas son of John of Birne, Richard Malesouer, William de Cayteforthe, William Baulin's man, Walter Fikais, John son of Hoby, and Adam Norais, as to whether it will be to the damage and prejudice of the King or anyone else, if Sir William le Vavasour grants four marcs worth (*marcatas*) of land and rent to a chaplain celebrating divine service in the chapel of St. Leonard at Heselwode, and to His successors for ever, out of his lands in Heselwode and Cokesforthe. They say that it will not be so, for he does not hold his lands of the King, but he holds his land in Heselwode of Sir Henry de Percy, and in Cokesforthe of the Earl of Lincoln, and he has sufficient other land in those townships to fully satisfy, etc.

LXXII. DEAN AND CHAPTER OF ST. PETER'S, YORK.
*Seisin of the Hay of Langwath.*ᵇ *Inq. p. m.*

[27 EDW. I. No. 90.]

[m. 1]

Writ dated at Boxle, 7 Sept., 27 Edw. I. (1299), directed to Geoffrey Russel and Lambert de Trikingham, keepers of the archbishopric of York during the vacancy of the see. The chapter of St. Peter's, York, had shown that the dean of that Church and the same chapter long ago demised Langwath Hay, which they had acquired by grant from the prior and convent of Wartre, to former archbishops in succession, namely, William de Wykewane, John le Romeyn and Henry de Newerk, the late archbishop, during the life of each archbishop, for a buck of grease and a doe of fermeson (*pro uno damo tempore pinguedinis et una dama tempore fermesone*) to be paid yearly by each archbishop to the dean and chapter, so that after the death of each archbishop the Hay might revert entirely to the dean and chap'er. Further that the dean and chapter had seisin of the said Hay at each vacancy of the archbishopric after the death of the said William and John in accordance with an ordinance (*juxta quandam ordinacionem*) made between Walter Gyffard, formerly archbishop of York, and the dean and chapter ; and that they ought to have seisin of the same in the present vacancy of the archbishopric and in subsequent vacancies in accordance with the said ordinance.

Nevertheless the persons addressed had taken the Hay with its appurtenances into the King's hands amongst the lands and tenements of the archbishopric after the death of the said archbishop Henry, and unjustly detained them from the chapter, to their damage, etc., and contrary to the form of the ordinance. The keepers of the archbishopric are therefore directed in the usual manner to make inquisition by the oath of good and loyal men of their bailiwick.

ᵃ Hazelwood and Cocksford, south of Tadcaster.

ᵇ Langwith, in the parish of Wheldrake and wapentake of Ouse and Derwent, from which wapentake the jurors come.

[m. 2]

A N inquisition taken at York on Wednesday after the feast of St. Edmund the archbishop, 27 Edw. I. (18 Nov., 1299), before Geoffrey Russel and Lambert de Trykyngham, Keepers of the archbishopric of York during the vacancy, about Langwath Hay, by Walter de Hemelesheye, William Paumes, Richard de Fiskersgate, Henry son of Geoffrey of Kelkefeld, Robert de . . . telowe[a] of Naburne, Austin Coc of the same, William Helewys of the same, Hugh Freman of the same, Thomas in Brasitibus,[b] John de Cotyngwith, Ralph Murdok', and Robert Dryewode, who say on their oath that the dean and chapter of York acquired the said Hay to themselves and their successors and their church of St. Peter's, York, for ever. And they say that William de Wykewan, formerly archbishop of York, had only a tenement for the term of his life in the said Hay on lease from the chapter, nor had the said archbishop John nor archbishop Henry, who has now lately died, ever anything in the said Hay except only a tenement for the term of his life as aforesaid. They further say that the said dean and chapter had seisin of the said Hay at their suit against the King after the death of the archbishops William and John.

LXXIII. MASTER OF THE HOSPITAL OF ST. LEONARD'S, YORK. *Inq. ad q. d.*

[27 EDW. I. No. 96.]

Writ dated at Temple Lyston, 18 July, 27th year (1299).[c]

I NQUISITION taken before the sheriff of Yorkshire, and the mayor and bailiffs of the city of York, on Tuesday the feast of St. Matthias the apostle, 27 Edw. I. (24 Feb., 1298-9),[d] as to a certain lane near the wall of the Hospital of St. Leonard's, by virtue of the King's writ directed to them, whether or not it would be to the King's damage or the injury of the city, or anyone else whomsoever, if the King grant to the venerable father W., bishop of Coventry and Lichfield, master of the said Hospital, that he may block up (*obstruere*) a lane which leads from Blake Street (vico de Blaykestrete[e]),

[a] A hole in parchment here.

[b] Perhaps Drasitibus.

[c] On the back of the writ:—Arrayamentium istius brevis continetur in inquisicione huic brevi attachiata.

[d] There is some mistake in the date of the inquisition. The feast of St. Matthias, 27 Edw. I., fell on Tuesday, Feb. 24, 1298-9, which is earlier than the date of the writ.

[e] In the writ, vicus de Bleykstrete.

near the wall of the Hospital, to the street which leads to Bootham Bar (portam de Buthum), and enclose it with a wall for the enlargement of the court of the same Hospital, and may hold it so enclosed to him and his successors, masters of that Hospital, for ever. The Jury, namely, John *le Specer*, James *le Flemenge*, George *le Flemenge*, Clement de Pontefracto, Vincent Verdenelle, Ralph de Lincoln, Nicholas *le Cordewaner*, William de Carleton, Gaceus Flour, Robert de Neuland, Thomas de Wyteby, and William de Useburn, say that the enclosure will not be any damage to the King or injury to the city or anyone else.[a]

LXXIV.   JOHN DE ESHTON, *alias* ESTON, *for* THE ABBOT AND CONVENT OF FURNESS. *Inq. ad q. d.*

[27 EDW. I.   No. 103.]

Writ dated at Westminster, 27 March, 27th year (1299).[b]

INQUISITION made Thursday after the feast of the Translation of St. Thomas the Martyr, 27 Edw. (9 July, 1299), before J. de Byron, sheriff of Yorkshire, by William de Cesterhunt,[c] Alan de Catherton, John de Kygheley, Hugh de Halton, Adam de Wikeliswrth junior, William de Brigham, Constantine Fauuel, William de Lytton, William Everad, John son of Robert of Preston, William de Chofeld, and William de Skipton, clerk, sworn whether or not it would be to the damage or prejudice of the King or others if the King grant to John de Estone that he may grant and assign a lake in Eston to the abbot and convent of Furneys and their successors for ever. They say on their oath that the King would lose wardship, reliefs, and escheats, when they happen, but there will be no damage to anyone else, inasmuch as the soil lying on all sides, as the water is withdrawn, is common to the different neighbouring men of the district.[d]

It is held of the King as lord of Skipton Castle by knight service appertaining to 30s. rent, where £100 makes a knight's fee, by grant of the King made to the said John, as is witnessed in the charter which he has of the King.

---

[a] License granted 2 April, 1299.   See *Patent Rolls*, 27 Edw. I., m. 33.

[b] Per ipsum regem, nunciante W., Coventrensi et Lychfeldensi episcopo (*In dorso*).

[c] The same jurors as in No. LXXVII.

[d] Eo quod solum jacens circumquaque, sicut aqua se retrait (*sic*), est (*communis*) diversis hominibus viscinis (*sic*) patrie.   Some word seems to be omitted, and *communis* appears the most likely.

The lake contains 90 perches in length and 50 perches in breadth, each perch of 20 feet, and it is scarcely worth 30*s.* a year in all its issues as extended. The same John has in the manor of Eston land worth 20 marcs by the year, sufficient to perform all customs and due services, and to bear all other charges which it bears or is wont to bear. He never was put or ought or was wont to be put on assises, juries, or other recognitions for the said lake. The country will be in no way burdened or charged (*gravatum nec honeratum*) on account of the said grant and assignment. Dated at Skipton in Cravene.[a]

LXXV. WALTER SON OF THOMAS OF BARKESTON. *Slain at Dunbar.*

[27 EDW. I. No. 107.]

[m. 2]

Writ dated at Westminster, 20 Oct., 25th year (1297).

[m. 3]

INQUISITION taken at Schyrburne, before the sheriff of Yorkshire, on the eve of St. Thomas the Apostle, 26 Edw. I. (20 Dec., 1297), on the articles contained in the writ, by John de Lacy, Thomas Gates (*ad portam*), Warin de Fenton, Adam de Mykelfeud, John de Ledesham, William Chambers (*de Camera*), William Overwater (*ultra aquam*), Robert Chambers of Fenton, William Forester of Wystowe, William Hubard, William Clerk of Drax, and Geoffrey Clerk of the same, who say on their oath that Walter, son of Thomas of Barkestone, held in the township of Barkestone on the day on which there was the battle between the King of England and the Scots (*Schottis*) at Dunbar, of the archbishopric of York, a messuage and eleven acres of land and some other tenements in Barkestone, by homage and the service of the fourth part of a knight's fee, a service of 15*s.* 10*d.* a year, and doing suit every three weeks at the court of the archbishopric at Schirburn. Because the said Walter son of Thomas was helping the Scots (*in vi et auxsilio cum Schotis*) as the enemy of the King and kingdom on the day of the said battle at Dunbar against the King of England and his army then there, the sheriff seized the messuage and eleven acres of land in the King's hand, as he was previously ordered with respect to seizing lands of this nature. As to the value of the messuage and eleven acres of land, they say that they are worth

a The license was granted 12 Sept., 1299. See *Patent Rolls*, 27 Edw. I., p. 436.

beyond the services due to the archbishopric 16*d.* only. The jurors, being asked what are the other tenements held of the archbishopric, say that Alice, widow of Thomas, father of the said Walter, holds a messuage and twenty-four acres of land in Barkestone in dower of the inheritance of Walter, which ought to have reverted to Walter if he had stood in fealty to the King of England (*si ad fidelitatem domini regis Anglie stetisset*).

Asked[a] also if Walter is now dead or alive, they say they do not know, but they well know that Walter was in the said battle, and afterwards adhered to the Scots, and never afterwards returned to the fealty of the King of England. If he is still alive he is in intercourse with the Scots and in entire agreement with their wickedness, and strives and works as far as he can for the invasion of England, which God forbid.

Dorso. This escheat of the war (*que est de guerra*) belongs to the King, saving the service due to the lord of the fee, because he was, and is, if he is alive, a public enemy of King and kingdom.

He may have it of the King's gift, although it is an escheat of the war and belongs to the King, yet he does this of especial favour.

[m. 1]

Petition (*in French*) from the archbishop to the King for a grant of the messuage and eleven acres of land mentioned above.[b]

LXXVI. MASTER THOMAS DE ABERBURY,[c] *for* THE DEAN AND CHAPTER OF ST. PETER'S, YORK. *Inq. ad q. d.*

[27 EDW. I. No. 111.]

Writ dated at Westminster, 22 April, 27th year (1299).

INQUISITION taken before the sheriff of Yorkshire on Friday next after the feast of the Blessed Mary Magdalen, 27 Edw. I. (24 July, 1299), by John de Meningthorp, Clement Green (*de viridi*) of Seterington, Hugh

[a] Quesitus eciam si idem Walterus modo mortuus sit vel superstes, dicunt quod ignorant, set dicunt quod bene sciunt quod idem Walterus fuit in predicto conflictu et post adesit (*sic*) Schottis, nec uncquam se postea fidelitati domini regis Anglie reddidit. Et dicunt quod si superstes sit, adhuc cum Schottis conversatur et totaliter eorum nequicie consentit, et quantum in ipso est pro terra Anglicana invadenda, quod absit, nititur et operatur.

[b] The grant was made to the archbishop on 10 April, 1299 (*Calendar of Patent Rolls*, 1292-1301, p. 407).

[c] So in the writ. Called Alberbirs in the inquisition

Palmer of the same, Thomas Mills (*ad molend'*) of the same, Geoffrey de Sutton, Robert son of Nigel of Wyverthorp, William Maungevileyn, Robert Dreng of Sutton, William Slette of Warrom, Adam de Fynmer, Roger Palmer of Fridaythorp, and Walter Travers of the same, sworn, if the King should grant that Master Thomas de Alberbirs may give or assign a messuage, six tofts, and two carucates of land with the appurtenances in Multhorp[a] to the dean and chapter of St. Peter's Church, York, and their successors, to the finding of a chaplain to perform divine service in the same church for the souls of the successors of the said Mr. Thomas for ever or not, and to make the usual inquiries in relation thereto.

The said messuage, tofts, and land are held of Sir John fitz Reginald by knight service, where ten carucates make one knight's fee, and are worth 60s. a year. He has no other tenements in the said county to perform services and customs. As to suits, views of frankpledge, aids, tallages, ransoms, watchings, contributions, amercements, nothing, but for fine of wapentake 12½d. a year.

In dorso. Let it be done for a fine of 60s., and let him pay forthwith, and let the fine be enrolled in the rolls of Chancery.

LXXVII. JAMES DE ESTON,[b] *for* THE PRIOR AND CONVENT OF BOLTON. *Inq. ad q. d.*

[27 EDW. I. No. 117.]

Writ dated at Arundel, 27 June, 27th year (1299).

STAYNCLYF'. Inquisition taken on Thursday next after the feast of the Translation of St. Thomas the Martyr, 27 Edw. I. (9 July, 1299), before J. de Byroun, sheriff of

---

[a] Mowthorpe in the parish of Kirkby Grindalythe.

[b] On 7 Nov., 1278, the King at Westminster granted to John de Aston the manor of Tornton by Pickering', together with the homages and services of four knights' fees belonging to the same manor, extended at £67, the hamlet of Appeltrewik', member of the castle of Skipton-in Crauene, with its chief messuage and half a carucate of land, extended at £16 12s. 6d.; the hamlet of Broughton, also a member of the same castle, extended at £13 2s. 10d., excepting the suits of freemen doing suit at the court of Skipton ; the hamlet of Bradeley (Kildwick parish), member of the same castle, extended at 23s., with the like exception ; the lake of Eston, extended at 30s.; 10 acres of land called Simonesflat, with a piece of meadow, extended at 12s. 8d.; and three acres of land in Eyleshou towards Aston [12d.], to hold as the equivalent of £100 worth of land which had been granted him for the hereditary right he claimed in the earldom of Albemarle, and in all lands, etc., in England, Normandy and elsewhere, which belonged to Alina de Fortibus and her ancestors, and which he had released to the King. John was to do the service of one knight's fee (*Charter Roll*, 6 Edw. I., No. 5).

Yorkshire, by William de Cestreund,[a] John de Kygheley, Alan de Catherton, Hugh de Halton, Adam de Wickeleswurth junior, William de Brygham, Constantine Fauuel, William de Lytton, John son of Robert of Preston, William Everard, William de Shefeld, and William de Skiptone, clerk, sworn to enquire if it be to the damage or prejudice of the King or others, if he grant to James de Eyston that he may give and assign his manor of Apeltrewike with its appurtenances to the prior and convent of Boulton for ever. They say it is to the damage and prejudice of the King, inasmuch as the King loses the sixth part of the service of one knight's fee beyond 10d., as in wards, reliefs, and escheats when they happen, but it is not to the damage or prejudice of others. The manor is held of the King by knight service, because the King enfeoffed Sir John de Eyston of the said manor with other lands and rents to the value of £100, to hold of the King by the service of one knight's fee for all service, suits, exaction, and demand whatsoever, as is witnessed in the King's deed about the gift.[b] John de Eyston gave the manor to his brother James de Eyston, to hold of the King for ever by the due and accustomed services. The service of that manor is the sixth part of a knight's fee, besides 10d., as is aforesaid. The yearly value of the manor beyond its issues is extended in the King's gift made to the said John at £16 12s. 6d., but in these times it is not worth the extent. No tenements remain to the said James in respect of which he can perform services. As to performing services, as in suits, views, aids, tallages, watchings, fines, ransoms, amercements, contributions, and other charges whatsoever, they say that the said manor was never charged with such services before the time of the said James, because that manor was in the hands of the Earl of Albemarle, and afterwards in the hands of the King, up to the gift made by the King to the said John. As to whether the said James may be placed in assizes and juries and other recognitions or not, they say not, because he has not the wherewithal (*non habet unde*), and in so much the country is charged. Given at Skipton in Craven.

Dorso. Let it be done for 100 marcs.

---

[a] Jurors same as in No. LXXIV.

[b] Licence granted on 1 April, 1300 (*Calendar of Patent Rolls*, 1292-1301, p. 506, See also p. 610).

LXXVIII.   SIMON GUMER, *alias* GOMER, *for* THE WARDEN
AND FRIARS MINORS OF SCARBOROUGH.   *Inq. ad q. d.*

[27 EDW. I.   No. 120.]

Writ dated at Westminster, 2 April, 27th year (1299).

THE King by the above writ ordered the sheriff of Yorkshire to inquire if he should grant leave to Simon
Gumer of Scardeburgh' to give and assign to the Warden
(*gardiano*) and Friars Minors of Scardeburgh' a messuage
with its appurtenances near their church of Scardeburgh',
for the purpose of enlarging theîr area and burying ground
(*ad largicionem aree sue et cimiterii sui*) there, and to make
the other usual inquiries.

INQUISITION made thereupon at Scardeburgh on Tuesday
next before the feast of the Apostles Philip and James,
27 Edw. I. (28 April, 1299), by Henry Sampson, Simon de
Folketun, Simon Sage, Robert Ham(onde), Almeric Codde-
lyng', John Ithun, John Stacy, Geoffrey de Folketun, Robert
son of Nell', Eustace Feryman, John Lynbrinner,[a] and Robert
Smith (*fabrum*), who say that if the said Simon gives or
assigns the said messuage to the said Warden and Friars,
it is not to the damage or prejudice of the King or others.
The messuage is held of the King, and pays 6*d.* yearly to
the King for gabulage, and in so far it is to the damage
of the King. The messuage is worth 10*s.* a year in all its
issues. One burgage remains to Simon beyond the said
gift, which burgage is sufficient to bear all customs and
services as well for the messuage so given as for the burgage
retained, and to sustain all else which they sustained or were
wont to sustain, as in suits, views of frankpledge, aids,
tallages, watchings, fines, ransoms, amercements, contributions, and other charges whatsoever. Simon can also be
put upon juries, assises, and other recognitions of whatsoever kind, as he was wont to be put before the gift and
assignment. The country will not be charged or injured more
than usual after the said gift and assignment by the default
of the said Simon.[b]

[a] Lymbrinner in *North Riding Records*, N.S., iv., p. 138.

[b] Licence granted to Simon Gumer on May 18, 1299 (*Calendar of Patent Rolls*,
1292–1301, p. 416).

LXXIX. JOHN, SON AND HEIR OF ROGER DE MOUBRAY. *Extent of Lands held in wardship by William de Hamelton.*

[27 EDW. I. No. 145.]

> Writ dated at York, 24 Nov., 27th year (1298), tested by J. de Metingham, addressed to the Sheriff, ordering him to have extended and valued the lands and tenements which William de Hamelton, guardian of certain parts of the lands of John, son and heir of Roger de Mounbray, holds in his bailiwick of the said inheritance, who [was called to warranty by]ᵃ Hugh de Eland, whom Henry de Knyueton and Joan, his wife, call to warranty, and who warranted to them the third part of a messuage and the moiety of a carucate of land, and 28s. rent in Butterwyke and Ouston, co. Lincoln, extended at 23s. 4d. a year, which Roesia, widow of Roger de Mounbray, claimed in dower against him before the Justices at York.

HOVINGHAM and Threske. Inquisition taken on Thursday after the Epiphany, 28 Edw. (13 Jan., 1299-1300), about the lands and tenements which William de Hamelton holds in his wardship of the inheritance of John, son and heir of Roger de Moubray, by John de Besingby, Roger Raboc, Robert de Colton, John son of Absolon, Robert Cowe, Robert Forester, William Talenace, Robert Yole, Robert de Nidde, William de Schalton, Walter le Talyur, and Richard de Kilburne. William de Hamelton holds the manor of Houingham, worth 13s. 4d. a year; a dovecote, 2s.; in demesne, 9 score and 7 acres of arable land (6d.); 50 acres of meadow (18d.); in bondage, 15 bovates of land, £10; 14 cottages, 49s.; from farms of free tenants in money and rents (*in den' et denarratis*), £4 12s. 6d.; a watermill, 23s. 4d. At Threske, 15 score acres of arable land (5d.), 10 acres of meadow (3s.), 14 acres of meadow (2s. 6d.), 20 acres of meadow (18d.); agistment in moor and wood and approvement (*approwamentum*) of pannage, 41s.; a boon rent (*redditum de precaria*), 8s.; a free court, 40s.; rent of assise from free men and bondmen ....., £8 16s. 5d.; rent of 8 pound of pepper, 8s.; 8 pound of cumin and one pound of incense, 9d. In two mills and one bakehouse, in toll of market, and in pleas of the borough, £13.ᵇ

In dorso. Sum, £49 14s. 4d., the third part whereof £13 4s. 7d.

ᵃ Some omission here.

ᵇ In duobus (molen)dinis et uno furno, in theoloneo mercati et in placitis burgi, xiij/i.

LXXX. WILLIAM SON OF HELEWYSE, DAUGHTER OF GILBERT DE SKUPTON', AND OTHERS. *Extent of lands claimed against John Sampson and Mary his wife.*

[27 EDW. I. No. 150.]

Writ tested by J. de Metingham and dated at York, 8 Feb., 27th year (1298–9), ordering the Sheriff to extend and have valued a messuage and two bovates of land with their appurtenances in Nune-Appeltone, which William son of Heleuyse, daughter of Gilbert de Skupton, William son of Matilda, and Adam son of Alice, claimed in the King's court before his Justices at York, as their right against John Sampson and Mary, his wife, for which the same Mary and John called to warranty Richard Wascelyn of Brunneby,[a] who holds no land in the county. He is directed to make the usual return.

AN extent and valuation made at Nun-Apilton of one messuage and two bovates of land in Nun-Apilton, by Henry de Colton, Michael de Knapton, Henry de Coupmanthorpe, Thomas Ayre, Nicholas de Castilford, William son of Ralph, William Smith (*fabrum*) of Merston, Thomas Broket, Henry Fraunsays, Henry Belle, and John son of Henry of Colton, who say that the said messuage and bovates of land are worth 26s. 8d. a year in all issues.

LXXXI. HOSPITAL OF ST. MARY MAGDALEN, PLUMTREE, NEAR BAWTRY. *Vacancy and value.*

[27 EDW. I. No. 151.]

Writ tested by John de Metingham and dated at Canterbury. . . . . . Sept., 27th year (1299), and directed to Geoffrey Russel and Lambert de Trikyngham, keepers of the archbishopric of York, states that the King wished to be certified whether the hospital of St. Mary Magdalen of Plumtre by Bautre, alleged to be vacant, is of the patronage of the archbishopric [so that if the King presents some fit priest to it during the present vacancy], he can do so without inflicting injury on any one. The keepers are therefore directed to make inquiry as to how long it has been vacant, what it is worth in all its issues, and who is the patron.

AN inquisition taken at Plumtre before Geoffrey Russel and Lambert de Trikyngham, keepers of the archbishopric of York during the vacancy of the see, on Friday, the feast of St. Leonard, 27 Edw., the 28th year commencing (6 Nov., 1299), by William Foreman (*dictus prepositus*) of Scroby,[b] Hugh Clerk of the same, Richard Neel of the same, William Grubbe of the same, Nicholas de Plumtre of the same, Peter son of Daud of the same, John *le Forester* of

---

[a] Burnby.

[b] These jurors occur again in No. 87, which is another inquisition relating to the same matter.

Plumtre, Roger Calle of the same, William Alinote of the
same, Hugh Leveryk of the same, Robert Amice of
Raveneshelf, and Geoffrey son of Robert of the same. As
to the vacancy in the hospital named in the writ the jurors
are quite ignorant, inasmuch as Roger, who for eight years
past has been in possession (*possessioni incubuit*) of the
hospital, is still alive, and collected the last profits for his
own use and spent them in his own name.[a] Although he
does not continually reside in the same hospital, yet he
sometimes (*alternis vicibus*) comes there. They have no
information as to his resignation or deprivation. It is worth
20s. a year in all its issues. They say positively (*precise*)
that it is of the patronage of the archbishopric of York.

LXXXII. NICHOLAS DE MEYNELL.[b] *Inq. p. m.*

[27 EDW. I. No. 156.]

[m. 1]

Writ dated at Canterbury, 28 May, 27th year (1299), and addressed to Master
Richard de Havering', Escheator beyond Trent.

[m. 2]

Similar writ to the same Escheator, dated the day following.

[m. 3]

INQUISITION of the lands and tenements which were
Nicholas de Menil's on the day he died, made at Tresk
on 6 July, 27 Edw. (1299), by the oath of John de Blaby,
Robert Guer, John de Menil, and Robert de Furneux,
knights, John de Redmershil, John de Gouton, John son of
John, Adam de Leke, John Morgan, William de Mundeville,
William *le Venur*, Ralph de Lestre, William de Moubray,
John . . . . . . , John de Kirkeby, Walter le Graunte, Robert
Oliver, John Maunsail, Thomas de Aldewerke, Thomas
Blaunfronte, John gener Dauid, and Thomas de Yolton.
Nicholas held in chief the manor of Castel Levington,[c] which

[a] Ultimos fructus ad usus suos collegit et nomine suo distraxit.

[b] Son and heir of Stephen de Meynell, of Whorlton in Cleveland. A pedigree
of the family is given in the *Guisborough Chartulary* (Surtees Society), ii., 78n.
On p. 67n an account is given of the above-named Nicholas de Meynell. The
parentage of his wife Christiana is unknown. The order to give seisin of his
father's lands to Nicholas, son and heir of Nicholas de Meynell, is dated at Chilton
in Kent, 21 July, 1299 (*Rot. Fin.*, 27 Edw. I., m. 10).

[c] In the parish of Kirk Levington. Castle Levington, as "alia Leuctona," was
given to Robert de Bruis some time after Domesday, probably in the reign of
Henry I. At the time (1284-5) of *Kirkby's Inquest* (p. 130) it had become part of
the Meynell fee, but in 1302-3 the Percies of Topcliffe were the chief lords (*Ibid.*,
p. 239). The history of the mesne tenants is far from clear. A family called
Feugers seem to have held it for a long time, but they disappear about 1280,
possibly in consequence of Andrew de Feugers borrowing money from the Jews
(*Calendar of Patent Rolls*, 1281-1292, p. 25). At a later period it belonged to
members of the family of Percy of Kildale (*Whitby Chartulary* (Surtees Society),
ii., 704n).

was for long of the fee of Brus, by the service of finding one serjeant on horseback (*servientem equitem*) in the King's army for forty days at his own expense. Cristiana, who was Nicholas's wife, still surviving, was jointly enfeoffed with him in the said manor by the charter of John de Lithgrayns and the royal confirmation, to hold to them and the heirs of Nicholas of the King by the same service. The manor yields yearly £ . . . . in all outgoings. Nicholas held nothing of the inheritance of Cristiana his wife.

He held in his demesne as of fee the manors of Werlton, Semer, Eston, and Aldewerke,ᵃ of the archbishopric of Canterbury, by the service of doing the office which pertains to the butlership in the archbishop's hostel on the day of the enthronization of the archbishop.ᵇ The manor of Wherleton is worth yearly in all its issues £24, the manor of Semer £16, the manor of Eston £22, and the manor of Aldewarke £9 10s. He also held in his demesne as of fee two bovates of land in Pottehowᶜ of the said archbishopric by the said office of butlership, worth yearly 20s. Also the manor of Bovingtonᵈ of the same by the same service, worth £24 a year.

Nicholas, son of Nicholas de Meynel, is the next heir of the said Nicholas, and was of the age of twenty-four years at the feast of St. Nicholas last past (6 Dec.).

[Same membrane]

INQUISITION of the knights' fees and advowsons of churches which were the said Nicholas's on the day he died, made on the day, place, and year abovesaid, by the same jurors. William de Boketon held four carucates of land of the said Nicholas in Boketonᵉ of the fee of the archbishopric of Canterbury by knight service, where twenty-four carucates of land make one knight's fee. Walter de Buketon held four carucates of land in Bentonᶠ of the same fee. Osbert de Arches held two carucates of land in Newsomᵍ of the same fee. William de Siwardby held of the same fee four

ᵃ Whorlton, Seamer and Eston in Cleveland, and Aldwark in the parish of Alne.

ᵇ Per servicium faciendi officium quod ad panetariam pertinet in hospicio archiepiscopi Cantuariensis die intronisacionis ejusdem archiepiscopi.

ᶜ Potto, Whorlton parish.

ᵈ Boynton, near Bridlington.

ᵉ Buckton, near Bridlington.

ᶠ Bempton.

ᵍ The vill of Neusom or Newsholm, now depopulated, nearly adjoined that of Bempton on the south-west (*Kirkby's Inquest*, 54*n*).

carucates and two bovates of land in Siwardby.[a] Robert de Bovynton held two carucates of land in Bovynton and three carucates of land in Thorp.[b] Theobald de Bryggham held three carucates of land in Briggham. John de Hesellarton held two and a half carucates of land in Louthorpe. Robert de Hesellarton held two and a half carucates of land in Louthorpe. John de Hesellarton held one carucate of land in Alburne.[c] William de Erghum held one carucate of land in Erghum.[d] John de Hessellarton held seven carucates of land in Hessellarton. Laurence de Etton held a carucate of land in Etton. All the abovesaid tenants held of the said Nicholas the abovesaid tenements by the quantity of service of a knight's fee, where twenty-four carucates make one knight's fee.[e] Each carucate of the same is worth 40s.

Robert de Pothow held three carucates of land in Pothow.[f] William de Traneholm held a carucate of land in Traneholm.[f] John de Meynill held six carucates in Rungeton.[g] Hugh de Meynil held six carucates in Hilton and seven bovates in Hoton.[h] John de Meynill held two carucates in Mydelton.[i] Matthew de Semer held one and a half carucates of land in Semer. Robert de Brathwayth held a carucate in Brathwayth.[j] Robert de Scotherskelf' held two bovates in Scothereskelf'.[k] Henry de Neuby held half a carucate in Neuby.[l] Hugh de Lellum held half a carucate in the same vill. Hugh de Lellum held three bovates in Tunstall.[m] Gilbert de Tunstall held a carucate in Tunstall. Hugh de Tunstall held five bovates in the same vill. Robert de Pothow and the others held the aforesaid tenements of the

[a] Sewerby, Bridlington parish. Of the same fee is repeated after each of the entries following.

[b] Thorpe, Rudston parish.

[c] Awburn, Carnaby parish.

[d] Erghum, or Argam, which has long ceased to exist, stood a little to the south of the road leading from Burton Fleming to Grindale, and about a mile from the latter village (*Kirkby's Inquest*, 54*n*). A different place from Arram in the parish of Atwick in Holderness, formerly Erghom. The Christian name is supplied from *Kirkby's Inquest*.

[e] Per quantitatem servicii feodi militaris unde, etc.

[f] Potto and Trenholme, Whorlton parish.

[g] East Rounton.

[h] Hutton Rudby.

[i] Middleton-on-Leven.

[j] Braworth, in the township of Skutterskelfe, parish of Hutton Rudby.

[k] Skutterskelfe.

[l] Newby, Seamer par.

[m] Great Ayton par.

said Nicholas by the amount of the service of a knight's fee, where twelve carucates make one knight's fee. Each carucate of the same is worth 26s. a year.

The prior of Briddellington held six carucates of land in Briddelington, the prior of Wartre . . . . carucates in Frydaithorp' and three carucates in Middelton[a]; the prior of St. Andrew's, York, three carucates in Middelton ; the abbot of Rievaulx (de Ryvalle), four carucates of land in Brochton[b] in frankalmoign. Each carucate worth 40s. a year.

The advowson of the church of Ruddeby, with the advowson of the free chapel of Wherleton, belonged to the said Nicholas. The church of Ruddeby was worth 200 marcs a year, and the chapel 15 marcs.

[m. 7]

Writ dated at Northaluerton, 1 Dec., 28th year (1299), and directed to the same Escheator, informing him that although the King had taken the homage of Nicholas, son and heir of Nicholas de Meinill, for his father's holdings, this was in no wise to interfere with the assignment of dower to Nicholas's widow, Cristiana, who was as yet undowered, and who had had assigned to her the morrow of Hillary then next on which to receive her reasonable dower in Chancery.[c]

[m. 5]

INQUISITION of the knights' fees which were Nicholas de Meynill's on the day he died, made at Killum on 23 Feb., 28 Edw. (1299–1300), by the oath of Nicholas de Bovyngeton, John de Burton, Richard Astyn, William son of Stephen, Ralph Helard, Roger de Lunde, Anselm Dryng, Walter Martyn, Hervey de Wyndduseme, John Hernysog, Thomas de Pokethorp', and Robert Bridde of Pokethorp', who say that Robert de Bovyngeton held a carucate and two bovates in Bovyngton, and three carucates in Thorpe by the service of the third part of one knight's fee, worth yearly £13 6s. 8d. William de Sywardeby held four carucates and two bovates in Sywardeby, and five carucates in Burton, by the service of three parts of one knight's fee, worth £30 a year. Theobald de Bryggeham held three and a half carucates in Bryggeham by the service of a fourth part of one knight's fee, worth £10 a year. Ingeram de

---

[a] In the wapentake of Harthill, called below Middelton by Baynton.

[b] Little Broughton, near Stokesley (Kirkby's Inquest, 136n).

[c] Note at back:—This writ was delivered to me on the . . . . day of December, and on Thursday the eve of the Nativity of the Lord next following (24 Dec.) I made known to Nicholas, son of Nicholas de Meynyll, deceased, at Wherleton, in the presence of William de Salcok, John son of Geoffrey of Wherleton, Ralph Sturmy of Fayceby, and John de Ellerker, and also of other free and lawful men, that he should be in the Chancery of the Lord King on the day contained in the writ according to the form of the writ.

Bovyngeton held a carucate in Bovyngton by the service of the twelfth part of one knight's fee, worth 66s. 8d. a year. William de Bovyngeton held half a carucate of land in the same vill by the service of the twentieth part of one knight's fee, worth 33s. 4d. a year. William de Erghom held a carucate in Erghom, and a carucate and a half in Neusom, by the service of the sixth part and the twenty-fourth part of one knight's fee, worth £8 6s. 8d. a year. Thomas de Hale held four carucates in Buketon by the service of the third part of one knight's fee, worth £13 6s. 8d. a year. Thomas de Poynton[a] held five bovates of land in Fraysthorp' by the service of the forty-eighth part of one knight's fee, worth 16s. 8d. a year. John de Hessellarton held ten bovates in Hessellarton, and two bovates in Yedingham, and two carucates in Louthorp', and a carucate in Bovyngton, and half a carucate in Alburne, and half a carucate in Neusom, by the service of half a knight's fee, worth £20 a year. Robert Bard' held half a carucate and a half in Hesellarton, and half a carucate in Yedingham, by the service of the eighth part of one knight's fee, worth 100s. a year. William de Colevile held five bovates and a half in Hesellarton, and two carucates and two bovates in Fridaythorp', and a bovate in Yedingham, by the service of the fourth part of one knight's fee, worth £10 a year. Agnes de Preston held four and a half carucates in Thurkelby in Krendale[b] by the service of the third part and the twenty-fourth part of one knight's fee, worth £16 a year. William de Ros held six carucates of land in Middelton by Baynton by the service of half a knight's fee, worth £20 a year. Thomas son of Geoffrey held five bovates in Hessellarton and Yedingham by the service of the twenty-fourth part of one knight's fee, worth 33s. 4d. a year. Robert de Hessellarton held two and a half carucates in Louthorp, and half a carucate in Aleburn', by the service of the fourth part of one knight's fee, worth £10 a year. John de Burton and Joan his wife held four carucates in Attyngewyk'[c] by the service of the third part of one knight's fee, worth £13 6s. 8d. a year. The prior of Briddelington held six carucates in Briddellington and six carucates in Frydaythorp by the service of half a knight's fee and the sixth part of a knight's fee, worth £26 13s. 4d. a year. The prior of Malton held half a carucate in

---

[a] This name is wrongly altered to Boynton in *The Lay Subsidy Roll* for 25 Edw. I. (1297), p. 140, where Thomas de Poyngtona is the chief taxpayer in Fraisthorpe.

[b] Thirkleby, Kirby Underdale par.

[c] Atwick in Holderness.

Hesellarton by the service of the twenty-fourth part of a knight's fee, worth 33s. 4d. a year. Laurence de Etton held a carucate in Etton by the service of the twelfth part of a knight's fee, worth 66s. 8d. a year. The prior of Wartre held half a carucate in Fraisthorp in frankalmoign, worth 20s. a year. Robert de Bovyngeton and the others held the aforesaid fees of the said Nicholas on the day he died, as of the same Nicholas's manor of Bovyngton.

[m. 4]
> Writ dated at Blithe, 17 Jan., 28th year (1299-1300), and addressed to the same Escheator, informing him that the inquisition already sent was insufficient, as no mention was made of the fee held in chief, or of the services due for the same. He is now ordered to remedy this omission.[a]

[m. 6]

INQUISITION of knights' fees and advowsons of churches, which were Nicholas de Meynill's on the day he died, made at York 8 Feb., 28 Edw. (1299-1300), by the oath of William de Mundeville, Adam de Kyrkeby, John de . . . . , Adam de Leeke, Nicholas de Lunde, Thomas de Ottryngeton, William de Smytheton, John de Malteby, Richard de Fenton, John de Fyntres, and John son of Richard of Thorneton, who say that Nicholas de Meynill and Cristiana his wife held jointly in their demesne, as of fee, the manor of Castellevington of the King in chief, by the service of the fourth part of one knight's fee, worth in all issues £20 a year. Cristiana is now seised of the manor. John Wake held two carucates in Aton in Clyveland by the service of the sixth part of one knight's fee, worth 8 marcs a year. John de Meynill of Rungeton held four carucates in Rungeton, two carucates in Hoton, and four bovates in Pottehou, by the service of half a knight's fee and the twenty-fourth part of a knight's fee, worth 26 marcs a year. Hugh de Meynill, of Hilton, held six carucates in Hilton and four bovates in Hoton by the service of half a knight's fee and the twenty-fourth part of a knight's fee, worth 26 marcs a year. Robert de Scotherschelf' held a carucate in Scotherschelf'[b] by the service of the twelfth part of one knight's fee, worth four marcs a year. Robert de Pottehou held three carucates in Pottehou by the service of the fourth part of one knight's fee, worth 12 marcs a year. Robert Gower held two carucates of land in Carleton by the service of the sixth part of one knight's fee, worth 8 marcs a year. Robert Bret held a carucate in the same

[a] *Dorso :*—xxiiij^to die Jan. apud E. v^us l.m. Thome de Salcok' in Northtriding.
[b] Skutterskelfe, Hutton Rudby par.

vill by the service of the twelfth part of one knight's fee, worth 4 marcs a year. William de Traneholme held a carucate in· Traneholme by the service of the twelfth part of one knight's fee, worth 4 marcs a year. Robert de Braithewath held a carucate of land in Braithewath by the service of the twelfth part of one knight's fee, worth 4 marcs a year. John de Meynill, of Middelton, held two carucates of land in Middelton by the service of the sixth part of a knight's fee, worth 8 marcs a year. Robert de Tunstall held a carucate of land in Tunstall by the service of the twelfth part of one knight's fee, worth 4 marcs a year. Matthew de Semer held a carucate and a half in Semer by the service of the twelfth and the twenty-fourth parts of one knight's fee, worth £4 a year. Henry de Neuby held half a carucate in Neuby by the service of the twenty-fourth part of a knight's fee, worth 2 marcs. Hugh de Lellum held half a carucate in Neuby and three bovates in Tunstall by the service of a twenty-fourth, a forty-eighth, and a ninety-sixth part of one knight's fee, worth 46s. 8d. a year. Hugh de Tunstall held five bovates in Tunstall by the service of a twenty-fourth and a ninety-sixth part of one knight's fee, worth 33s. a year. Alexander le Mareschalle held two bovates in Hoton by the service of a forty-eighth part of a knight's fee, worth 13s. 4d. a year. John, son and heir of Alan de Walkyngham, held two bovates in the same vill by the service of the forty-eighth part of one knight's fee, worth 13s. 4d. a year. The advowson of the church of Ruddeby and the advowson of the free chapel of the manor of Wherelton belonged to the said Nicholas on the day he died. The church of Ruddeby is worth 250 marcs a year, and the said chapel 20 marcs a year, according to their true value.

LXXXII a. THOMAS DE LONGEVILERS, BROTHER AND HEIR

OF JOHN DE LONGEVILERS. *Proof of age.*

[Curia Regis. 28 EDW. I. No. 158.]ᵃ

NOTINGHAM. The sheriff was commanded that, whereas Thomas de Longevilers, brother and heir of Roger de Longevilers, deceased, who held of the King in chief, said that he was of full age, and demanded from the King that the lands and tenements which were of his inheritance, and were in the wardship of the King's relative, Edmund, Earl

---

ᵃ The Roll for Trinity Term, 28 Edw. I. (1300).

of Cornwall, by grant from the King, should be restored to him, in consequence of which the King granted him a day for proving his age before him wherever he shóuld be, who was born at West Markham, in the said county, and baptized in the church of the same vill, to summon the Earl and Mr. Richard de Havering', the escheator *ultra*, who were warned to attend by William Freman, of Markham, and Robert *le Seriaunt*, of the same. The sheriff comes, and the Earl by his attorney, Gilbert de Holm, but show no reason why the proof of age should be delayed.

William de Bevercotes, knight, aged 50 and upwards, distant from West Markham half a league, where the heir was born, examined about his age, says he is of full age, namely, 21 years and upwards, and was so on Monday the morrow of Easter last (11 April). Asked how he knows this, says he has a son named Thomas[a] born before (*antenatum*), who was born two years before the birth of the said heir, which John was 23 years at Palm Sunday (*Pascha floridum*) last (3 April). The heir was baptized in the church of All Saints, West Markham, and Thomas Barbot and William *le Taillour* were his godfathers, and a certain lady, Ivetta de West-Markham, his godmother. The heir's mother was purified in the said church on a Saturday, about three weeks after the heir's birth.

Henry de Sutton, living at Walesby, aged 44, distant from West Markham ten leagues, says the heir has a sister, Ellota, whom the same Henry was at one time to have married, according to an arrangement (*per prelocucionem*) made between the heir's father and the same Henry's uncle (*avunculum*), and he says that a certain day was fixed between them for carrying out this business, namely at West Markham on Tuesday the morrow of the said heir's nativity, since which day 21 years have elapsed on Tuesday in Easter week last past. As they could not agree about the marriage, Henry married a certain Isabel, now his wife, at the feast of the Purification next following, since which time 21 years will have elapsed at the feast of the Purification next (2 Feb.).

Roger Crescy, of Est Markham, living there, aged 38, distant from West Markham one league, says the chaplain who baptized the heir was called John *le Neyr*. Knows the fact because he was with John de Lysours, knight, who married the mother of the said heir after his father's death, namely at the feast of the Blessed Mary Magdalen (22 July),

---

[a] A mistake for John.

and he says that 21 years will have elapsed at the said feast last past, and that the heir was then aged ten years old and more, as he learnt from trustworthy persons.

Simon de Caldewelle, living in Laxton, aged 40, distant from West Markham two leagues and more. His father died at the feast of Peter's Chair (22 Feb.), before the heir's birth. His father held a meadow of the heir's grandfather (*avo*), wherefore he himself after his father's death went to the grandfather for the purpose of doing what was due for the meadow, and he found the grandfather at West Markham in the Easter week after his father's death, and there saw the heir's nurse and others of the grandfather's household talking about the birth of the heir. Twenty-one years have elapsed on Easter week last.

William de West Markham, living in the same, aged 45. At that time he was (*stetit*) with his uncle Robert, whose daughter was the heir's mother, and he says he was present in the vill when the heir was born and in the church when he was baptized; and ever afterwards he stayed, and still stays, in the same vill.

William de Eyville, of Egmanton, living in the same, aged 51, distant from West Markham one league, knows because he has a daughter, Elena, born on Palmsun eve (*vigilia Palmarum*) before the heir's birth, who was 21 on Palmsun eve last (2 April). Besides[a] at that time he was seneschal of some portions of the lands of John de Eyville in those parts, and at the same time the heir's father was seneschal of the household (*hospicii*) of the said John, and he then went to the same father to ask leave of the said John to go to his wife, who was then lying in childbirth.

William son of Maude of Egmanton, living there, aged 60, has a son John, born on Palm Sunday before the heir's birth, who will be 21, etc.

John de Dodington, living in Tokesford, aged 45, distant from West Markham half a league, knows it from the statement (*relatu*) of the heir's mother, who told it him once at Fletburgh, when he came there for some land he had acquired from John de Lysours, who married the heir's mother after his father's death.

Nicholas *le Clerk*, of Tokesford, living there, aged 40. His father Robert died on the first Sunday in Lent before

---

[a] Preterea dicit quod ipse fuit senescallus tunc temporis quarundam parcium terrarum Johannis de Eyville in partibus illis, et quod eodem tempore fuit pater predicti heredis senescallus hospicii dicti Johannis, et tunc adivit ipsum patrem petere licenciam a dicto Johanne quod posset adire uxorem suam que tunc jacuit in puerperio.

the birth. He also married his wife the year following his father's death.

John de Lanum, living in Laxton, aged 36, distant from West Markham two leagues, has a younger brother, Gilbert, born the week before the heir's birth.

William de Bildewath, living in Bughton, aged 50, distant from West Markham two leagues, had a younger brother Thomas, who died, and was buried in the church aforesaid the same day the heir was born.

Roger son of Henry of West Markham, living there, aged 40, was in the vill the day the heir was born, and his wife Ivetta was the godmother, and all the time afterwards he stayed there, and does so still.

The heir being asked whether he was married or not, says no. On this the Treasurer gives evidence that the lord King had offered the heir one of the daughters of Adam de Cretingges, deceased, and that the heir, on seeing the said daughters, agreed to marry the eldest. And whereas the said Thomas has sufficiently proved his age before the lord King, and as it also appears by the appearance of the heir's body that he is of full age, namely twenty-one years, and has also agreed to the said marriage offered him by the King, as is aforesaid, therefore let the said heir have seisin of the lands and tenements falling to him from his inheritance.

LXXXIII. JOHN DE DANTHORPE,[a] *an idiot. Extent of lands.*

[Esc. ultra Trentam. Series I. File 50.]

[m. 5]
    Writ dated at York, 27 June, 28th year (1300), and addressed to Mr. Richard de Haveryngg', Escheator *ultra*, or his subescheator in Holdernesse.

[m. 6]
DANTHORP. Extent made before Mr. Richard de Haveryngg on Saturday after the Translation of St. Thomas, 28 Edw. (9 July, 1300), by the King's writ, of the manor of Danthorp, which belongs to John de Danthorp, an idiot (*fatui*), son

[a] An inquisition was taken on Friday before the Conversion of St. Paul, 21st year (23 Jan., 1292-3), at Neweton in Allerdale (co. Cumberland), before Thomas de Normanville, Escheator beyond Trent, concerning the lands in the King's hand by reason of the idiotcy (*racione fatuitatis*) of the same John of the inheritance of the John de Danthorppe in Alneburgh. Thomas de Luscy was chief lord of the lands in question. Of his relationship and of what family the same John was sprung (*de parentela et de qua gente idem Joh. sit oriundus*), the jurors say that the said John de Danthorppe was son and heir of Sir John de Danthorppe, knight, and the same John was son of Sir Alan de Danthorppe, knight. The mother of the said John was daughter of Sir Robert de Carlaton, knight (*Inq. post mort.*, 21 Edw. I., No. 210, and *Calendarium Genealogicum*, ii., 477). In the account of Thomas de Normanville, Escheator beyond Trent, from Michaelmas, 12 Edw. I. (1284), to

and heir of Sir John de Danthorp, deceased, by John de Fyttelyngg', Simon de Lund', Henry de Wyueton, Peter de Hyldeyerd, Simon de Sprottele, Nicholas Warde, Nicholas Haukyn, Robert Ingeram, Peter de Byltone, William Leueneht, Thomas de Ros, and William Ysac'. A capital messuage, with herbage and fruit of garden, and with herbage of a close before the gate, 20s. A close called Millecroft, 3s. In demesne, 15 bovates of land and two parts of one bovate, at 10s. the bovate. A bovate of land in bondage, which Walter Stute holds, 10s. A toft called Abbitoft', 2s. A toft called Dundraghetoft, 2s. Sir Walter de Faukunbergge holds in Danthorp a toft and bovate of land, and yields for all service at Martinmas and Whitsuntide, 6s. 8d. William Leueneht holds a toft and bovate of land, and yields at the same terms, for all service, 2s. William Ysac' holds a toft and bovate of land, and yields, etc., 12d. Laurence son of Thomas of Humbeltone, holds a toft, and yields at Christmas, for all service, 1d. Roger *de le Croft* holds a toft and bovate, and yields at Christmas, for all service, 1d. William Smith (*faber*) holds a toft and two acres of land on either side the vill (*ex utraque parte ville*), and yields at Christmas 1d.

Sum, £10 3s. 6d.

Dorse :—Holdernesse. Extenta de Danthorp'. Dominis Thesaurario et Baronibus de Scaccario per subescaetorem regis in Holdernesse. Manerium contentum, etc., committatur Johanni de Kirkeby clerico pro x marcis regi reddendis ad scaccarium ad totam vitam idiote, et de residuo extente inveniat eidem idiote racionabilem sustentam suam. In rotulo memorandorum de anno xxviij° inter commissa.

LXXXIV. THOMAS DE WESTON.[a] *Inq. p. m.*

[28 EDW. I. No. 35.]

[m. 1]

Writ of *Diem clausit extremum* of Thomas de Weston, dated at Stepney (Stebenheth'), 5 May, 27th year (1299), and addressed to Mr. Richard de Havering', Escheater *ultra*.

INQUISITION made at Harewode of the lands and tenements which belonged to Thomas de Weston, on Sunday after the feast of St. Luke the Evangelist, 27 Edw. (25 Oct., 1299),

Michaelmas in the year following, he renders account of £10 from the issues of the lands which were John de Danthorpe's in Danthorpe, whose son and heir is in the King's custody as he is of unsound mind, and no more because the mill is thrown down, and he made payments for his clothes and shoes (*pro robis et calciatur'*) (*Escheators' Accounts ultra Trentam* §). The same entry occurs in the account for the year following (*Ibid.*). On 11 June, 1293, the King granted to Adam by Richard de Skyteby, Robert Attetounende of Harewode, William de Budeby, Robert de Lofthus', Robert son of Angnes of Langwathby, Robert de Dychton, Robert Trayst', Robert Petypas, William de Fenton, Serlo de Ecop', and Richard de Stoketon. The said Robert and Cristiana his wife, still surviving, were jointly seised of the lands and tenements in Wirdeley[b], within the manor of Harewode hereunder written, which lands and tenements the same Thomas and Cristiana jointly acquired by the feoffment of the different feoffees hereunder written, to hold to them and the heirs and assigns of the same Thomas of the chief lords of Harewode, which is in the King's hand by the death of Isabel de Fortibus, late Countess of Albemarle, namely of the grant of Henry Underwode, a messuage, 40 acres of land, which Agnes widow of the said Henry holds in dower of the grant (*ex reddicione*) of the said Thomas and Cristiana, the said messuage and 9 acres of land, at 6*d.* an acre. Total, 15*s.* 6*d.* Of the grant of Adam *le Hunter*, 18 acres of land (6*d.*); sum, 9*s.* Of the grant of Henry son of John Clerk of Wirdeley, 18 acres (6*d.*); sum, 9*s.* Of the grant of William son of Richard of Wiggedon, half a toft, an acre of land, and a rood, 12*d.* Of the grant of Robert son of Robert Undrewode, 5 acres and a rood of land (6*d.*); sum, 2*s.* 7½*d.* Of the grant of Alice Engepas, daughter of William Mannoys of Wirdeley, and of Richard Cobbler (*sutoris*) her husband, a messuage (8*d.*), 3 acres and 2 roods of land (6*d.*); sum, 2*s.* 5*d.* Of the grant of William Wolpak', half an acre of land, 3*d.* Of the grant of Robert de Hoperton, two messuages (12*d.*), and 12 acres of land (6*d.*); sum, 7*s.* Of the grant of John de Holm, 3½ acres of land (6*d.*); sum, 21*d.* Of the grant of Robert de Lofthus' and Juliana his wife, seven selions of land, 10*d.* Of the grant of Robert de Stoketon and Margaret his wife, three selions of land, 4*d.*

They also acquired two tofts and two bovates of land in Wytheton,[c] containing 14 acres, of the feoffment of Robert de Broghton, to be held of Thomas de Westetouht by

de Skyrewyth, his watchman (*vigili nostro*) the custody of the lands of John de Danethorp, an idiot from birth, in Alneburgh, co. Cumberland, to hold for the life of the said John, on condition that he pay 40*s.* a year for his maintenance to the kinsman of the idiot, who by consent of his friends shall have custody of him. *Calendar of Patent Rolls*, 1292–1301, p. 22.

[a] From the Cumberland inquisition taken at Cokermuthe on the Epiphany, 28 Edw. I. (6 Jan., 1299–1300), it appears that Weston had acquired lands in that county, namely, the lordship of Great Clifton, from John de Plumlaund, and property in Little Clifton from Thomas de Ireby.

[b] Weardley.

[c] Weeton in the parish of Harewood.

paying 6d. at Martinmas, and by doing suit for this and the other lands and tenements aforesaid at the court of Harewode every three weeks, and paying the sheriff of Yorkshire, for the King's use, 6½d. at Michaelmas ; worth 6s. 8d.

John, son of Richard de Weston, brother of the said Thomas, is his heir, and is of the age of 30 years and upwards.

They also acquired from Henry son of Robert Underwode the homage and service of Richard de Goldesburg', and an annual rent of a pound of cumin; the homage and service of Robert de Burghdon, and an annual rent of 6d.; the homage and service of Robert son of Robert of Wyrdeley, and an annual rent of 16d.; the homage and service of Robert Clerk of Harewode, and an annual rent of 4d.; and the homages and services of Margaret, daughter of John Drinkewel', and Elena, daughter of Henry Shepherd (*bercar*), and an annual rent of 4d. To be held in fee of the chief lords of the manor of Harewode, by the service of doing suit at the manor court of Harewode every three weeks.

-- —

LXXXV.   EDMUND, EARL OF CORNWALL.[a] *Inq. p. m.*

[28 EDW. I. No. 44.]

[m. 33][b]

.... Boroughbridge on Monday next after the feast of the Epiphany, ... Edw. (11 Jan., 1299–1300) .... skyp, Jordan Casse, John de Mildeby, Thomas Coning, Ralph *le Clerk,* Thomas ...... edale, Walter Gamel, and Richard *atte West Lythe.* Edmund held the day on which he died [the manor of Aldborough (*Vetus Burgus*)],[c] as a member of the honour of Knaresburgh, which honour the said Edmund held of the King in chief .... a certain garden where formerly was the site of the manor, containing 2½ acres, worth 3s. There are ...... 6d. Sum, £8 9s. 9d. Thirty-seven acres of meadow (2s.) ; sum, 78s. Free .... and render their rents at Easter and Michaelmas, namely

---

[a] Edmund of Almaine, son of Richard, Earl of Cornwall and King of the Romans, and Sanchia, third daughter and co-heir of Raymond Berenger, count of Provence, and grandson of King John, was born in Dec., 1250, succeeded to the carldom of Cornwall in 1272, and died 1 Oct., 1300. He married Margaret de Clare, daughter of Richard, Earl of Gloucester.

[b] The condition of many of the membranes belonging to this inquisition is most deplorable. Owing to a lavish use of galls at the beginning of the century they have become utterly illegible. The version printed above is taken from the *Add. MSS.* 15662, fo. 257. See also *Add. MSS.* 26719, fo. 23b, and *Add. MSS.* 26727, fo. 11b. It has been collated with the original where legible.

[c] Supplied from the printed calendar.

William Hall (*de aula*), a messuage and 10 bovates of land
. . . . Ralph Casse, a messuage and 4 bovates of land,
4*s.* 6*d.*, whose works are worth by the year 3*s.* 1*d.* William
de Minskip . . . . . . by the year, 18½*d.* Juliana *atte Grene*,
a messuage and 4 bovates of land, 2*s.* 8¾*d.*; works, 4*s.* 1*d.*
. . . . . . by the year, 12*d.* . . . . asteis, a messuage and 2
bovates of land, 16*d.*; works, 18*d.* Jerome de Ethelingthorp,
a messuage and 4 bovates, ... 11*d.*; works, 3*s.* 1*d.* John
de Linton, a messuage and 6 bovates of land, 4*s.* 10*d.*;
works, 2*s.* 5*d.*, and gives for the custody of one foal, 12*d.*
Elias de Tanfeld, a messuage and carucate of land, 3*s.* 3*d.*
for all things. John *atte Hil*, a messuage and 4 bovates of
land, 2*s.* 9½*d.*; works, 3*s.* 1½*d.* William Tasckard, a messuage
and 2 bovates of land, 16*d.*; works, 19*d.*; and gives yearly
for a certain waste there, 18*d.* Ralph Manipe, a messuage
and bovate of land, 8½*d.*; works, 9¼*d.*; for food of dogs, 6*d.*
Richard de Walrethwait, a messuage and bovate of land,
8½*d.*; works, 9¼*d.* William de Gaithill, a messuage and bovate
of land, 8½*d.*; works, 9¼*d.* Ralph *atte Grene*, a messuage
and four bovates of land, 3*s.* 7*d.*; works, 3*s.* 1*d.* Richard son
of Richard, a messuage and 4 bovates of land, (*omission*);
works, 3*s.* 1*d.* Walter Gamel, a messuage and two bovates
of land, 13*d.*; works, 18½*d.* Ralph Bothe, a messuage and
3 bovates of land, 2*s.* 3½*d.*; works, 2*s.* 8¾*d.* John Casse, a
messuage and two bovates of land, 15*d.*; works, 18½*d.*;
and for waste, 6*d.* There are there the bond-tenants (*bondi*)
underwritten, some of whom hold more and some less land,
and pay their rents at the terms above written, namely :—
Ralph de Linton, a messuage and 2 bovates of land, 17*d.*;
works, 2*s.* 5½*d.* Walter Gamel and Richard son of the
Foreman (*prepositi*) hold and render the same. Richard de
Cathale, a messuage and bovate of land, 8½*d.*; and does half
the service that the said Richard does. Ralph son of
Ralph, a messuage and bovate of land, 8½*d.*; works, 14¾*d.*
Robert de Burgo, Oliver de Burgo, and Richard *atte West
Lythe*, each of whom holds a toft and bovate of land, 8½*d.*;
works, 14¾*d.* Gilbert son of Geoffrey, a messuage and 3
bovates of land, 2*s.* 1½*d.*; works, 3*s.* 7½*d.* From rent of John
Bulling for waste, 16*d.*; and of Robert Gamel for waste,
4*d.* From rent of 7 cottagers, holding at the will of the
lord, at the said terms, 6*s.* 9*d.*; works, 3*s.* 3*d.* The township
(*villata*) of Aldborough (*Veteris burgi*) gives to the tallage
at Michaelmas 40*s.* There are five bond tenants there, who
hold at the will of the lord 5 bovates of land of the lord's
demesne, each of whom renders at the terms aforesaid 10*s.*,
and the works of each of them are worth by the year 2*s.* 9½*d.*

Sum, £23 2*s.* 9¾*d.*

MINSKIP. In demesne, 2 tofts, 2s. 111 acres of arable land (4d.); sum, 37s. Free sokemen, some of whom hold more and some less land, and pay their rents at the terms aforesaid, namely Ralph son of Adam, William de Gaithill, William son of Geoffrey, Richard son of Ralph, each of whom holds two bovates of land, and renders by the year 13d.; works, 18½d. Sum, 10s. 6d. Of the same tenure, Alan de Walkingham, Ralph son of Alan, and William Britt, each of whom holds a bovate of land and renders 6½d.; and works, 9¼d. Sum, 3s. 11½d. Richard *le Vavasur*, a free tenant (*liber tenens*), holds 12 bovates of land, 6s. 5d.; works, 8s.; and gives for the custody of the dogs and foals, 12d. Sum, 15s. 5d. Thomas son of Alexander, a free tenant, 6 bovates of land, 3s.; works, 4s. 0½d.; for the custody of the foals, 12d. Sum, 8s. 0½d. Free tenants, Alan . . . . . , William Tankard, Alan Bracket, and William Spakeman, who hold 8 bovates of land and render yearly in common, 4s. 4d.; works, 11s. 2d.; and give in common, for the keeping of dogs, 6d. Sum, 11s. Richard son of Alan, a free sokeman, 2 bovates of land, 13d.; works, 18½d. John son of Stephen, a free tenant, 6 bovates of land, 2s. 8d.; works, 3s. 2d. Two sokemen, Robert son of Richard and John son of Michael, each two bovates of land, 6½d.; works, 9¼d. Sum, 2s. 7½d. A messuage and 3 acres of land of the lord's demesne, let to farm yearly for 18d. Agnes, daughter of Ralph, a free tenant, a toft and 2 acres of land, 2d. Robert son of Thomas, Richard son of Adam, and John son of Gilbert, free tenants: Robert holds 3 bovates of land, 18d., works 2s. 4¾d.; Richard, a toft and 3½ acres of land, 17d., works 3d.; and John, a bovate of land, 6½d., works 9¼d. Alan de Walkingham, a free tenant, holds a bovate of land, and renders for all things 12d. Richard son of Ughtred, a bovate of land, 6½d.; works, 9¼d. The aforesaid Ralph son of Adam and Richard son of Ralph give each of them for the food of the dogs (*putura canum*), 6d. Sum, 12d. The township (*villata*) of Minskip gives to tallage at Michaelmas, 20s. The said Thomas son of Alexander gives, for the keeping of foals, 12d.; and from the land of John Woderove, for the keeping of foals and dogs, 18d. Sum, £6 13s. 10½d.

BOROUGHBRIDGE (*Ponsburgi*). There are burgesses who hold their burgages by doing suit therefor at the court of Boroughbridge thrice in the year, and they do not render any rent for the same. There are certain wastes and escheats, the tenants of which hold them by the letting of the bailiffs of the late Earl of Cornwall at the will of the lord, and render therefor by the year at the said terms,

35*s*. 1¼*d*. Three watermills, which every year want great repairs, worth yearly £20. Toll and freight (*fraght*) of the said borough, by land and water of Yor, £20. The fishery in the waters of the Yor and Use, £12. Stallage (*stallagia*) in the waters aforesaid, £8. Pleas and perquisites of courts, as in amercements and other casualties, 100*s*.

Sum, £66 15*s*. 1½*d*.

BURTON.[a] John de Walkyngham holds the town (*villatam*) of Burton at 4*s*. 4*d*. a year, at the terms aforesaid; works, 13*s*. 4*d*.
Sum, 17*s*. 8*d*.

DONESFORD.[b] Robert de Donesford, 4 bovates of land, 2*s*. 2*d*.; works, 8*d*.
Sum, 2*s*. 10*d*.

BRANTON.[c] Free tenants: Roger de Hunsynghoure, John Scayf, Henry *atte Gate*, and Robert de Rippeley, who hold ten bovates of land in common, and render at the said terms, for all things, 4*s*. 10*d*.
Sum, the same.

GRAFTON. Six bovates of land in demesne, containing 30 acres (6*d*.) Sum, 15*s*. Free tenants, some of whom hold more and some less land, and pay their rent at the terms aforesaid, namely:—Richard son of Godfrey, two bovates of land, 3*s*. for all things. John son of Richard, two bovates of land, 5*s* for all things. William son of Thomas, two bovates of land, 6*s*. Alan Russel, a cottage, 12*d*.
Sum, 30*s*.

MILDEBY.[d] Free tenants (*liberi tenentes*), some of whom hold more and some less land, and pay their rent at the terms aforesaid, namely:—John son of Alan Walkingham, 2 tofts and 6 bovates of land, 4*s*. 10*d*.; works, 19*d*.; also 3½ acres of land, 3*s*. 6*d*. John de Ouldeby, a messuage and 3 bovates of land, 2*s*. 5¼*d*.; works, 16¼*d*. George son of William Tankard, 3 tofts and 5 bovates of land, 4*s*. 0¾*d*.; works, 2*s*. 3¼*d*.
Sum, 21*s*. 1*d*.

ROUTHCLYVE.[e] A capital messuage, worth in herbage and fruit of the garden yearly 2*s*.; 250 acres of land in demesne, the price of 200 whereof at 6*d*., sum 100*s*., and of 50 at a penny, because the land is poor (*debilissima*) and lies uncultivated; 18 acres of meadow in divers places (3*s*.). Sum, 54*s*. A wood, containing in circuit half a league, the pasture whereof is common, and is worth in the sale of underwood yearly 2*s*. Three free tenants, namely:—Robert

[a] Humberton.
[b] Dunsforth.
[c] Branton Green.
[d] Milby.
[e] Roecliffe, in the parish of Aldborough.

de Burgo, Richard son of Alan, and Thomas Fruggy, of whom Robert holds a messuage and two bovates of land, 12*d*.; works, 2*s*. 2*d*.; and the aforesaid Richard and Thomas hold two tofts and 4 bovates of land, 2*s*. 6*d*.; works, 2*s*. 9½*d*. The underwritten bond tenants, some of whom hold more and some less land, and pay their rents at the terms above written, namely:—Peter son of Ralph, Agnes who was the wife of Stephen de Minskip. Stephen Punchard, Henry son of Stephen, John son of Robert, Ralph son of Stephen, Thomas Punchard, William Palky, Richard son of Henry, Henry son of Herbert, each of whom holds a messuage and two bovates of land and renders 12*d*., and the works of each are worth yearly 3*s*. 4½*d*. Sum, 43*s*. 9*d*. The said Stephen holds a messuage and bovate of land, 6*d*.; works for the same, 20¼*d*. Gilbert son of Auot, a messuage and bovate of land, 6*d*.; works, 20¼*d*. Richard son of Peter, a messuage and two bovates of land, 18*d*.; works, 3*s*. 4½d. William Broun, a messuage and three bovates of land, 18*d*.; works, 5*s*. 0⅔*d*. Jerome son of Gilbert, a bovate of land, 6*d*.; works, 20¼*d*. William Tuchet, a messuage and two bovates of land, 5*s*. 3*d*.; works, 3*s*. 4½*d*. The said Gilbert son of Auot, a toft and bovate of land, 6*s*. 8*d*.; works, 20¼*d*. The said Stephen Punchard and Henry son of Gilbert give two (*blank*), remitted 6*d*. From the rent of William son of Richard of Minskyp, for a bovate of land, 10*s*. 6*d*. Alan Sele, Ralph son of Alan, Alexander son of Mariot, and Adam son of William hold two bovates of land, and render in common 2*s*. 2*d*. for all things. Adam Bracket, William Tankard, and William Spakeman, free tenants, give for their works, from six bovates of land, 3*s*. 10½*d*. in common. Rents of cottagers holding at the will of the lord, at the terms aforesaid, 17*s*. 1*d*., whose works are worth yearly 2*s*. 7*d*. From the tenants of William de Stopham in Est Westwyke, for the easement of a road to their pasture, 18*d*. A fishery, worth 12*d*. The town (*villata*) of Routheclive gives for tallage at Michaelmas 10*s*. Perquisites of court, as in amercements and other casualties, 6*s*. 8*d*.

Sum, £15 15*s*. 2¾*d*.

Sum of the whole, £116 2*s*. 5*d*.

And the said jurors say that the lord King Edward, cousin of the said Edmund, is the next heir of the same Edmund, and is of the age of fifty years and upwards.

Dorso. Amount of the sums of all the extents in the county of York in the custody of the escheator beyond Trent, £376 2*s*. 8*d*.

[m. 34]

INQUISITION on the lands and tenements which belonged
to Sir Edmund, Earl of Cornwall, made at Knaresburgh
on Monday, the morrow of the Circumcision, 29 Edw. (2 Jan.,
1300–1301), by the oath of Nicholas de Burton, William
· · · · · , Thomas Turpyn,[a] · · · · · · · , a very full extent of the
manor, castle, and honour of Knaresburgh, held in chief for
two knights' fees, with the parks and forest, in which is an
iron mine. There are 239 acres of land, 39 acres of meadow,
40 acres of pasture, and 4 parks, Bilton, Hay, Hawray,
Castleparke. Extent of the manor of Skrivene. Feryngesby
hamlet, 234 acres in demesne. Doglofthouse hamlet, John
de Walkingham holds one carucate in socage. Erkendale
Lofthouse hamlet, Nigel de Loftus holds 14 bovates in
socage. Burepere hamlet, certain cottars at the will of the
lord. Hoperton, Thomas Bewelt holds 2 carucates in socage.
Coningesthorpe,[b] extent, 13 bovates in socage. Walkingham.
Thorescrosse, 4 bovates in socage. Staveley, 3 carucates in
socage. Kirkestanleye. Brereton. Erkenden Loftus. Roudon
hamlet. Stocton hamlet. Ripeley hamlet. Rosthurst[c] hamlet.
Beckwith hamlet. Panhalle hamlet. Clifton Elesworth
hamlet. Foston[d] Bestaine hamlet. Timble Brian hamlet.
Timble Percy hamlet. Thorescros hamlet, extent. Pateside
hamlet. They are all free tenants. Thornethwait extent.
Derlemoneswith extent. Fellesclife extent. Birscate[e] hamlet,
extent. Hamesthwaite extent.

[m. 35]

Clinte[f] hamlet, extent. Killingholme[g] hamlet, extent.
Sprotesby[h] hamlet, extent. Bilton hamlet, extent. All these
are members of the castle of Knaresburgh.

[a] From this point the MS. becomes illegible. What follows is taken from the
printed index (*Cal. Inq. post mortem*, i., 159), supplemented and corrected from a
copy in Add. MSS. 26719, fo. 23*b*. The following is the list of the places printed
in the Official Calendar :—Brereton, Brearton between South Stainley and
Knaresborough ; Erkenden Loftus, Arkendale and Loftus Hill ; Roudon, Rowden,
one mile south of Hampsthwaite ; Stocton (*sic*), Scotton ; Ripeley, Ripley ;
Rosthurst, Rosnersey or Rosnerses, perhaps Rossett Moor south of Harrogate ;
Beckwith, in the parish of Pannall ; Clifton, in the parish of Fewston ; Elsworth,
not identified ; Foston, Fewston ; Bestaine, not identified ; Timble Brian, Little
Timble ; Timble Percy, Great Timble ; Thorescrosse, Thruscross ; Pateside, not
identified ; Thornethwaite, Thornthwaite, five miles west of Hampsthwaite ;
Derlemoneswith, probably near Darley ; four parks called Bilton, Hay, Hawray
(Harrogate), and Castle Park.

[b] Coneythorpe, 1½ miles N.W. of Allerton Mauleverer.

[c] Rosnersey or Rosnerses in the Add. MSS.

[d] Foxton (*Ibid*).

[e] Birstwith.

[f] One and a half miles west of Ripley.

[g] Killinghall.

[h] Spruisty, between Killinghall and Bilton.

[m. 39]

Writ of *certiorari* addressed to Richard de Havering', Escheator *ultra*, date at Nettleham, 28 Jan., 29th year (1300-1).

INQUISITION of the knights' fees and advowsons of churches which belonged to Edmund, late Earl of Cornwall, made at ˙Knarr' on Monday after the feast of the Purification of the B.M., 29 Edw. I. (6 Feb., 1300–1), by Henry *del Hil* of Burton, William de Knarr', Henry ate Gate, Robert Clerk of Knarr', William Clerk of Skrevyn, William de Skakel-thorp, Walter *le Porter*, John Telous', Thomas son of Walter, Ralph Warde, Thomas Turpyn, and John de Boneye. Henry son of Hugh holds 15 carucates of land in Staveley and Farnham by the service of one knight's fee and a quarter, worth £30 a year. Peter Bekard holds six carucates of land in Burton[a] by the service of half a knight's fee, worth £12 a year. Henry *de Boys* holds twelve carucates in Great Useburne[b] by the service of one knight's fee, worth £24 a year. William Fossard holds a carucate in Little Cathale[c] by the service of the eighth part of one knight's fee, worth 40s. a year.   Total, £68.

He had no advowsons of churches within the honour of Knaresburgh or elsewhere within the bailiwick of Mr. Richard de Havering, escheator *ultra*.[d]

LXXXVI.   GILBERT DE ISELBEK'.   *Extent of Lands.*

[28 EDW. I. No. 57.]

Writ of *certiorari* dated at York, 13 Dec., 28th year (1299), and directed to Richard de Haverynge, Escheator *ultra*, as to the lands of Gilbert de Iselbek', deceased, which the Escheator has lately taken into the King's hands, because Walter, son and heir of the said Gilbert, is an idiot. The Escheator is to make an extent of the said lands and return it without delay before the Barons of the Exchequer at York.

Dorso:—xxvij die Jan. a E. v[i] l.m.

INQUISITION of the lands and tenements which belonged to Gilbert de Yselbek' on the day he died, made at Thirsk in Yorkshire on Monday after the feast of the Purification

---

[a] Humberton.

[b] Great Ouseburn.

[c] Little Cattal.

[d] In the inquisition for Lincolnshire [m. 43], taken on Sunday after All Saints, 28 Edw. I. (6 Nov., 1300), it is stated :—" Richard Malebyse held of the earl one knight's fee in Neubo in Lincolnshire, and Acastre and Aton in Yorkshire, worth £20 a year," meaning Acaster Malbis, and Little Ayton in Cleveland near Roseberry Topping. " Newbo, in the neighbourhood of Grantham, was the site of a religious foundation, but though the name would suggest a comparatively late origin, the county map of the present day has no record of it, and the very site of the convent is a matter of conjecture " (Streatfield's *Lincolnshire and the Danes*, p. 252).

of the B.M., 28 Edw. I. (8 Feb., 1299–1300), by the oath of
Robert de Foxoles, William de Norton, John de Neuby,
William son of the Clerk, Adam de Buggeden, William de
Silton, John Fraunceys, Robert Clare, John Gra of Yselbec,
William son of Gilbert of Crakehale, John Gelle of Hoton,[a]
and William Knyght. Gilbert had at Yselbec[b] a chief
messuage, worth half a marc a year. He had in demesne
68 acres of arable land at 8*d*., total 45*s*. 4*d*.; 5½ acres of
meadow at 3*s*., total 16*s*. 6*d*. He had in bondage two bovates
of land paying 24*s*. a year, payable half yearly at Whitsuntide and Martinmas. He had two pence a year rent from
a free tenant there. There is no other approvement there,
but he had at Dalton a toft and croft worth 3*s*. a year, and
4*s*. a year of assize rent from the grange of St. Peter's.

Total, £4 19*s*. 8*d*.

Dorso. Let a commission be made for Henry Tuke, as
long as it shall be in the King's custody, for £6 a year.[c]

LXXXVII. HOSPITAL OF THE BLESSED MARY MAGDALEN,
PLUMTREE BY BAWTRY. *Lands belonging to the
Hospital.*

[28 EDW. I. No. 58.]

Writ dated at Durham, 4 Dec., 28th year (1299), and directed to Geoffrey
Russel and Lambert de Trikyngham, keepers of the archbishopric of
York. Whereas the hospital of the Blessed Mary Magdalen of
Plumptre by Bautre is vacant by the resignation of Roger *le Porter*,
chaplain, the late warden (*custodis*), and belongs to the King's gift by
reason of the archbishopric being in his hand, the keepers are ordered
to take into the King's hand and keep safely the hospital with the
lands and tenements, books, chalice, and ornaments of the chapel of the
same, and to cause an inquiry to be made as to the value of the lands.

Dorso :—We have taken into the King's hand the hospital named in
the writ, with all the lands and tenements, but we have not found any
books, chalice, or ornaments of the chapel of the same hospital. The
value of the lands of the same appears by the inquisition made
according to the form of the writ, which we send you together with the
writ.

INQUISITION taken at Plumtre on the eve of the Epiphany,
28th year (5 Jan., 1299–1300), before the keepers of the
archbishopric of York, in the time of the vacancy of the
same, by John *le Forster*, William Foreman (*prepositum*),
Roger Galle, Thomas son of Ralph, Adam Shepherd

[a] Sand Hutton, near Thirsk.

[b] Islebeck, in the parish of Kirkby Knowle, is about three miles south of
Thirsk. Dalton, in the parish of Topcliffe, is near by.

[c] Grant made to Henry Tuk, the King's yeoman, on 1 April, 1300 (*Calendar of
Patent Rolls* (1292-1301), p. 501).

(*bercar'*), Nicholas de Plumtre, William Grubbe, Richard Neel, Hugh Clerk, Robert Amys, Geoffrey son of Robert, and Hugh son of Alice. There belong to the hospital a bovate and a half of land and 12*d.* rent in the vill of Marton, and meadow in the marsh of Schaftworthe, the arable land worth 9*s.* a year, the meadow 7*s.*, and the easement of pasture 3*s.* The chief messuage of the same hospital and the half bovate of land, with the meadow, are held of the archbishopric of York in frankalmoign, and the bovate of land is held of the lord of Marton by the service of a pound of pepper only. The burden of that rent of pepper ought to be compensated for by the benefit of a turbary, called Cnapewelleheued.[a] So that hospital is worth, in all issues, 20*s.* a year, and was founded for a chantry of one chaplain.

LXXXVIII. WILLIAM DE HAMELTON, DEAN OF YORK.
Inq. ad q. d.
[28 EDW. I. No. 70.]
Writ dated at Holmcoltran, 4 Oct., 28th year (1300), and directed to the Sheriff.

INQUISITION taken before the mayor and bailiffs of the city of York on Monday after Martinmas, 28 Edw. (14 Nov., 1300), by Benedict *le Éspecer*, Gilbert de Arnale, Thomas de Benigburgh, Robert de Grimeston, Gaudin *le Orfeuer*, Adam de Pokelinton, Adam de Munketon, Robert de Mikelgate, William de Barneby, Robert Foreward', Robert de Burbrigge, and Robert Blaunchecote, whether it would be to the damage of the King or the hurt of the city of York or of anyone else, if the King grant leave to William de Hamelton, dean of the church of the Blessed Peter of York, to enclose a path, containing sixty feet in length and four in breadth, leading from a street called Petergate, below the dean's kitchen, to the churchyard of the same church, for the enlargement of his piece of land (*placee*) there, and to hold it thus enclosed to himself and his successors, deans of the same church. The jurors say it will be to no one's hurt, but that it is to the great safety of the said street and of the parts adjoining, as well as of the close of the said churchyard, as evildoers who have entered the city of York for the purpose of committing crime at night, have been

---

[a] "Dicunt insuper quod onus redditus illius debet compensari cum comodo unius turbarie que vocatur Cnapewelleheued." The custody of the hospital was granted on 21 April, 1300, to Nicholas de Mistreton, the King's clerk (*Calendar of Patent Rolls* (1292-1301), p. 510).

wont frequently to hold meetings and gatherings in the same path on account of the darkness of the place, from which meetings and gatherings murders and fires have often happened to persons dwelling within the said city.[a]

Dorso. Let it be done for a fine of half a marc, to be enrolled in the Exchequer.

LXXXIX. MILES DE STAPELTON *for* THE PRIORESS AND NUNS OF MARRICK. *Inq. ad q. d.*

[28 EDW. I. No. 71.]

Writ dated at Westminster, 28 March, 28th year (1299-1300), and addressed to the Sheriff.

Dorso:—This writ was returned to the bailiff of the liberty of Richmond, who answered as appears by the inquisition attached to this writ.

INQUISITION taken on Saturday, the eve of Whit-Sunday, 28 Edw. (28 May, 1300), by Hugh de Langeton, Thomas de Goremire, John son of Dene of Neuton, Roger Lardaunt, Adam de Kirkeby, Henry de Cuton, Adam son of John of Fletham, Henry Payn of Fletham, Thomas Walbert of Scurueton, Thomas Northiby, Adam Webster (*textor*) of Fletham, and Hugh de Anderby, about four acres of land in the vill of Fletham in exchange between Sir Miles de Stapelton and the prioress of Marrig. They say the exchange is equal, so that no hurt can arise to the King or anyone else. Sir Miles holds the said land of Sir William Giffard, and Sir William of the Earl of Richmond, and the Earl of the King. The prioress holds her land of the heirs of Sir Henry son of Conan, and the heirs of the Earl, and the Earl of the King.

Dorso. Let it be done for a fine of 20s. Let them also be enrolled at the Exchequer.[b]

[a] "Eo quod malefactores civitatem Ebor. ingressi causa male perpetrandi de nocte in eadem conventicula et congregaciones in eadem semita propter obscuritatem loci frequenter facere consueverunt. De quibus conventiculis et congregacionibus pluribus infra dictam civitatem commorantibus homicidia et incendia sepius accederunt." Licence granted on 27 Nov., 1300 (*Calendar of Patent Rolls* (1292-1301), p. 558). Licence granted on 9 Jan., 1300, for life, to the dean to hunt with his own dogs the fox, hare, badger, and cat throughout the forest of Galtres, except in the fence month; on condition that he take no deer, nor course in the warrens of the King or others (*Ibid.*, p. 562).

[b] Licence granted on 30 June, 1300, to Sir Miles de Stapelton, to assign in mortmain to the prioress and nuns of Marrick four acres of land in Fletham, in exchange for four acres of land there, which are under his manor of Kirkeby (*Calendar of Patent Rolls* (1292-1301), p. 523).

XC. The Prior and Friars Preachers of York.
Inq. ad q. d.
[28 Edw. I. No. 83.]

Writ dated at Market Weighton (Wighton), 21 Nov., 28th year (1299), and addressed to the Sheriff.

INQUISITION taken before the bailiffs of the city of York on Sunday after the feast of St. Eadmund, King and martyr, 28th year (22 Nov., 1299), by Alan Fox, William Sleht, William Lengeteyll', William de Brunneby, Peter *le Lorymer*, Richard de Cathale, Thomas Ammory, Richard de Bilburg', John Attegatende, James *le Mareschale*, Robert de S. Leonardo, and Thomas *le Brewester*. It will not be to the King's loss or harm, or of others, if he give leave to the prior and friars of the order of preachers of York to have a vacant piece of ground (*placeam vacuam*) in York adjoining their area towards the water of Use, for the enlargement of their area. The piece of land is vacant, and worth nothing by the year in issues. It contains in length 4 score feet and in breadth 4 score feet.

Dorso. Let it be done.[a]

XCI. Abbot and Convent of Thornton. *Inq. ad q. d.*
[28 Edw. I. No. 88.]

Writ dated at Carlisle, 4 July, 28th year (1300), and addressed to Richard Oysel, bailiff of Holdernesse.

INQUISITION made at Raueneshereodde, the day of St. Margaret the virgin, 28 Edw. (20 July, 1300), by Gilbert Enne, Robert de Cotes, Roger Fysk', Geoffrey Campioun, Peter Bateman, William Waker, Stephen Moring', William Colyn, Adam Attehill', Peter Goldsmith (*aurifabrum*), William Attehill', and Richard Broun. It is not, etc., if the King grant to the abbot and convent of Thornton a piece of ground in Raueneshereodde,[b] which they had of the grant of Isabella de Fortibus, late Countess of Albemarle, for her life, and which after her death was taken into the King's hand. It contains in breadth 4 score and 9 feet, and[c] in length from the way called Neugate towards the south it contains towards the Humber 12 score feet and upwards,

---

[a] Licence dated 1 May, 1300 (*Calendar of Patent Rolls* (1292–1301), p. 512).

[b] In writ, Raueneserod.

[c] Et in longitudine a via que dicitur Neugate versus austrum continet versus Humbriam xij[xx] pedes, et ultra versus boream quantum super flumen pot' acquirere.

towards the north as much as they can acquire on the river, saving the common way leading to *le Kaye*. It is only worth a marc a year. It is in the King's hand, and he can give it to whomever he will without doing harm to anyone.

Dorso. Let it be done for a fine of ten marcs.[a]

XCII. WALTER DE LANGETON, BISHOP OF LICHFIELD AND COVENTRY, MASTER OF THE HOSPITAL OF ST. LEONARD, YORK. *Inq. ad q. d.*
[28 EDW. I. No. 90.]
Writ dated at Caerlaverock (Karlauerok), 10 July, 28th year (1300).

INQUISITION made by Richard Oysel, King's bailiff of Holdernesse, at Raueneserodde, Monday the feast of the Decollation of St. John the Baptist, 28 Edw. (29 Aug., 1300), by Peter *atte See*, William Broun, William Wytte, Robert *del Cotes*, Henry Helward, John de Maltebate, Simon *atte Se*, Peter *le Quyte*, William Waker, Gilbert Tryour, John *atte See*, and Richard Broun. It is not, etc., if the King grant leave to the venerable father, William de Langeton, Bishop of Coventry and Lichfield, master of St. Leonard's Hospital, York, to grant to the hospital a plot of his waste land in the vill of Raueneserodde, to hold by charter at rent (*per cartam arentatam*), payable yearly at the Exchequer by the bailiff of the town. It contains in length 220 feet, and in breadth 120 feet. Rent to the King, 3s. a year.[b]

XCIII. WILLIAM DE THORNETOFT, *for* THE CHAPEL IN THE VILL OF YOKEFLEET. *Inq. ad q. d.*
[28 EDW. I. No. 92.]
Writ dated at Skelton (Cumberland), 24 June, 28th year (1300), and addressed to the Sheriff.

INQUISITION taken at Houeden, before the sheriff of Yorkshire and the seneschal of the liberty of Houeden, on Saturday after the feast of St. James the Apostle, 28 Edw. (30 July, 1300), by Thomas de Portington, William de Belassise, Thomas Vergon, Robert Bataylle, John de Yucflet, William son of Henry, John de Cotenesse, Gilbert son of William, Adam son of Henry, John *atte Gate*, William

---

[a] Licence granted 16 July, 1300 (*Calendar of Patent Rolls* (1292-1301), p. 528).

[b] Licence dated 25 Sept., 1300 (*Ibid.*, p. 536).

Westiby, Adam Pigaz, and Stephen Lucy, who say that it is not to the hurt of the King or others if he grant leave to William de Thornetoft to give a messuage, 40 acres of land, and 10s. rent in Yucflet, to a chaplain celebrating divine service every day in a chapel built in the same vill in honour of the most blessed Virgin Mary, so that the services owing to the lords of the fee be done in the proper way. Premises held of the prior and priory of Finkehale, which is a cell of the priory of Durham, and pay the priory of Finkehale 26s. 8d. a year, worth five marcs a year. Donor has sufficient lands, etc., left over for doing the services due from the lands granted and retained.

Dorso. Let it be done for a fine of 40s., made at the Exchequer, and let it be enrolled at the same place.[a]

XCIV. SIMON DE BARNEBY, *chaplain, for* THE PRIORESS OF NUN APPLETON. *Inq. ad q. d.*

[28 EDW. I. No. 120.]

Writ dated at York, 16 Nov., 27th year (1299).

INQUISITION taken before the Sheriff on the morrow of St. Katherine, 28 Edw. (26 Nov., 1299), by Henry de Rockelay, Thomas de Sayville, R . . . . . de Ryale, Peter de Boseuille, Robert his brother, Matthew de Ofspringes, Richard Danyel, Roger son of Richard of Bretton, Thomas Dulle, Richard de Berlay, Roger Hechley, and Hugh at the cross of Berneslay. It is not to the loss of the King or others if he grant leave to Simon de Barneby, chaplain, to give four bovates of land and ten marcs rent in Wirkesburgh[b] to the prioress and convent of Apelton, except that Sir Henry de Lascy, Earl of Lincoln, has ward of it, and relief when they happen, inasmuch as the land and rent are held immediately of the Earl for the fourth part of half a knight's fee. It pays 11d. a year to the fines of the Wapentake of Stayncros, which wapentake is in the Earl's hand. Worth 12 marcs a year, the four bovates being worth two marcs a year exactly. Donor has enough still remaining to. support all burdens.

Dorso. The prioress of Appeltone has made a fine with the King for herself and convent at the Exchequer, to enter upon and hold the tenements named in the writ. Therefore

---

[a] Licence dated at Aberford, 27 Nov., 1300 (*Ibid.*, p. 557).
[b] Worsborough.

let a charter from the King be made about the licence for the fine aforesaid. Per rotulum memorandorum de anno xxviij.[a]

XCV. RICHARD DE LASCY *for* THE PRIOR AND CONVENT OF BRIDLINGTON. *Inq. ad q. d.*

[28 EDW. I. No. 130.]

Writ dated at Rokingham, 25 April, 28th year (1300).

INQUISITION made at Rudestan before Robert Ughtrede, the sheriff, on Monday after the Ascension, 28 Edw. (23 May, 1300), by Richard de Torny of Rudestan, Hugh de Karliolo, Thomas de Poynton, Norman de Kernetteby, Ralph de Foxholis, Simon Fribois of Rudestan, Walter Martin of Louthorp', John Hirnyng' of Thirnom, Anselm Dreng' of the same, William son of Stephen of the same, William Bellard of Staxton, and Walter Percy of Burton. It is not to the King's loss if he give leave to Richard de Lascy to grant pasture for 300 sheep in Folketon, and 50 cartloads of turves in the marsh (*marisco*) of the same Richard, to be dug and led away by the men of the prior and convent, to the prior and convent of Bridelington. Held of John, baron of Craistok', by the service of 16s. a year for all service, the baron holding of Sir Robert de Tatissale, and Robert of the King. Pasture worth 3s. a year. Each cartload of turves from the said marsh, to be dug and led at the costs of the prior and convent, is worth a penny.

Dorso. Let it be done for a fine of 100s., and enrolled at the Exchequer in the roll.[b]

XCVI. ROGER DE MOUBRAY, *deceased. Forestership of Hovingham.*

[28 EDW. I. No. 145.]

Writ dated at York, 13 June, 28th year (1300).

INQUISITION on the forestership (*forestaria*) of Hovingham, with its appurtenances, taken at York before Mr. Richard de Hauerynges, escheator *ultra*, on 20 June, 28 Edw. (1300), by the oath of John de Besingby of Ridale, Roger Abbot, Robert de Colton, Adam Torny, John Absolon of Calueton,

---

[a] Licence granted on 8 March, 1300 (*Ibid.*, p. 492). Simon de Barneby was the parson of Wheldrake in 1294 (*Ibid.*, p. 94).

[b] Licence granted at Dunipace (Stirlingshire), Sept. 30, 1301 (*Ibid.*, p. 610).

John de Wathe, Robert de Kirkham, Walter de Scouesby, Richard *le Mareschal*, Richard de Houthorpe, John de Etton, and William de Wathe. Roger de Munbray[a] long before his death granted to Ralph de Kirketon by his charter the forestership of Hovyngham, with its rights and appurtenances, and with the trees blown down by the wind, and the branches and the bark (*ramis et tanno*) of all the trees which were given away, with a quarter of corn (*frumenti*) every ten weeks, to be received from Roger's manor of Hovingham, and a robe of the suite of Roger's squires (*de secta armigerorum ipsius Rogeri*), or 20*s.* instead of the robe, at Christmas, at the manor of Hovyngham every year, to be held for life, paying one penny yearly at Christmas. Ralph was in full and peaceable seisin of the forestership aforesaid from the time of the making of the deed to the day of Roger's death, when John de Lithegreynes, then the escheator, took into the King's hand the lands and tenements of which Roger died seised. Ralph was in seisin of the forestership for seven years and upwards before Roger's death. The forestership is worth 40*s.* a year. Ralph on the Christmas after the making of the deed received the robe, and afterwards every year up to the day of Roger's death 20*s.*, instead of the robe. The forestership is in the wardship of Edmund, Earl of Cornwall, amongst other wardships granted him by the King.[b]

XCVII.   HENRY LE MERCER AND OTHERS *for* THE PRIOR AND CONVENT OF WATTON.   *Inq. ad q. d.*

[28 EDW. I. No. 139].

Writ dated at Carlisle, 3 July, 28th year (1300).

INQUISITION taken before Sir Robert Ughtrede, the sheriff, at Bralken (*sic*)[c] on Wednesday, the feast of St. Wilfrid the Bishop, 28 Edw. (12 October, 1300), by William de Raventhorpe, Adam *Stabeler* of Skirne, Thomas de Wymthorpe, Thomas de Kyllingwyke, Hugh de Colvyl, William *Stabeler*, Walter de Cotom, Richard de Skirne, Roger Locke, John de Bracken, William de Hoton, and Richard de Wynton. It is not to the hurt of the King or others if he

---

[a] Moubray in the writ.

[b] *Ancient Petitions*, No. 10,022. Rauf de Kirketon says in his petition to the King that Moubray's grant consisted of "la foresterie de Houingham a tenir a terme de sa vie, pernaunt vynt souz pur une robe e cynk' quarters de furment par an." Endorsed:—"Le roi le voet bien, qil eit le purport de sa chartre."

[c] Bracken in the parish of Kilnwick.

give leave to Henry *le Mercer* to grant a messuage and two bovates of land in Hugat[a]; to Isabel de Messingham to grant ten acres of land in Traneby; to Geoffrey Dote of Watton to grant five acres of land in Kyllingwyke by Watton; to Henry Lolke[b] to grant a messuage and three acres of land in the same; to William Fimmer to grant a messuage and a bovate of land in Esthorp; and to Geoffrey Agillon to grant 20s. rent in Besewyke to the prior and convent of Watton. The premises in Hugat held of the prior and convent of Watton by a yearly service of 4d., and worth 6s. 8d. The premises in Traneby held of the prior by a yearly service of 12d., worth 3s. a year. The premises in Kyllingwyke granted by Geoffrey Dote held by a yearly service of 6d., worth 18d., and those by Henry Locke of the same prior by a yearly service of 6d., worth 18d. The premises in Esthorpe held of the prior by a yearly service of 12d., worth 4s. The 20s. rent comes from half a carucate of land in Besewyk held of Peter de Mauley by the service of 5d. to the fines of the wapentake of Herthille. Henry has 40s. worth of land, Isabel 60s., Geoffrey 6s., Henry 4s., and William de Fymmer 100s., beyond the grants aforesaid.

Dorso. Because he has made a fine with the King for 20 marcs, which he has paid at the Exchequer, for having entry upon the within named lands, let a charter be made for him for the fine aforesaid.[c]

XCVIII. HENRY, COUSIN AND HEIR OF HENRY SON OF CONAN OF KELKEFELDE.[d] *Proof of age before the King at York, Hilary Term*, 28 Edw. (1299–1300).

[28 EDW. I. No. 161.]

THE sheriff was ordered that, whereas Henry, cousin and heir of Henry son of Conan, deceased, who held by knight service of the heir of Marmaduke de Twenge, deceased, a tenant in chief, under age and in the King's custody, said he was of full age, and demanded of the King

[a] The modern names of these places are, Huggate, Tranby, Kilnwick, Easthorpe in the parish of Londesbrough, and Beswick.

[b] It should be Locke.

[c] Licence granted at Carlisle on 16 Oct., 1300 (*Calendar of Patent Rolls* (1282–1301), p. 540).

[d] An account of the family of FitzConan will be found in the *Guisbrough Chartulary*, ii., 183n. Kelfield, which the family assumed as their surname, is in the parish of Stillingfleet. The name of the heir's father, which is not given, was Conan.

that the lands and tenements which were of his inheritance, and were in the custody of William *le Latimer*, senior, by grant from the King, up to the lawful age of the said heir, should be restored to him, in consequence of which the King granted him a day for proving his age before the King in the octaves of St. Hilary wherever he should be, who was born at Sokeburne and baptized in the church of the same vill, he should summon a jury of knights, etc., by whom the truth might be known.

The heir and the jurors come, but not William, though warned to attend by Adam de Fulthorpe, Geoffrey de Everlay, Richard Qursy, and Nicholas de Thornholm.

William of York, 60, living at Lesingby,[a] distant from Sokeburne, where the heir was born, eleven leagues, says the heir is of full age, namely 21 years and upwards, inasmuch as he was 22 years old on Monday after the feast of St. Lambert the Bishop last past (24 Sept., 1299). Asked how he knows this, says he has a daughter Emma, born in the quinzaine of St. Michael next after the feast of St. Lambert, who was 22 years old on the quinzaine of St. Michael last. He says also that Henry son of Conan, grandfather of the heir, at the time of his nativity was living at Leverton,[b] five leagues distant from Lesyngby, and that immediately after his birth messengers came to the said Henry son of Conan informing him of the birth of the heir, and asked him to come to the heir's baptism, who, being detained by infirmity, could not come, but ordered that they should give the child his name, whether male or female. He was baptized at Sokeburne, in the parish church there, and the chaplain who baptized him was called Gilbert. His godfathers were William, the parson of the same church, and Thomas, the parson's clerk; and Elizabeth, the lady of the same vill, was his godmother.

John de Kyrkebi in Clyvelaund, 60 and upwards, living there, distant from Sokeburne 11 leagues, says the second godfather was John Brien, not Thomas Clerk. He holds his lands of John de Euer, his lord, who was born on the same day as the heir, which John proved his age two years ago. He agrees that Henry, the grandfather, sent and ordered that the heir should bear his name, whether male or female.

Robert de Fenton, 50, living at Marton in Cliflaund, 8 leagues distant from Sokeburne, has a son Stephen surviving, who was born on the eighth day after the heir's birth, and was 22 on Monday after the feast of St. Lambert last. He

[a] Lazenby, near Redcar.
[b] Liverton, near Loftus-in-Cleveland.

came to Sokeburne on the morrow of the baptism of the same heir, that is on the Tuesday after his birth, and he himself was at that time bailiff to Marmaduke de Twenge at Yarm, whither rumours came at once after the heir's birth, and he spoke with the messenger going and returning from the heir's grandfather, who told him of his birth.

John de Fymtres, 40, living at Marton in Clifland, 8 leagues distant from Sokeburne, has a son Robert born on All Saints' after the heir's birth.

Walter de Hemelsay, 60, living at Hemelsay,[a] 50 leagues distant from Sokeburne, says the heir was six years old at the time of his grandfather, Henry's death, and that 16 years have elapsed since that date.

John de Skipwyth, 60 and more, living at Skipwyth, 30 leagues from Sokeburne, had a son born at Easter after the heir's birth.

Robert de Pontefracto, 50, living at Wylesthorpe,[b] 26 leagues distant, says the heir was six years old when his grandfather died, and that he himself was a friend and acquaintance of the grandfather (*de amicicia et noticia predicti avi*).

William *le Cerf*, 40, living at Catherton,[c] 40 leagues and more distant, says that Conan, father of the said Henry, was of so tender an age at the time when the heir's mother was pregnant with him, that it was commonly said that the same Conan could not raise issue, on account of which after the heir's birth there was a great deal of talk on the subject in the district.

Henry de Colton, 40 and upwards, living at Colton,[d] 50 leagues and more distant, had a firstborn son Henry, now dead, who was born the same day as the heir.

Michael de Cnapton, 60, living at Cnapton,[e] 40 leagues and more distant, says the heir was with his grandfather at the time of his death, and he then saw the heir, who was six years old.

Thomas *in le Wylies*, 60, living at Cotoum,[f] 40 leagues distant, says he was at the court of the wapentake between Use and Derwent, where Henry the grandfather was, when rumours came to him about the heir's birth.

[a] Gate Helmsley.

[b] Wilstrop, Kirk Hammerton parish.

[c] Catterton, Tadcaster parish,

[d] In the Ainsty.

[e] Knapton, in the parish of Acomb, near York.

[f] East Coatham, near Redcar.

Henry *de Cruce*, 36, living at Catherton, 40 and more leagues distant, only knows by hearsay. (*De certa sciencia ignorat, nisi per relatum aliorum.*)

And because the said Henry has sufficiently proved his age before the King, and it also appears by the appearance of the body (*per aspectum corporis*) of the same Henry that he is of full age, that is 21 years and upwards, therefore let the said Henry have seisin of the lands and tenements falling to him from his inheritance, etc. And this record is sent to Chancery, etc.

XCIX.   RICHARD DE HALSAM.   *Inq. p. m.*

[29 EDW. I. No. 3.]

Writ addressed to Master Richard de Haveringe, Escheator this side Trent, and dated at Beverley, 11 June, 29th year (1301).

INQUISITION taken at Hedone on Thursday after the feast of St. John the Baptist, 29 Edw. (29 June, 1301), on the lands and tenements of Richard de Halsam, by William Arnalde, Nicholas de Thorne, Robert Ouste of Holem, Michael *le Aumener*, Richard Noryeby (Northeby), John de Northorpe, Thomas son of Robert of Preston, Robert Ingeram, Nicholas Haukyn, John Aldelote, Richard de Ederewyke, Symon de Rungetofte. Richard held in the vill of Halsam a toft containing 2½ acres of land, worth 2s. 6d. a year; also half a bovate of land, worth 4s. 6d. a year. All held of the King of the barony of Albemarle, by the service of the thirtieth part of one knight's fee. He also held of Thomas, son of Ralph of Wellewyke, in Frismareys (*Frismarisco*),[a] 2½ acres of arable land, by the free service of 2d. a year, each acre worth 12d. a year. Nicholas, the son of the said Richard, is his next heir, and is aged 22 years and upwards.[b]

C.   JOHN DE GOUSLE, *alias* GOUSEL.

[29 EDW. I. No. 9.]

The King, by a writ dated at Toucestre, 14 March, 29th year (1300-01), ordered the Escheator *ultra* to make inquisitions on the lands and tenements of John de Gousle, who held by knight's service of the heir of Peter de Gousle, deceased, a tenant-in-chief in the royal custody, and who had died.

[a] Swallowed up by the Humber.

[b] The King, on 13 March, 1301-2, when still at Beverley, ordered the Escheator, on getting proper security, to give seisin to Nicholas, son and heir of Richard de Halsham, of his father's lands (*Rot. Finium*, 30 Edw. I., m. 13).

INQUISITION on the lands and tenements of John de Gousel, made at Beford on Thursday after the Ascension, 29 Edw. (18 May, 1301), by Thomas Gelle, Thomas de Frisemersk', Robert de Catefosse, William *Attegrene*, Alan Markaund, Walter son of Richard, Ralph son of Emma, Roger de Leset, Peter Saym, Thomas Fisker, Ingeram de Beford, and Thomas Borel. John held nothing of the heir of Peter de Gousel. However, he held certain lands and tenements in Beford in Holdernesse of the daughter and heiress of Ralph de Gousel, under age and in the King's custody, who died long ago, son and heir of Peter de Gousel, deceased, by the service of the fortieth part of one knight's fee, and by rendering annually to the said heiress for *Castelward* and *Schirefgeld* 6d. A capital messuage, worth, in fruit and herbage of the garden, 3s. 4d. In demesne 6½ bovates of land, 8s. a bovate. William *Attegrene*, a free tenant, holds a toft and bovate of land, and renders 5s. at Whitsuntide and Martinmas. Two natives, John Prat, holding a toft and half a bovate of land, and rendering yearly at the same terms, 6s., and Alice Prat, holding a toft and a bovate of land, and rendering at the same terms, 11s. A cottar (*cotarius*), Simon de Gousel, holding a toft with a croft, and rendering yearly at the said terms, 6s. Sum, £4 3s. 4d.

He also held two bovates of land in the same vill of Beford of the Abbot of Meus (*Melsa*) by the service of the 112th part of a knight's fee, value of a bovate, 8d. Sum, 16s.

Peter de Gousel, brother of the said John, is his next heir, and is of the age of 26 years and upwards.[a]

CI. JOHN DE ESHTON, *alias* ESTON.[b] *Inq. p. m.*

[30 EDW. I. No. 13.]

[m. 3]

Writ directed to the Escheator *ultra*, dated at Durham, 20 June, 29th year (1301).

[m. 4]

INQUISITION on the lands and tenements of John de Eston, made at Gergrave, on Sunday after the feast of the Blessed Peter and Paul, 29 Edw. (2 July, 1301), by Everard

---

[a] Order to the Escheator to give seisin to Peter, brother and heir of John de Gousel, of the lands and tenements of his brother, dated at Kenilworth, 1 June, 1301 (*Rot. Finium*, 29 Edw. I., m. 8).

[b] John de Eshton, or Eston, derived his name from Eshton, in the parish of Gargrave. He had been one of the claimants to the estates belonging to the earldom of Albemarle, alleging he was descended from a certain Avicia, daughter of William le Gros, and sister of Hawisia, who married William de Forz or Fortibus, and carried the earldom into that family. A Coram Rege Roll for Michaelmas Term,

Fauuel, John de Heton, Henry de Marton, Elyas de Stretton, Adam son of William of Brohcton, Richard de Fauuelthorp, Alan de Catherton, Henry son of Beck', William Everarde, Robert Forbrace, John de Lofthous, and Richard de Plumlaund. John de Eston held nothing of the King in chief on the day he died, but at one time he held the manor of Eston of the King by homage and service. At that time Robert de Eston, brother of the said John, came and brought a writ for an agreement (*tulit breve de convencione*) against the said John at the eyre (*itinere*) at Lincoln, in 56 Henry III. (1271–2), before Ralph, Abbot of Croyland, and his associates, before whom John acknowledged the manor to be the right of the same Robert; and for this acknowledgment Robert granted the manor to John for life at an annual rent of a penny, and by doing the services due to the chief lord of the fee. There is a capital messuage, with 23 bovates of land (6s.), worth £6 18s.; 9 tofts, 17s. 1d., at different values; a watermill, alienated by the said John after the fine was levied, worth 40s. a year; a bovate of land in Uttelay, with approvements from the waste (*cum appruamentis vasti*), 13s. 4d. John, son of Robert de Eston, is John de Eston's nearest heir, [a]if any inheritance may come to him, inasmuch as he claims the manor of Eston by the death of Robert his father under the fine levied, and is of the age of 25 years.[b]

[m. 1]

    Writ directed to the same Escheator, ordering him to ascertain to whom the reversion of the lands and tenements of John de Eshton belonged. Dated at Berwick-on-Tweed, 16 July, 29th year (1301).

[m. 2]

INQUISITION on the lands and tenements of John de Eston, made at Gergrave, on Tuesday, the feast of St. Peter *ad vincula*, 29 Edw. (1 Aug., 1301), by William de Cestrehunte, Elias de Stretton, Richard de Fauuelthorpe, Adam son of

4 Edw. I. (1276), quoted by *Dodsworth* (cxliv., 22), gives the pedigrees of the claimants to this property. Avicia, through whom Eston claimed, was the daughter of William le Gros by a nun, and was therefore a bastard. There must have been something in the claim, as the King gave John de Eston land to the value of 100*li.* a year in Thornton near Pickering and Skipton, in consideration of his releasing his right to the earldom of Albemarle and the barony of Skipton. The other claimants were the four sisters of Peter de Brus III., John de Sunningham, and Philip de Wivelesby.

[a] Si hereditas aliqua sibi accedere poterit, quia manerium de Eston' cum pert. clamat per decessum Roberti, patris sui, per finem levatum.

[b] The King having taken the homage of John, son and heir of Robert de Eshton, long deceased, for the lands and tenements which John de Eshton, deceased, held on the day that he died, of the grant of the said Robert, ordered the Escheator on receiving security for his relief to give him seisin. Lynliscu, 21 Dec., 1301 (*Rot. Finium*, 30 Edw. I., m. 16).

William of Broghton, John de Lofthuse, William Everarde, Robert de Gergrave, Alan de Catherton, Henry son of Beck', William son of the same Henry, John de Heton, and Eustace de Heton. John de Eston held the manor of Eston of John, son and heir of Robert de Eston, late brother (*quondam fratris*) of John de Eston, for life, of the grant of the said Robert de Eston, by a fine levied between the said Robert and John de Eston before Ralph, late Abbot of Croylande, and his associates, Justices Itinerant in the county of Lincoln, 56 Henry III. (1271-2), by the service of rendering to the said Robert and his heirs one penny a year for all service; saving a watermill out of the said manor, which John, son of Hugh, held on the day John de Eston died, in fee of the gift of Hugh de Ledes, to whom the said John de Eston gave the said mill by his charter after a fine had been levied. There is there a capital messuage, worth 6s. a year, but it does not suffice for the maintenance of the houses. There are 23 bovates of land in demesne, each bovate worth, with the meadow belonging to it, 6s.; also 9 tofts, each toft worth 2s. a year. John St. John holds the mill for the term of his life by lease (*ex dimissione*) from the said John, son of Hugh, rendering to John de Eston, deceased, half a pound of cumin at Christmas for all service, which is worth 1d.

Sum, £8 2s. 1d.

John de Eston held in his demesne as of fee three acres of wood (2d.) in Eleshowe of the King, as of the Honour of Skipton Castle, by homage and knight service, and rendering nothing a year. Sum, 6d. The reversion belongs by the fine aforesaid to John, son and heir of the said Robert, who now ought to hold those lands and tenements of the King in chief, as of the Honour of Skipton Castle (by reason of the escheat of the lands and tenements which belonged to William de Fortibus, late Earl of Albemarle, deceased, now in the hands of John St. John by the King's grant), by homage and knight service, as much as pertains to ten carucates of land, where fourteen carucates of land make a knight's fee, and by doing suit at the knights' court (*ad curiam militum*) of the lord of the Honour of Skipton every three weeks.

John, son of Robert de Eston, late brother of the said John de Eston, is the nearest heir both of the said John de Eston and the said Robert, late brother of John de Eston, and is aged 25 years. Sum total, £8 2s. 7d.

CII. JOHN DE BLABY.[a] *Inq. p. m.*

[29 EDW. I. No. 15.]

Writ dated at Linliscu, 17 Nov., 29th year (1301).

INQUISITION on the lands and tenements of John de Blaby, made at Bageby, on St. Andrew's day, 30 Edw. I. (30 Nov., 1301), by . . . . gton, Adam son of Robert of Bageby, Adam son of William, Thomas son of Robert, William Knyt, John de Welleberhe, Thomas de . . . . , ... de Turkelby, and William son of Walter. Sir John de Blaby held the manor of B[ageby of the heir] of Sir Roger de Moubray, who is under age and in the King's custody, by the service of the tenth part of a knight's fee, ... about two acres, and is worth in fruit and herbage 3s. 4d. In demesne, 60 acres of land . . . . Sum, 30s. Three acres of meadow (12d.) Sum, 3s. A wood with its profits, as in not giving underwood (*ut in subbosco non dando*), worth . . . . . . Adam de Bugedene holds two bovates of land by homage and fealty. Adam de Carleton holds two bovates of land by homage and fealty. . . . . of land by homage and fealty. Robert de Buscy holds five bovates of land, and renders yearly at Christmas 2d. William Botus holds one bovate . . . . Peter Haasketh holds two bovates of land, and renders yearly a pound of pepper, and is extended at 12d. Thomas son of Robert holds one bovate at . . . . . . , namely at the feasts of the Purification, St. John the Baptist, and St. Michael the Archangel. Sum of the rent of the free tenants, 7s. 3d. Twelve cotters (*coterelli*) . . . . . , at two terms, Martinmas and Whitsuntide. Sum, 24s. John de Blaby had £10 rent of the grant [of Roger de Moubray],[b] to be taken for all the life of the said John of the mill and market (*foro*) of Trescke, at two terms of the year, Martinmas and Whitsuntide . . . . He also held certain lands and tenements in Marton of Richard de Malebys by the service of the twelfth part of a knight's fee . . . . in demesne 6 score acres of arable land, (6d.) Sum, 60s. A windmill, 13s. 4d. a year . . . . There is no other approvement (*appruamentum*) there. Sum of Marton, 79s. 4d.

Joan, the first-born daughter of the said John de Blaby, wife of Adam de Horrewrth', aged 36; Alice, another of the

---

[a] A Leicestershire man who came from Blaby, near Leicester, which continued in the possession of the main line of the family till the time of Henry VI. The grandmother of the John de Blaby, whose *Inq. post mortem* is given above, was Amicia, sister of William and Hugh Malbis, through whom property at Bagby and Marton-in-Cleveland came into her husband's family (*Guisborough Chartulary* (Surtees Society), ii., 8n, 19n).

[b] See p. 78.

daughters of the same John, wife of Robert de Pothowe, aged 34; Christiana, the third daughter, wife of William de Snaynton, aged 33; Elizabet, the fourth daughter, wife of John Dautrey (*de Alta ripa*), aged 30; Cecily, the fifth daughter, wife of Robert Gower, aged 28; and Eustachia, the sixth daughter, not yet married, aged 22, are the nearest heirs of the same John.[a]

CIII. PETER DE NUTTLE *alias* NUTTELE.[b] *Inq. p. m.*

[29 EDW. I. No. 21.]

Writ directed to Master Richard de Haveryng, the Escheator, and dated at Lugwardyn, 26 April, 29th year (1301).

INQUISITION on the lands and tenements of Peter de Nuttele, made at Nuttele[c] on Friday, the morrow of the Ascension, 29 Edw. (12 May, 1301), by Henry de Wytheton, John de Rihil, William de St. Quintin, John de Fitlyng', Simon *du Lunde*, Simon de Sprotle, Nicholas Warde, Thomas de Ros, Nicholas Haukin, Michael *Laumener*, Robert son of Alice, and Thomas Humbelton. The said Peter held in his demesne as of fee lands and tenements in Nuttele of the King in chief, as of the Honour of Albemarle, by the service of the twenty-fourth part of a knight's fee. A capital messuage, worth in fruit of the garden and moat (*fossat'*), with a dovecote, 13s. 4d. Fourteen bovates of arable land in demesne (10s.). Sum, £7. In a close 5 acres of pasture, and in another close three acres of pasture (2s.). Sum, 15s.

Sum of the said sums, £8 9s. 4d.

The said Peter and Isabella, his wife, who is still surviving, were jointly enfeoffed, and held lands and tenements in Preston and a windmill and half an acre of pasture in Nuttele of the King in chief as of the said Honour, by the service of the thirtieth part of a knight's

---

[a] Dec. 14, 1301. Lynliscu. The King ordered the Escheator to give seisin of John de Blaby's lands and tenements to Adam de Horreworth, who married Joan, to Robert de Pothou, who married Alice, to William de Snaynton, who married Cristiana, to John de Alta ripa, who married Elizabeth, and to Robert Gower, who married Cecilia, daughters and heiresses of the said John de Blaby, who held of the heir of Roger de Moubray, deceased, a tenant in chief, under age and in the King's custody, and to make a lawful partition of the said lands, Adam and Joan receiving the *einescia hereditatis*, and Agnes, John's widow, having her dower assigned (*Rot. Finium*, 30 Edw. I., m. 16).

[b] Over age in 1275 (Vol. i., 154).

[c] Nuthill, near Hedon-in-Holderness.

fee. A bovate and acre of land at Preston, 20s. 6d. The mill is worth nothing a year, because there is no suit to it. The said half acre of pasture, 2s.   Sum, 22s. 6d.

The said Peter and Isabella obtained (*perquisivienent*) for themselves from different feoffees lands and tenements in Preston, Sprotle, and Garton, of which the same Peter and Isabella were jointly enfeoffed and seised, to be held of the lords below written, namely, a croft in Preston of ...... Passemer, by the service of 8d. a year for all service to be rendered to the same John, worth 5s. a year; of Simon *du Lunde* an acre of land in Sprotle, doing no service, worth 3d. a year; of John de Carleton six tofts, five bovates, and three parts of a bovate of land in Garton, by the service of the thirtieth part of a knight's fee, each toft with the bovate worth 13s.   Sum, 76s. 8d.

Sum of the sums of the value of the lands and tene-ments, of which the said Peter and Isabella were jointly enfeoffed as above, £4 19s. 2d.

John, son of the said Peter, is his nearest heir, and is of the age of 23 years.[a]

CIV. DRAX. *Extent of manor.*[b]

[29 EDW. I. No. 29d.

No writ.

...... in money, 5s. .... four hundred 4 score and 6 acres of land and 3 roods, each acre of which pays to the same lady[c] 4d. yearly .... of St. Michael 2d. for all secular services, saving to the said lady suit of court every three weeks.

Sum of acres of the freehold (*de libero tenemento*), 486 acres and 3 roods.

Sum of the money, £9 8s. 11d.

Sokemen in the soke of Drax (*sockemanni in soka de Drax*) hold of the said lady 281¼ acres and half a rood, each acre of which pays yearly to the said lady 5¼d., at certain terms of the year, namely, at Easter 2d., in the name of a fixed rent (*nomine certe firme*) ; and at Michaelmas 2d., in the name abovesaid ; and at the Purification 1¼d., in the name of tallage, for all secular services, saving to the said lady suit of court as above.

---

[a] Order to the Escheator to give seisin to John, son and heir of Peter de Nuttle, dated at Eversle, 14 June, 1301 (*Rot. Finium*, 29 Edw. I., m. 8).

[b] Extents of this manor, made in the time of Henry III., are printed in Vol. i., 123-129. See also Vol. ii., 55, 61.

[c] Some member of the Paynel family.

Sum of acres, 281¼ acres and half a rood.

Sum in money from fixed rent, £4 13s. 10½d.

Sum in money from tallage, 31s. 9½d.

Bondage holdings of old bovates (*bondag' de veteribus bovatis*). The same sokemen (*sokemanni*) hold there of the same lady 26 bovates of land of the old bovates, each bovate of which contains 6 acres, and pays to the said lady 5½d. a year at the terms above written, and all the said bovates jointly pay the lady 47½ fowls at Christmas and 220 eggs at Easter and Martinmas, and *merchet* and *lecherwite*.

Sum of the acres, 7 score and 16 acres.

Sum in money from fixed rent, 52s.

Sum in money from tallage, 14s. 6½d.

Sum of fowls, 47½ fowls.

Sum in money from fowls, 3s. 11½d.; price of a fowl, 1d.

Sum of eggs, 22s.

Sum in money from eggs, 6½d.; price per hundred, 3d.

Rent of mill belonging to the lady, 4s. 4½d.

Free rent of the court, 5s.

Rent of oats. Thirty quarters of oats by *estrick'*, of annual rent, 30s.; price per quarter, 12d.

Sum total of the acres, 8 hundred 4 score and 13½ acres.

Sum total in money, according to the true extent, in demesnes, gardens, fisheries, rents of lands, both of freemen and bondmen, and of oats, fowls, and eggs, rent of mill, suit of court, £22 7s. 8½d.

CV. JOHN DE WYVILLE. *Inq. p. m.*

[29 EDW. I. No. 42.]

Writ[a] directed to the Escheator, and dated at Newerke, 6 June, 29th year (1301).

INQUISITION on the lands and tenements of John de Wyvyle, made at Slengesby, on Sunday, the feast of St. Barnabas the Apostle, 29 Edw. (11 June, 1301), by Richard *le Mareschal*, Robert de Colton, Roger Raboc, William de Besingby, Richard de Holthorp, Thomas son of Idonia, Nicholas Dod, John de Wathe, Richard de Holme, William de Wathe, Thomas de Foston, and Walter de Scouesby. The said John held certain lands and tenements in his demesne as of fee in Slengesby, Northolm, and Colton,[b] of John, son and heir of Roger de Mubray, under age and in the King's custody, by the service of one knight's fee.

[a] The writ to Walter de Gloucestria, the Escheator *citra*, is of the same date.

[b] Slingsby near Malton, and North Holme and Colton near Kirby Moorside.

SLENGESBY. A capital messuage, worth 20s. a year and
no more, on account of the charges for the maintenance of
the houses there (*propter reprisas pro sustentacione domorum
ibidem*). In demesne, 18 acres of arable land (5s.) Sum,
£4 10s. In demesne, 18 acres of meadow (15d.) Sum, 22s.
6d. There is no several pasture there, whereby the lord
as regards agistment is not able to receive any money
from it.[a]

Free tenants. Gilbert de Briddesale, two tofts, at Martinmas and Whitsuntide, 12d.; Geoffrey de Craumvyle, a toft,
2d. at the same terms; Geoffrey *le Keu*, a toft, 16d.; Hugh
de Carleton, a toft, 2s.; Thomas de Wyvile, 8 bovates of
land, rendering at the feast of the Nativity of St. John the
Baptist a chaplet of roses (*unum capell' rosarum*); William
de Yeland, half a carucate of land, rendering at Easter a
pair of gilt spurs or 6d.

Sum of the rent of the free tenants of Slengesby, 5s.

Bonders (bondi) who render their rents at the two said
terms. William *le Moinier*, Henry Nod, John Fraunces,
Isabella Fraunceys, John son of Emma, Geoffrey *le Provost*,
and John son of Thomas, each of whom holds a toft and
two bovates of land, and renders at the said terms 20s., and
in the time of mowing (*falcacionis*) 2s. Two bonders, Alan
Melifray and Geoffrey *le Moinier*, of whom Alan holds a toft
and two bovates of land, and renders at the said terms,
Martinmas and Whitsuntide, 6s. 8d., and in the time of
mowing 2s.; and Geoffrey *le Moinier* holds two bovates, and
renders at the said terms 16s., and in the time of mowing
2s., as the time of mowing shall come sooner or later.[b]

Sum of the rent of the bondmen of Slengesby, £9 0s. 8d.

Cottars (cotarii). Thomas Hugun, William Kyng, Roger
le Keu, Thomas Whinfel, John Oxehirde, and Hugh *le
Vaysur*, each of whom holds a toft, and renders at the said
terms 4s. Also Alice Fatting', Walter *le Keu*, and William
le Batur, each of whom holds a toft, and renders at the said
terms 2s. 6d.; Juliana Everarde, William *le Bercher*, Agnes
Shouferyn, Walter Gunnyld, Alan Petyt, Alice Moubray, and
William Hodelyn, each a toft at 2s.; Robert de Marton, a
toft at 2s. 2d.; Gervase *le Fossur* and Thomas Wodecok, each
a toft at 3s.; Thomas Purde, a toft at 2s. and an oven (*furnum*)
at 3s.; Robert Gaythirde, a toft at 2s.; Stephen Bate and
Isabella Catous, each a toft at 18d.

Sum of the rent of the cottars of Slengesby, 63s. 8d.

[a] Item non est ibi pastura separalis per quod quantum ad agistamentum nullum
denarium inde potest recipere.

[b] Prout tempus falcacionis evenerit cicius vel tardius.

Two watermills under one roof, 40s.; and a windmill, 13s. 4d.   Sum, 53s. 4d.

Two small woods, one called *le Frythe*, 5s., and the other Thurkelwode, 3s. 4d.   Sum, 8s. 4d.

Pleas and perquisites, 4s.

Sum of the sums of Slengesby, from the fee of the heir of Roger de Mubray, deceased, from the tenements which are held of the same heir, £22 7s. 6d.

NORTHOLM. The said John held 4s. rent in Northolm from four bovates of land, held of the said heir by the said service, which James de Northolm holds.

COLTON. A messuage and 30 acres of waste land, which are worth nothing.

SHIREBURNE.[a] He held of the said heir 37s. rent by the service aforesaid, to be taken from three carucates of land which the heir of Robert de Everingham holds there.
                                                                          Sum, 37s.

Sum of all the preceding sums from the fee of the said heir, from the lands and tenements which the said John held of the same heir, £24 8s. 6d.

The said John held of the heir of John Wake three bovates of land (5s.) and six acres of meadow (15d.) in Slengesby, by doing homage and suit at the said heir's court of Buttercrambe every three weeks.   Sum, 22s. 6d.

The said John held of the Archbishop of York two marcs rent in Nonewykethornes[b] by doing homage and suit at the Archbishop's Court of Ripon every three weeks, to be taken from the hamlet (*hamclotto*) of Nonewykethornes, which Walter de Nonewykethornes holds.   Sum, 26s. 8d.

Sum of all the sums aforesaid, £26 17s. 8d.

William, son of the said John, is his nearest heir, and was of the age of twenty-six years at Easter last past.[c]

---

[a] Sherburn, in the East Riding.

[b] Nunwick Thornes is adjacent to Nunwick, near Ripon, but the name is not now used (*Kirkby's Inquest*, p. 212n).

[c] The Northants inquisition was taken at Welleford, on Friday after St. Barnabas' Day, 29 Edw. I. (16 June, 1301). He held the manor of Welleford in that county of the heir of Roger de Moubrai. Heir aged 24 and upwards. On 27 June, 1301, the Escheator was ordered to give the heir seisin of his father's lands in Northants., saving the dower of Matilda, John's widow (*Rot. Finium*, 29 Edw. I., m. 7).

CVI.   WALTER, BISHOP OF COVENTRY AND LICHFIELD, *for*
THE PRIOR AND CONVENT OF BOLTON   *Inq. ad q. d.*

[29 EDW. I. No. 72.]

Writ directed to the Sheriff of Yorkshire, and dated at Donypas, 14 Oct.,
29th year (1301).

INQUISITION made before Simon de Kyme, the sheriff, by William de Hewedene, John de Boulton, Elias de Thressckefeld, Richard Fauuell, Adam Fauuell, William Couuel, William Desert, Robert Bucke, Robert son of Geoffrey of Bradeley, Richard de Heton, Alexander de Esteburne, and William son of William of Skipton. It will not be to the loss or prejudice of the King or of others, if he grant leave to Walter, Bishop of Coventry and Lichfield, Master of the Hospital of St. Leonard of York, to give 2s. rent in Appeltrewicke to the prior and convent of Boulton, in exchange for 3s. rent in York, but only to the loss of the prior and convent of Boulton, inasmuch as they lose 12d. a year rent. The messuage in Appeltrewike, out of which the 2s. rent comes, is held of the said prior and convent in frankalmoign. The messuage in York, out of which the 3s. rent comes, is held of the Master of the Hospital of St. Leonard of York in frankalmoign.

CVII.   ROGER DE MOUBRAY, *deceased.*[a]

[29 EDW. I. No. 47.]

[m. 7]

Writ directed to Master Richard de Havering, Escheator *ultra*, and dated at Canterbury, 27 May, 29th year (1301).

[m. 10]

INQUISITION on the knights' fees and advowsons of churches which were Roger de Moubray's, made at York, on Friday after St. Mark's day, 29 Edw. (28 April, 1301), by Henry Ulf, Elyas de Stretton, John de Preston, Richard Cordewan[er], Robert Buke, Gregory de Pathenale, Gregory de Burton, Richard de Linghou, John de Thorneton, Robert son of Edward (Ed'i) of Clapham, William de Mirwro, and Benedict de Stubbe. Alan de Catherton held of the said Roger the manor of Coldeneuton[b], in the wapentake of Steyncleve, by the service of half a knight's fee, worth £10 a year. William Greindorge held the manor of Flasceby, in the same wapentake, by the service of one knight's fee,

---

[a] See No. LVI.

[b] Bank Newton, in the parish of Gargrave.

worth 100s. a year. John de Haveryngton held the manor of Ostwike,[a] in the wapentake of Yucros, by the service of the fourth part of a knight's fee, worth £40[b] a year.

Sum of the value of the fees aforesaid, ...

---

m. 13]

INQUISITION on the knights' fees and advowsons of churches which were Roger de Moubray's, made at York, on 8 May, 29 Edw. (1301), by William de Casteley, Adam de Wynkesle, William Graffard, Richard son of Ranulph of Kyrkeby, Robert de Colton, Roger Raboc, Robert Fox, Henry de Hasham, Henry de Colton, William son of Ranulph of Thocwit, John Groo of Cawode, and William de Cawode. William de Aldefeld held of Roger de Moubray three carucates of land in Aldefeld and Stodley,[c] by the service of the fourth part of a knight's fee, worth £6 a year. Agnes, daughter of John de Stodley, held three carucates of land in Stodley, by the service of the fourth part of a knight's fee, worth £6 a year. John, son of Alan of Walkyngham, held two carucates and two mills in Azerle and Kyrkeby,[d] by the service of the sixth part of a knight's fee, worth £10 a year. Roger de Beltoft and Thomas de Beltoft held two carucates of land in Azerle and Kyrkeby, by the service of the sixth part of one knight's fee, worth £4 a year. John de Walkyngham held a carucate in Brathwait,[e] by the service of the eighth part of a knight's fee, worth 40s. a year. Richard Foliot held one and a half carucates in Wynkesle,[f] by the service of the 36th part of one knight's fee, worth 60s. a year. Robert de Nonewick the younger held a carucate in Ketelismor,[g] by the service of the 20th part of one knight's fee, worth 20s. a year. The abbot of Fountains held three carucates of land in Swettem, Carlemor, and Kyrkeby,[h] by the service of a 50th part of a knight's fee, worth 30s. a year; also two carucates in Growelthorpe,[i] by the service of the eighth part of one knight's fee, worth £4 a year. Isabella *la Grace* and Thomas

---

[a] Austwick, in the parish of Clapham, and wapentake of Ewcross.

[b] One would expect 40s., but the same amount occurs below.

[c] Aldfield and Studley, near Ripon.

[d] Azerley and Kirkby Malzeard.

[e] Braithwaite Hall, in the township of Azerley.

[f] Winksley, near Ripon.

[g] *Letelismor.* Kexmoor, two miles west of Kirkby Malzeard.

[h] Swetton, Carlesmoor, and Kirkby Malzeard.

[i] Grewelthorpe.

de la Crestene[a] held two carucates in Granteley, by the service of the sixth part of one knight's fee, worth 40s. a year. Alan *le Oyselour* held a carucate in Kyrkeby, by the service of the 96th part of a knight's fee, worth 5s. a year. Henry Be[au]fiz held half a carucate in Grouwelthorpe, for the service of the 24th part of one knight's fee, worth 20s. a year. The prior of Newburgh (*Neubourg*) held a carucate in Mikilhawe,[b] by the service of the twelfth part of a knight's fee, worth 40s. a year. John de Bellew (*Bella aqua*) held three carucates of land in Grenehamerton, a carucate in Quixley, a carucate in Usburne,[c] two carucates in Allerton, a carucate in Hoperton, a carucate in Clarton, two carucates in Weteneuton,[d] by the service of the 17th part of one knight's fee, worth £22 a year. William Lovel held four carucates in Broutton,[e] by the service of two parts and a half of one knight's fee, worth £8 a year. Ivo de Etton held a carucate and a half in Southholm,[f] by the service of the 60th part of one knight's fee, worth 60s. a year. Nicholas de Barton held a carucate in Barton,[g] by the service of the twentieth part of a knight's fee, worth 40s. a year. Juliana de Besingby held half a carucate in Holm, by the service of the 40th part of one knight's fee, worth 20s. a year. John de Wyvyle held seven carucates in Slengesby, by the service of one knight's fee, worth £[15] a year. Joan Wake held five carucates in Slengesby, by the service of the fifth part of a knight's fee, worth £10 a year. Ernulph de Percy held three carucates in Friton,[h] by the service of half a knight's fee, worth £6 a year. Matthew de Loveyne held two carucates and seven bovates in Friton,[h] by the service of half a knight's fee, worth £6 a year; also two carucates in Holthorpe,[h] by the service of the 14th part of a knight's fee, worth £4 a year. Ivo de Etton held two carucates in Gilling, by the service of the tenth part of one knight's fee, worth 40s. a year. Walter Barn held one carucate in Gilling, by the service of the twentieth part of a knight's

---

[a] Perhaps Crescene. Probably the same person as Thomas de la **Cressener**, mentioned below.

[b] Micklehow, about a mile south of Fountains Abbey, now called How Hill.

[c] Green Hammerton, Whixley, and Little Ouseburn.

[d] Allerton Mauleverer, Hopperton, and Clareton. Wet Newton would seem to be Newton Kyme.

[e] Broughton-in-Ryedale.

[f] South Holme, in the parish of Hovingham.

[g] Barton-le-Street.

[h] Fryton and Howthorpe, in Hovingham parish.

fee, worth 40s. a year.[a] John de Wyvyle held three carucates in Colton, by the service of the fourth part of one knight's fee, worth £4 a year. Joan Wake held . . . . carucates in Calueton,[b] by the service of half a knight's fee . . . . . . Walter de Teye held . . . . . carucates in Stayngreve,[c] by the service of a knight's fee, worth 40s. a year. Joan Wake held . . . . . . in Mosecotes,[d] held by the service of . . . . . part of a knight's fee, worth £6 a year. Milo de [Stapelton and] Agnes de Bulford[e] held . . . . in Wymbelton,[f] by the service of a knight's fee, worth . . . . . . Joan Wake held . . . . . in [Kirkeby] Moresheved, Gillingmore . . . . . , by the service of ten knights' fees, worth . . . . Robert *le Conestable* held two carucates of land in Buterwyke, by the . . . . of a knight's fee, and worth . . . . s. Richard Malebise held . . . . Halmby[g] . . . . . , worth £6 a year . . . . in the vill of Walton . . . . Ranulph de Albo monasterio (*rest illegible*).

---

m. 9]

INQUISITION on the knights' fees and advowsons of churches which were Roger de Moubray's, made at Lemyng, on Thursday after St. Barnabas' day, 29 Edw. (15 June, 1301), by Hugh de Langgeton, Roger *le Ardant*, Henry de Couton, William Des, Thomas de Gormyre, Roger *le Porter*, Henry son of Henry, Henry son of Hugh of Couton, Elyas son of Adam, Alan de Kyrclyngton, John de Middelton, and John de Ravenestwaith. John de Wauton held of Roger de Moubray the manor of Massam, in the wapentake of Hange, by the service of one knight's fee, worth £10 a year. Margaret de Nevyle held four carucates of land in Hoton Lunggevilers, in the wapentake of Gilling, by the service of the third part of one knight's fee, worth £8 a year. Hugh son of Henry held two carucates of land in Westapilgarth,[h] in the same wapentake, by the service of the sixth part of one knight's fee, worth £4 a year.

Sum of the value of the aforesaid fees, £22.

[a] From here the document is very difficult to decipher.

[b] Cawton, in Gilling parish.

[c] Stonegrave.

[d] Muscoates, in Kirkdale parish.

[e] Bowforth, in Kirby Moorside parish.

[f] Wombleton, in Kirkdale parish.

[g] Hawnby.

[h] West Applegarth, near Richmond.

[m. 11]

INQUISITION on the knights' fees and advowsons of churches which were Roger de Moubray's, made at Treske, on Friday after St. Barnabas' day, 29 Edw. (16 June, 1301), by the oath of Roger Raboc, William Talenace, William Koke, Ralph de Kyrketon, William de Sutton, William de Scefeld, Roger de Stapilton, William *le Hunte*, Ralph Crane, ... de Kilburne, William *le Tannur*, and Robert Yol. Simon de Stotevyle held of Roger de Moubray three carucates of land in Langlethorpe,[a] by the service of the fourth part of a knight's fee, worth 100s. a year. John Pecche, three carucates of land in Hundesburton,[b] by the service of the fourth part of a knight's fee, 100s. a year. Ralph de Nevyle, six carucates of land in Kepwike, by the service of half a knight's fee, £10 a year. John de Ruddestan, six carucates of land in Hayton, by the service of half a knight's fee, £10 a year. Thomas, heir of Nicholas de Grendale, five carucates of land in Garton-on-the-Wolds (*super Waldas*), by the service of half a knight's fee, £10. John de Evyle held the manors of Kilburne, Thorneton-on-the-Hill[c] (*super le Hul*), and Athelingfleth,[d] by the service of two and a half knights' fees, worth £50 a year. William de Buscy, the manor of Thurkilby, and the vills of Osgoteby and Silton,[e] by the service of one knight's fee, £20. Thomas *de la Rivere*, the manor of Brandesby and the vills of Steresby and Braffirton, by the service of one knight's fee, £20. Brian, son of Alan, a moiety of the vill of Baynton,[f] by the service of half a knight's fee, £10. Walter de Carleton, three carucates of land in Carleton and Yselbeke,[g] by the service of the third part of a knight's fee, £4 a year; also three carucates of land in Hoton,[h] by the service of a fourth part of a knight's fee, £4 a year. William de Norton, a carucate of land in Carleton, by the service of the twelfth part of a knight's fee, 20s. a year. Joan Talenace, two bovates of land in Treske, by the service of the sixtieth part of a knight's fee, 13s. 4d. a year. John de Blaby, the manor of Baggeby, by the service of the fourth part of a knight's fee, £4 a year. William *le Gra*, the manor of Sandhoton,

[a] Langthorpe, near Boroughbridge.

[b] Humberton.

[c] In the parish of Coxwold.

[d] Adlingfleet.

[e] Thirkleby, Osgodby, and Nether Silton.

[f] In the East Riding.

[g] Carlton Miniot and Islebeck.

[h] Sandhutton, in Thirsk parish.

by the service of half a knight's fee, worth £10 a year. William de Vescy of Kildare, the manor of Brumton,[a] by the service of one knight's fee, worth £20 a year; also the vills of Soureby and Brakenberou,[b] by the service of one and a half knights' fees, worth £30 a year; also the vills of Langeton and Wyntringham,[c] by the service of two knights' fees, worth £40 a year; also the vills of Suthcaue, Hesel, and Swanysland,[d] by the service of three knights' fees, worth £60 a year; also the manor of Neusom in Spaldingmor,[e] by the service of one knight's fee, worth £20 a year; also the manor of Malton, by the service of two knights' fees, worth £40 a year.

Sum of the value of the fees aforesaid, £373 13s. 4d.

Roger de Moubray had no advowson of a church on the day he died.

-- --- -- -- -- --- --- --- --

[m. 12]

INQUISITION on the knights' fees and advowsons of churches which were Roger de Moubray's, made at Malton, on Saturday after St. Barnabas' day, 29 Edw. (17 June, 1301), by Robert de Bucketon, John de Menythorpe, Thomas de Middelton, Thomas of the Green (de viridi), Ralph de Barkethorpe, Thomas Lovel, William de Langton, William de Levenyng, Hugh Palmer, Thomas ...... land, Thomas Wacelyn, and William de Thoroldby. William de Vescy of Kildare held of Roger de Moubray six carucates of land in Wellom, Sut[ton], Norton, and Cnapton,[f] by the service of half a knight's fee, worth £8 a year. Matthew de Loveyne held two carucates in Norton and Sutton, by the service of the fourth part of a knight's fee, worth 53s. 4d. a year. William of York (de Eboraco) held a carucate of land in Norton, by the service of the eighth part of one knight's fee, worth 30s. a year. Ernulph de Percy held a carucate in Norton and Sutton, by the service of the eighth part of a knight's fee, worth 30s. a year. John de Wivyle held eleven carucates in Sledmere, by the service of one knight's fee, worth £20 a year.

Sum of the value of the fees aforesaid, £33 13s. 4d.

He had no advowson of any church.

---

[a] Brompton (Pickering Lythe).

[b] Sowerby by Thirsk and Breckenbrough.

[c] In the East Riding.

[d] Swanland.

[e] Newsholme, in the parish of Wressell.

[f] Welham, Sutton, Norton, and Knapton, in the East Riding, near Malton.

[m. 14]

Knights' fees assigned in dower to Roesia, who was wife of Roger de Moubray.[a] One third of a fee in Hoton Lungevilers, held by Margaret de Neville, extended at £8. One sixth of a fee in West(a)pilgarth, held by Hugh fitz Henry, extended at £4. Half a fee in Coldeneuton, held by Alan de Catherton, extended at £10. One fee in Flasceby, held by William Grayndorge, extended at 100s. Half a fee in Wellom, Sutton, Norton, and Knapton, held by William de Vescy of Kildare, extended at £8. One fee in Sledmer, held by John de Wyville, extended at £20. One fourth of a fee in Langelethorp, held by Simon de Stoteville, extended at 100s. One fourth of a fee in Hundesburton, held by John Pecche, extended at 100s. Two and a half fees in Kilburne, Thornton super le Hull', and Athelingflete, held by John de Eyville, extended at £50. One fee in Thurkilby, Osgodeby, and Silton, held by William de Buscy, extended at £20. One third of a fee in Carleton and Iselbeck, held by Walter de Carleton, extended at £4. Half a fee in Sandhoton, held by William *le Gra*, extended at £10. One fee in Brumpton, held by William de Vescy of Kildale (*sic*), extended at £20. Two fees in Langeton and Wyntringham, held by the same William, extended at £40. The fourth part of a fee in Aldefelde and Stodleye, held by William de Aldefelde, extended at £6. The fourth part of a fee in the same vill of Stodleye, held by Agnes, daughter of John de Stodleye, at £6. The sixth part of a fee in Azerle and Kirkeby, held by Roger de Beltoft and Thomas de Beltoft, extended at £4. The sixth part of a fee in the same vills, held by John, son of Alan de Walkyngham, extended at £10. The seventeenth part of a fee in Grenehamerton, Quixleye, Usburne, Hoperton, Clarton, and Weteneuton, held by John de Bella aqua, extended at £22. One fee in Slengesby, held by John de Wyville, extended at £15. One fifth of a fee in the same vill, held by Joan Wake, extended at £10. Half a fee in Fryton, held by Ernulph de Percy, extended at £6. One fourteenth of a fee in Holthorp, held by Mathew de Loveyn, extended at £4. One tenth of a fee in Gillyng, held by Ivo de Etton, extended at 40s. One fourth of a fee in Colton in Rydale, held by John de Wyville, extended at £4. One half of a fee in Calveton, held by Joan Wake, extended at £12. One tenth of a fee in Buttrewyke, held by Robert *le Conestable*,

---

[a] The membrane is quite illegible. Roesia de Moubray had dower assigned to her by writ, dated at Peebles (Pebbles), on 2 Aug., 1301 (*Close Roll*, 29 Edw. I., m. 5). The parcels assigned in dower are set out above. From the inquisition it appears that the dower in Lincolnshire amounted to £45 10s., and in Leicestershire to £58.

extended at 60s. One fee in Thorp Arches and Walton, held by John de Bella aqua, extended at £20. Half a fee in Wyhale and Esdyke, held by Ranulph de Albo monasterio, extended at £13 6s. 8d. One fourth of a fee in Helawe, held by Richard *le Waleys*, extended at 100s. One fourth of a fee in the same vill, held by William *le Vavassar* extended at 100s. One fourth of a fee in Scalleby, co. Lincoln, held by John de Saunton, extended at 100s. One fourth of a fee in the same vill, held by Richard Wacelyn, extended at 100s. One fee in Haxeye and Buttrewyke, held by Oliver de Buscy and Robert Takel, extended at £15. One tenth of a fee in the same vill of Haxeye, held by Roger Cook (*cocus*) of Westwode, extended at 10s. Two parts of a fee in Beltoft and Buttrewyke, held by Roger de Beltoft and Roger, son of Henry de Beltoft, extended at £20. Half a fee in Statherne, co. Leicester, held by Lambert de Trikyngham, extended at 100s. Half a fee in Gouteby, held by William Maureward, extended at £20. Half a fee in Burton S. Lazari, held by the Abbot of Vaudey (*de Valle Dei*), extended at £10. Half a fee in Wynordeby, held by John Chevercourt, extended at 60s. Half a fee in Lenthorp, held by the Abbot of Vaudey, extended at 60s. Half a fee in Aston, held by John de Perers, extended at £6. One fee in Thurstinton and Redeclyve, held by John Wake, extended at £11.

[m. 15]

EXTENT of the knights' fees which belonged to the said Roger beyond Trent on the day he died, and which on the occasion of his death were taken into the King's hand, namely:—[a]

Nottinghamshire.

One knight's fee in Egmanton, held by John de Eyvile, and extended at £30.

Three parts of one knight's fee in Serleby and Tortheworthe,[b] held by Hugh de Serleby, extended at £15.

Two knights' fees in Egrum, Starthorpe, Kelum, and Crumwelle,[c] held by James de Sutton, and extended at £40.

One knight's fee in Alkeleye[d] and Fynyngleye, held by Nicholas de Sancta Elena and Alice Tonkes, extended at £10.

Sum of the knights' fees in the county of Nottingham, £95.

---

[a] Sums of the value of the knights' fees in Lincolnshire, £137 10s.; Northants., £30; Rutlandshire, £50; Essex, £2; Warwickshire, £87 5s.; Leicestershire, £182. Sum total, £488 15s., the third part of which is £162 18s. 4d.

[b] Serlby in the parish of Harworth, and Torworth in that of Bawtry.

[c] Averham, Staythorpe in the parish of Averham, Kelham, and Cromwell.

[d] Auckley in the parish of Finningley.

11

Yorkshire.

One knight's fee in Massam, held by John de Wauton, extended at £[10].

The third part of one knight's fee in Hoton Lungevilers, held by Margaret de Neville, extended at £8 a year.

The sixth part of one knight's fee in Westapilgarth, held by Hugh, son of Henry, extended at £4 a year.

Half a knight's fee in Coldneuton, held by Alan de Catherton, extended at £10 a year.

One knight's fee in Flasceby, held by William Greyndoye, extended at 100s. a year.

The fourth part of one knight's fee in Oustwyke, held by John de Haveryngton, extended at £40.

Half a knight's fee in Wellom, Sutton, Norton, and Cnapton, held by William de Vescy of Kildare, extended at [£8].

The fourth part of one knight's fee in Norton and Sutton, held by Matthew de Loveyne, extended at 53s. 4d.

The eighth part of one knight's fee in the same vill of Norton, held by William of York (de Eboraco), extended at 30s.

The eighth part of one knight's fee in Norton and Sutton, held by Arnulph de Percy, extended at 30s.

One knight's fee in Sledmere, held by John de Wyville, extended at £20.

The fourth part of one knight's fee in Langelethorpe, held by Simon de Stoteville, extended at 100s.

The fourth part of one knight's fee in Hundesburton, held by John Pecche, extended at 100s.

Half a knight's fee in Kepwyk, held by Ranulph de Neville, extended at £10.

Half a knight's fee in Hayton, held by John de Ruddestan, extended at £10.

Half a knight's fee in Garton-on-the-Wolds (super Waldas), held by Thomas, heir of Nicholas de Grendale, extended at £[10].

Two and a half knights' fees in Kilburne, Thorneton-on-the-Hill (super Hulle), and Athelingeflete, held by John de Eyville, extended at £50.

One knight's fee in Thurkelby, Osgodeby, and Silton, held by William de Buscy, extended at £20.

One knight's fee in Brandesby, Steresby, and Braffirton, held by Thomas de la Ryvere, extended at £20.

Half a knight's fee in Baynton, held by Brian, son of Alan, extended at £10.

The third part of one knight's fee in Carleton and Iselbek, held by Walter de Carleton, extended at £4.

The fourth part of one knight's fee in Hoton, held by the same Walter, extended at £4.

The twelfth part of one knight's fee in Carleton, held by William de Norton, extended at 20s.

The sixty-fourth part of one knight's fee in Threske, held by Joan Talenace, extended at 13s. 4d.

The fourth part of one knight's fee in Baggeby, held by John de Blaby, extended at £4.

Half a knight's fee in Sandhoton, held by William *le Gra*, extended at £10.

One knight's fee in Brumpton, held by William de Vescy of Kildare, extended at £20.

One and a half knights' fees in Soureby and Brakenboru', held by the same William, extended at £30.

Two knights' fees in Langeton and Wyntringham, held by the same William, extended at £40.

Three knights' fees in Suthcave, Hesel, and Swannesland, held by the same William, extended at £60.

One knight's fee in Neusum in Spaldyngmore, held by the same William, extended at £20.

Two knights' fees in Malton, held by the same William, extended at £40.

The fourth part of one knight's fee in Aldefeld and Stodleye, held by William de Aldefeld, extended at £6.

The fourth part of one knight's fee in Stodleye, held by · Agnes, daughter of John of Stodley, extended at £6.

The sixth part of one knight's fee in Azerle and Kirkeby, held by John, son of Alan of Walkyngham, extended at £10.

The sixth part of one knight's fee in the same vills, held by Roger de Beltoft and Thomas de Beltoft, extended at £4.

The eighth part of one knight's fee in Braythwayt, held by John de Walkyngham, extended at 40s.

The thirty-sixth part of one knight's fee in Wynkesle, held by Richard Foliot, extended at 60s.

The twentieth part of one knight's fee in Ketelesmore, held by Robert de Nonewyke the younger, extended at 20s.

The fiftieth part of one knight's fee in Swettem, Carlemore, and Kirkeby, held by the abbot of Fountains, extended at 30s.

The eighth part of one knight's fee in Growelthorpe, held by the same abbot, extended at £4.

The sixth part of one knight's fee in Granteley, held by Isabella *la Grace* and Thomas *de la Crestene*, extended at 40s.

The ninety-sixth part of one knight's fee in Kirkeby, held by Alan *le Oysilur*, extended at 5*s.*

The twenty-fourth part of one knight's fee in Growelthorpe, held by Henry Beaufiz, extended at 20*s.*

The twelfth part of one knight's fee in Mikilhawe, held by the prior of Neuburgh, extended at 40*s.*

The seventeenth part of one knight's fee in Grenehamerton, Quixleye, Usburne, Allerton, Hoperton, Clarton, and Weteneuton, held by John de Bellew (*Bella aqua*), extended at £22.

Two parts and a half of one knight's fee in Brouton, held by William Lovel, extended at £8.

The sixtieth part of one knight's fee in Sutholm, held by Ivo de Etton, extended at 60*s.*

The twentieth part of one knight's fee in Barton, held by Nicholas de Barton, extended at 40*s.*

The fortieth part of one knight's fee in Holm, held by Juliana de Besingby, extended at 20*s.*

One knight's fee in Slengesby, held by John de Wyville, extended at £15.

The fifth part of one knight's fee in the same vill, held by Joan Wake, extended at £10.

Half a knight's fee in Fryton, held by Ernulph de Percy, extended at £6.

Half a knight's fee in the same vill, held by Matthew de Loveyn, extended at £6.

The fourteenth part of one knight's fee in Holthorpe, held by the same Matthew, extended at £4.

The tenth part of one knight's fee in Gillinge, held by Ivo de Etton, extended at 40*s.*

The twentieth part of one knight's fee in the same vill, held by Walter Barn, extended at 20*s.*

The fourth of one knight's fee in Colton in Ridale, held by John de Wyville, extended at £4.

Half a knight's fee in Calueton, held by Joan Wake, extended at £12.

The sixth part of one knight's fee in Stayngreve, held by Walter de Teye, extended at 40*s.*

The third part of one knight's fee in Mosecotes, held by Joan Wake, extended at £6.

Two parts of one knight's fee in Wymbelton, held by Miles de Stapelton and Agnes de Bulford, extended at 60*s.*

Ten knights' fees in Kirkeby Moresheued, Gillingmore, and Fadymor, held by Joan Wake, extended at £100.

The tenth part of one knight's fee in Buttrewyke, held by Robert *le Conestable*, extended at 60*s.*

One knight's fee in Scalton, Dale, and Halmby, held by Richard Malebise, extended at £6.

One knight's fee in Thorpe Arches and Walton, held by John de Bellew (*Bella aqua*), extended at £20.

Half a knight's fee in Wyhale and Esdyke, held by Ranulph de Albo monasterio, extended at £13 6s. 8d.

Half a knight's fee in Bykerton, held by John, son of Alan of Walkyngham, and John Gramari, extended at £10.

The fourth part of one knight's fee in Helawe, held by Richard de (*sic*) Waleys, extended at 100s.

The fourth part of one knight's fee in the same vill, held by William *le Vavassur*, extended at 100s.

Sum of the value of the fees in the county of York, £796 8s. 4d.

Sum of the sums of the value of the fees this side Trent, £891 8s. 4d., of which the third part is £297 2s. 9½d.

Sum of the sums of the value of fees, both this side Trent and beyond, £1,380 3s. 4d., of which the third part is £460 13s. 0½d.

CVIII. JOHN DE BELLA AQUA *or* BELLEWE.[a] *Inq. p. m.*
[29 EDW. I. No. 57.]

[m. 7]
Writ directed to Master Richard de Haveringges, Escheator this side Trent, and dated at Lynliscu, 11 Jan., 29th year (1300-01).[b]

[m. 2]
INQUISITION on the lands and tenements which John de Bella aqua held on the day he died, by the law of England, of the inheritance of Ladrana, formerly his wife, made at Estbrunne,[c] on Sunday after the feast of St. Luke the Evangelist, 29 Edw. (22 Oct., 1301), by Thomas de Cardole, Thomas de Wynthorpe, Henry de Birton, William

---

[a] John de Bellew married Laderina, or Ladarana, the youngest sister and co-heir of Peter de Brus III. See Vol. i., p. 147, where her share in the Brus inheritance is set out. Dec. 3, 1293. The King gave leave to John de Bella aqua, who had married Laderana, one of the heirs and coparceners of William de Lancaster, long dead, to pay, by annual instalments of £10, the sum of £62 5s. 6d., in which he was bound to the King for his share of William de Lancaster's debts (*Rot. Finium*, 22 Edw. I., m. 22). Laderina's mother, Helewisa, was one of the sisters and co-heirs of William de Lancaster. The different inquisitions concur in stating that the heirs to Laderina de Bellew's lands were Nicholas, son of her daughter, Isabel, who had married Miles de Stapleton, aged 15, and her other daughter, Joan, wife of Aucher, son of Henry, aged 24. Nov. 22, 1301. The Escheator was ordered to give seisin to Aucher, son of Henry, of the lands which came to his wife, Joan, from her mother, Laderana, wife of John de Bella aqua, saving the right of Nicholas, son and heir of Sibil, the other daughter and heiress (*Rot. Finium*, 30 Edw. I., m. 17). Sibil and Isabel seem to have been used as synonyms.

[b] On m. 1 is another writ to the same Escheator, dated at Pebbles, on 18 Aug., 29th year (1301).

[c] Eastburn, in the parish of Kirkburn, near Driffield.

Crisping, John de Lokinton, William Abel, Nicholas de Brunne, clerk, Richard de Rippele, John de Weteuuang, Robert Carpenter (*carpentarii*), Peter son of Reginald, and Thomas son of Serlo. John de Bella aqua held of the inheritance of Ladrana, formerly his wife, the vill of Tibethorpe of Sir William de Ros of Helmesle, by the free service of two hawks (*nisorum*) a year for all services. There are there 12 carucates and 3 bovates of land, held in *bondage*, of which William West holds 2½ bovates, and renders yearly 33s. 4d. at Whitsuntide and Martinmas. Henry de Kyrcham, 1 toft and 3 bovates, 40s. William, son of Andrew, 3½ bovates, 46s. 8d. Philip Coupstacke, 3 bovates, 40s. Robert Warpelou, 3 bovates, 40s. Peter, son of Reginald, 3 bovates, 40s. William Peronel, 2 bovates, 33s. 4d. Robert, son of Andrew, 3½ bovates, 46s. 8d. Robert, son of Andrew the younger, 2½ bovates, 33s. 4d. Richard Foreman (*prepositus*), 3½ bovates, 46s. 8d. John at the Cross (*ad crucem*), 3 bovates, 40s. Andrew, son of Henry, 2½ bovates, 33s. 4d. Adam Kay, 3 bovates, 40s. Ysabella at the Cross, 3 bovates, 40s. William Perisman, 2½ bovates, 33s. 4d. Alan, son of Tilli, 2 bovates, 26s. 8d. Robert, son of Richard, 2 bovates, 26s. 8d. Thomas Tepel, 2 bovates, 26s. 8d. Richard Carpenter, 2 bovates, 26s. 8d. Ysabella at the Houe (*apud Hov*), 2 bovates, 26s. 8d. Richard de Warrom, 3 bovates, 40s. Adam at the Hou, 3 bovates, 40s. Robert, son of William, 2½ bovates, 33s. 4d. William, son of Mabel, 2½ bovates, 33s. 4d. John Coupstac, 2 bovates, 26s. 8d. Walter, son of Cristiana, 3 bovates, 40s. Richard Pakoc, 2 bovates, 26s. 8d. Andrew, son of Mabel, 3 bovates, 40s. Geoffrey, son of Mabel, 3 bovates, 40s. Robert Carpenter, 4 bovates, 40s. Alice, wife of Peter, 2 bovates, 33s. 4d. He[a] also 3 bovates, 40s. Adam, son of Alan, 2 bovates, 26s. 8d. Roger Pakoc, 2 bovates, 26s. 8d. Robert, son of Peter, 2 bovates, 53s. 4d. Richard *ad le Mar*, 2 bovates, 26s. 8d. Robert Handing, 2 bovates, 26s. 8d. Robert *ad le Mar*, 2 bovates, 26s. 8d. Robert Carpenter, 2 acres, 5s. Robert, son of Cristiana, 1½ acres, 3s. 6d. William, son of Andrew, half a rood of land, 6d. Ysabella at the Cross, three feet of one toft (*iij pedes unius toftt*), 3d. Alice Pinder, the like part of another toft, 3d.

Sum by the year, £66 9s. 6d.

Cottages. Isabella Gruel, 1 cottage, 4d. Agnes Warpelou, 1 cottage, 2s. Avice Yngoli, 1 cottage, 2s. Adam Burre, 1 croft, 2s. Richard Foreman, 1 croft, 3s. Richard de Warrom, 1 croft, 12d. Richard Smith (*faber*), 1 cottage, 3s.

Sum by the year of the cottages and crofts, 13s. 4d.

[a] That is the husband.

Henry de Barton holds one toft freely at 18*d*. Half a windmill and watermill, £7. From the said bonders, by custom (*de predictis bond' ex consuetudine*), 7½*d*.
Sum, £7 2*s*. 1½*d*.
Sum total, £74 4*s*. 11½*d*., payable at Whitsuntide and Martinmas, by equal portions.

John de Bellew held in Estbrunne of the King, of the barony of Brunne, 4½ bovates, of which Peter, son of Robert, held 2 bovates, 26*s*. 8*d*.; Robert Biscop, 2½ bovates, 33*s*. 4*d*.
Sum, 60*s*.

He held of the said inheritance in Suthbrunne[a] of the King, of the said barony, 14 bovates, of which William at the Cross (*ad crucem*) held 2 bovates, 26*s*. 8*d*.; Richard, son of Alan, 2 bovates, 26*s*. 8*d*.; Richard *in le Wiligis*, 2 bovates, 13*s*. 4*d*.; Robert, son of Beatricia, 2 bovates, 33*s*. 4*d*.; Mabel the widow, 2 bovates, 26*s*. 8*d*.; William, son of Eda, 3 bovates, 40*s*.; Geoffrey Biscop, 1 bovate, 20*s*.   Sum, £9 6*s*. 8*d*.

Nicholas, son of Ysabella, daughter of the said John and Ladrana, late wife of Miles de Stapelton, deceased (*defuncte*), is of the age of 15 years and upwards; and Joan, the other of the daughters of the said John and Ladrana, is of the age of 24 years and upwards, and are the nearest heirs of the said John and Ladrana.
Sum of all the sums aforesaid, £86 11*s*. 7½*d*.

[m. 15]
INQUISITION on the lands and tenements which John de Bella aqua held of the inheritance of Laderana, formerly his wife, made at Thorp Arches, on Tuesday, the eve of St. Luke the Evangelist, 29 Edw. (17 Oct., 1301), by William de Tocwyth, Robert de Hawley, William *le Turnour*, Henry *de la Chaumbre*, Adam de Thorpe, William de Hornyngton, Alan de Folyfayt, Elias de Farwath, Robert of Pontefract, John Fairfax, William de Bugthorpe, and William de Walton. John de Bella aqua held of the said inheritance the manor of Thorp Arches of John, son and heir of Roger de Moubray, under age and in ward to the King, by knight service. There is a capital messuage, worth 13*s*. 4*d*. a year. Also 12 score acres in demesne (15*d*.). Sum, 14*s*. 7*d*. There are in different places, at the heads of the selions,[b] 3 acres of meadow (2*s*. 6*d*.) Sum, 7*s*. 6*d*. Pasture in the park, 14*s*. In the same park 30 acres of alder and hazel (*alneti and corlete*), of which each acre of underwood, if sold, is worth

[a] Southburn, in the parish of Kirkburn.
[b] Per diversa loca ad capita selionum.

4*d*. Sum, 10*s*. 8*d*. A foreign wood, containing about 50 acres (6*d*.) Sum, 25*s*. Two watermills under one roof for corn, worth ten marcs a year, out of which there are rendered to Simon de Creppinges five marcs a year. A fulling mill, 13*s*. 4*d*. In the river Wherfe, in the dam of the said mills, *heckes* for catching fish, 5*s*.   Sum, £26 2*s*. 2*d*.

Free tenants. Alan de Folyfayt, and Elena his wife, Isabella, Agnes, and Margaret, sisters and parceners of the same Elena, holding four tofts and five bovates by the service of the twenty-eighth part of a knight's fee, and rendering 13*s*. 4*d*.; also a close, 10*s*.; a toft and two acres, 1*d*., and doing 3 works (*opera*) in autumn, worth 3*d*. William de Letheley, 3 bovates, 20½ acres, and half a rood of land, 55*s*. 5½*d*. Richard *le Taillur*, 1 bovate, 15*s*. Robert de Farnlaye, 1 bovate and 9½ acres and half a rood of land, 23*s*. 7*d*. John son of Thomas, 1 bovate and 9½ acres of land, 19*s*. 9*d*. Richard *le Fullur* and Amia, his wife, Maude and Beatrice, sisters and parceners of the same Amia, 12 acres of land for one clove, doing 3 works in autumn, worth 3*d*. John, son of William of Walton, one bovate and 5 acres of land, 4*s*. 2¾*d*., and doing 3 works in autumn, worth 3*d*. Robert, son of William, 2 tofts, 1 bovate, and 6 acres of land, 3*s*., and doing 6 works in autumn, worth 6*d*. Agnes, daughter of Walter, 1 bovate and 5 acres of land, with one toft, 17*s*. 6*d*., and doing 3 works in autumn, worth 3*d*. William de Wyke and Agnes, his wife, 1 toft and 3 acres of land, 13*d*. Thomas *le Piskur*, 1 toft and 2 acres of land, 2*s*. 1*d*. Roger *le Seriaunt* and William, son of Henry, and Agnes, his wife, one toft and one bovate, doing 3 works in autumn, worth 3*d*. Beatrice, daughter of Ralph, the miller, and William, son of Alan Hasarde, her parcener, 1 toft and half a bovate of land, doing 3 works in autumn, worth 3*d*. John, son of Alan *atte Brigge*, 5½ acres and 1½ roods of land, 2*s*. 5½*d*. Robert *le Clerke* and Beatrice, his wife, Constance and Alice, sisters and parceners of the same Beatrice, 1 bovate of land, 15*s*. William, son of Thomas, 1 toft and 3 acres and 3 roods of land, 2*s*., and doing 3 works in autumn, worth 3*d*. Richard Smith (*faber*), 2 acres of land, 12*d*. William, son of Gregory, a toft, 10 acres, and 1½ roods of land, 5*s*. 1¼*d*., and doing 3 works in autumn, worth 3*d*. John Fayrfax, 1 close, 3*s*. 4*d*. William, son of Henry, 5 acres, 3*s*. 4*d*.

Sum of the rent and services of the free tenants of Thorp Arches, £9 19*s*. 10¼*d*.

Bonders. Robert de Wodehouse, Alice, who was wife of Henry Foreman, Isabella atte Brigge, and Alice, daughter of William Foreman, each a toft and 15 acres of land, 13s. 4d. They also hold in common a close containing 8 acres, rendering in common 2s. 8d. The said Alice, daughter of William, holds one acre of *Forlande*, 9d.

Sum of the rent of the bonders of Thorp Arches, 56s. 9d.

Cottars. Robert, son of Letitia, and William Swyteman, each a toft, 2s. The same William Swyteman, a close, 3d. William, son of Hugh, a toft, 18d. Thomas Mantel, a toft, 14d. Robert de Bykerton, a toft, 14d. Henry *le Peddere*, a toft, 18d. Alan, son of Adam of Fristegate, a toft, 18d. Alan, son of Alan of Brigge, a toft, 18d. Richard Dykelyn, of Clyfford, a toft, 14d. Robert de Shepeleye, a toft, 2s. 6d. Thomas Pate, a toft, 18d. Roger *le Seriaunt*, a toft, 3s.

Sum of the rent of the cottars of Thorp Arches, 20s. 9d.

WALTON. At Walton, which is a member of Thorp Arches, are 18 acres of meadow which may be mown (*falcabilis*), 18d. the acre. The pasture of the said meadow after the hay has been carried is worth 3s. Sum of the said meadow, 30s. Elias de Farewath, William Scot, and William, his parceners, hold 15 bovates, rendering one pair of gilt spurs, worth 8d., and one pair of white gloves, worth 2d., and four broad arrows without shafts,[a] worth 2d. apiece, for all service. John Fairfax holds 2 bovates, and renders a pound of cummin, worth 2d.

Sum of the whole of Walton, 31s. 2d.

Pleas and perquisites of the court of Thorp Arches, 2s.

Sum of all the preceding sums, £41 12s. 8¼d., out of which is paid for the mill of Thorp Arches as above 66s. 8d., and there remains clear £38 6s. 0¼d.

Simon de Kyme holds the manor of Neuton in the Wylghes[b] of the said manor of Thorp Arches by knight service, and the said Simon's tenants of the manor of Neuton are bound[c] to do for the lord of the manor of Thorp Arches a ploughing with seven ploughs for one day, at winter sowing, at Thorp Arches, and 18 works in autumn. These are not extended, because the expense of the manor exceeds the value of the works.

[a] iiij sagittas barbatas sine flechiis.

[b] Newton Kyme.

[c] Debent facere domino manerii de Thorp Arches aruram per vij carucas per j diem ad semen yemale apud Thorp Arches, et xviij opera in autumpno, et non extenduntur quia custus manerii excedit valorem operum.

Nicholas, son of Sibil, daughter of the said Laderana, late wife of Miles de Stapelton, of the age of 15 years, and Joan, the other daughter of the said Laderana, wife of Aucher, son of Henry, of the age of 24 years and upwards, are the nearest heirs of the said John de Bella aqua and Laderana.

[m. 16]

INQUISITION on the lands and tenements which John de Bella aqua held by the law of England of the inheritance of Laderana, formerly his wife, made at Carleton, on Wednesday next after All Saints, 29 Edw. (8 Nov., 1301), ... Henry de .. wy ...., Richard *le Clerk*, of Snayth, Peter *Atteyate*, William son of Agnes, Hugh son of Adam *le Clerk*, William son of Alice, William son of Adam of Hirst, John *de la Chapele*, William son of Walter, ... He held certain lands and tenements in ...... of Carleton of the said heritage of the King by the service of .... in herbage and fruit of the garden, 10s. In the common field (*campo*), called Northker, 75 acres of arable land ...., 25s. In the common field, called High Field (*altus campus*), 8 acres ...... *Le Merhs*, 6½ acres of arable land (12d.). Sum, 6s. 6d. Sum of the value of the whole of the arable land, 36s. 10d. In a place called Westmersch, 60 acres of meadow, ... Sum of the whole of the extent of the meadow, £9. In a place called *le Merchs*, 15 acres of several pasture (12d.). Sum of the pasture, 15s. .... 49 acres of land, rendering at Martinmas and Whitsuntide 18s. 1d., and at Christmas 1d. Henry son of Walter of Newland (*de nova terra*), 15 acres of land, 5s. at Michaelmas and Easter. John, son of Adam of Newland, 10 acres, ... William son of Adam of ..... 10 acres of land, 10s. 3d. at Martinmas and Whitsuntide, and at the Purification 3¾d. Roger son of Thomas, one toft, 9½ acres of land, 3s. 7d. at Michaelmas and Easter. Robert son of Thomas ...... *la chapele,* a toft, a bovate of land, and an assart, 13s. 4d. Thomas Belle, a toft and 3 acres of land, 4s. 6d.; also 3 acres .... at the Purification, 3½d. Peter *Attehalleyate*, 34½ acres of land, 14d. at Martinmas and Whitsuntide, and at Michaelmas and Easter .. d. Thomas *del* ...., one acre, 4d. .... 4d. Richard de Snayth, a toft and 23½ acres of land, 10s. 3d. at Martinmas and Whitsuntide, at Michaelmas and Easter 2d., and at the Purification 3d. William, son of John of Rosholm, ... 2s. 6d. ...... 14s. 2d. Henry de Cuwyke, a toft and 30 acres of land, 11s. 3d.; an acre of pasture, 4d. Alan Griffin of Hirst, 20 acres of land, 6s. 8d. Robert son of

William Cook (*coci*), ... William son of Walter, a toft
and 7 acres of land, 16*d*. at Martinmas and Whitsuntide, 2*s*.
10*d*. at Michaelmas and Easter, and 2½*d*. at the Purification.
John, son of Adam Miller, 7 acres of land, 5*s*. Thomas, son
of Adam ...... Ladrana, daughter of Adam of Breresdike,
2 acres of land, 8*d*. Edusa Everard, a toft and 9 acres of
land, 5*s*. 2½*d*. Robert, son of Alice, 4 acres of land, 20*d*.
Thomas, son of Roger, 16 acres of land, ... Henry Kyng,
3 acres of land, 14*d*. John Warner, of Snayth, 3 acres of
land, 12*d*. Thomas, son of Adam of Snayth, 13½ acres of
land, 6*s*. Alice *la Kydere*, 1 acre, 4*d*. ....., 5½ acres, 22*d*.
John, son of Thomas of Snayth, 2 acres and 3 perches of
land, 11*d*. William son of Agnes, 6 acres, 2*s*. 8*d*. William
de Neusom, 4 acres, ... Henry Everard, 2 acres, 8*d*.; also
a toft and a perch of land, 2½*d*. Roger *Forester*, 3 acres, 12*d*.
Thomas de Snayth, 14 acres, ...; 15½ acres, 4*s*. 11*d*.; a
toft, 12*d*. Hugh, son of Adam Clerk, a toft and 18 acres of
land, 9*s*. William Hebbe, 1½ acres and 1 perch, 7*d*.
William, son of Alice, 5 acres, 20*d*. The prior of Drax
renders 20*s*. 8*d*. a year. The lady of Sewardeby renders
20*s*. 1*d*. a year.

Sum of the aforesaid demesnes, £12 2*s*. 2*d*.

Sum of the rent of the said free tenants, £11 8*s*. 5*d*.

Other tenants of base tenure (*de bassa tenura*). William
son of Henry, 30½ acres and half a perch of land, and
renders yearly at Michaelmas and Easter 10*s*. 6½*d*., and at
the Purification 22*d*. He ought to reap in autumn for 3
days ...., because[a] he ought to do them at the food of the
lord once a day. He ought also to carry ten loads of corn
with his cart or waggon, at the lord's foods, and all the
carryings are worth 3½*d*. He also owes two carryings of
wood without food, and it is worth .... 1*d*. .... He ought
also to plough three days with one plough at the Lent
sowing, at the lord's food. Price of a day's ploughing, 2*d*.
Sum of the rent of the said William, 12*s*. 4½*d*. Sum of his
works, 12¼*d*. .... at the Purification 2*s*. 4*d*.; and does
works as the said William does. William de Cotes holds
18½ acres of land, and renders at Michaelmas and Easter
6*s*. 11½*d*., and at the Purification 2*s*. 4*d*., and does works and
services like the said William. .... 9½ acres and one
rood of land, and renders at Martinmas and Whitsuntide

---

[a] Quia ea facere debet ad cibum domini semel in die. Item debet cariare
x pondera bladi cum curru suo vel caretta sua ad cibum domini, et valent omnia
cariagia iij*d*. quad. Item debet ij cariagia bosci sine cibo, et valet .... j*d*. .....
Item debet arare cum una caruca per iij dies ad semen quadragesimale ad cibum
domini, precium arure diete ij*d*.

4s. 2½d., and at the Purification 13¼d., and does half the works the said William, son of Henry, does. Thomas Shotebrid holds a toft, 6½ acres and 1½ roods of land, and renders at Michaelmas and Easter 2s. 6d., at Martinmas and Whitsuntide 9½d., and at the Purification 8¼d., and does works like the said J. Roger Flemyng, 5 acres 3 roods of land, at Martinmas and Whitsuntide 7½d., at Michaelmas and Easter 18¼d., and at the Purification 5¼d. John, son of Thomas *le Juesne,* 11 acres of land, rendering at Michaelmas and Easter 4s. 6d., and at the Purification 14¼d. William Persone, 4 acres and one rood of land, rendering at Michaelmas and Easter 23d., and at the Purification 6½d. Hugh Casselove, 3 acres, rendering at Michaelmas and Easter 19½d.; also one rood of land, rendering at Martinmas and Whitsuntide 1d., and at the Purification 5d. And each of the said Thomas Shotebrid, Roger Flemyng, John, son of Thomas, William Persone, and Hugh, does the same works as the said John Joyelavedy does.

Sum of the rent of the said tenants of base tenure, £55 0s. 11d.

Sum of works of the same, 6s. 1½d.

Other tenants, natives. Robert and Roger Somer hold 2 acres and 3½ roods of land, rendering at Martinmas and Whitsuntide 14d., and at the Purification 4½d. Richard de Kelinton, one toft and half an acre of land, rendering at Martinmas and Whitsuntide 8d., and at the Purification 2¼d. Adam Nutebrun, 1½ roods of land, rendering at Martinmas and Whitsuntide 4d., and at the Purification ½d. Roger Nutebrun, 1 acre 1½ roods of land, rendering at Martinmas and Whitsuntide 11½d., and at the Purification 2d. Richard .....tel, ..., rendering at Martinmas and Whitsuntide 4d., and at the Purification ¾d. William Nutebrun, 1 acre and 1½ roods of land and one rood of meadow, etc., 12d. The heirs of William Flaundres, 2 acres ..... William son of Sibbe, a toft, 24 acres and 1 rood of land, rendering at Martinmas and Whitsuntide 13s. 1d., and at the Purification 3s. 3d. Adam Casselove, 7 acres of land, at Martinmas and Whitsuntide 3s. 7d., and at the Purification 10d. ..... 3 acres of land, rendering at Martinmas and Whitsuntide 17d., and at the Purification 3¾d. Osbert Kons, a toft and half an acre, rendering at the said terms 5½d., and at the Purification 2d. William, son of Peter, a toft, 19 acres ..., 6s. 5d., and at the Purification 19½d. Roger, son of Peter, 1½ roods, rendering at the said terms 3d., and at the Purification ¾d. John, son of Peter, 1½ roods, at the same terms 3d., and at the Purification ¾d. ...... a toft and 19½ acres of land, 7s. 11½d. at the same terms, and 2s. 4½d. at the Purification. Henry, son of John, 3 acres and 3 roods, 19d. at the same terms, and 1d. at Easter. Thomas, son of John, 2½ acres . . . . Ralph Osbern, one acre one rood, 4½d. at the said terms. Cecilia, daughter of Adam, 3½ acres, 16d. at the said terms, and 5½d. at the Purification. John Attewelle, 8 acres 2 roods . . . . . , 2s. 11d., and 11½d. at the Purification. Richard, son of Gilbert, William, son of Geoffrey, William Harding, John Frere, Adam de Byarn, Adam Somer, Thomas *le Caretter*, Elena Otteman, John Otteman, Thomas *le Mazun*, John Dellowe, John son of Margaret, Thomas son of Roger Persone, Alan de Wynandermer, Robert Forester, Thomas Horn, Richard de Cameslesford, Alan de Balne, John de Wintrington, William son of Hugh *le Cras*, Hugh Gayard, Henry son of Roger, Thomas *le Keu*, William de Lexinton, Thomas Rumfar, Walter Horn, Maude *le Madur*, Henry Whitserk, Roger son of William Hille, Robert son of Richard, Roger de Kent, William son of Richard Leyly, Maude daughter of Adam *le Madour*, William de Baghan, Roger *le Baileur* (3 *swathes* of meadow), Roger *le Glovere*, Richard *le Glovere*, John son of Roger Hardyng, John son of Adam Hard', Henry son of Thomas *le Juesne*, Edusa . . . . . . , William de Kent, John son of William de Kent, Roger son of Roger, John *le Baileur*, Roger son of William *le Baileur*, Maude widow of Henry, Robert Belle, John son of William Sibbe, ... son of Ralph de Cotes, Margaret Pin, Agnes Pin, Adam *le Clerk*, Roger Paramurs, William de Wynandermere, Thomas Belgl', John son of Adam of Cotes, Matthew *le Carpenter*, Cecilia Godgris, Stephen *le Petyt*, Maude widow of Richard Graffard, Simon son of John of Beverlay, John Pog, Henry son of Peter Snou, John *del Nes*, and Thomas his brother, Maude widow of William *le Forester*, William son of William Sille, Isold the widow, Cristiana the widow, John son of Robert *le Bailour*, John son of William.

Sum of the said tenants, £18 13s. 9d.[a]

[m. 8]

INQUISITION of the knights' fees and advowson of churches which John de Bella aqua held in chief beyond Trent on the day he died, of the inheritance of Laderana, late his wife, made at York, on Thursday, the eve of the Conversion of St. Paul, 31 Edw. (24 Jan., 1302-3), before the Escheator,

[a] The writing from this point becomes almost entirely illegible. Mention is made of two windmills at Draxebrigge and a passage over the river Ayr.

by Alan de Folifait, Henry de Cr . . . . , Adam de Thorp, William de Hornington, Robert de Haulay, William de Tocwyth, William *le Cerf*, Thomas de Ulskelfe, John Fairfax, William Faukes, William de Castelay, Nigel de Werreby, Robert de Gaylesthorp, William Graffard, Richard *le Clerk* of Carleton, William *le Mareschal* of the same, Peter *a la Porte*, and Richard son of Milisant.

Robert of Pontefract held of John de Bella aqua as of the said inheritance 7 carucates and 2 bovates in Wyvelesthorp, Tocwyth, and Hoton,[a] in demesne and service, by the service of half a knight's fee, of which the same Robert holds three carucates in Wyvelesthorp in demesne, worth £20 a year. Of the residue John de Creppinge and Robert de Clerevaus hold of the said Robert of Pontefract in Hoton 3 carucates; and William de Bugthorp holds half a carucate in Tocwyth, worth £7 a year. The prior of Helagh Park (*de Parco*) holds in frankalmoign two bovates in Tocwyth, worth 10s. a year; and the prioress of Synithwayt holds in frankalmoign half a carucate, worth 10s. a year.   Sum, £28.

John de Kirkeby held of John de Bella aqua one carucate and two bovates in Tocwyth in demesne, by the service of the 13th part of one knight's fee, worth 50s. a year.
                                                                Sum, 50s.

William de Bugthorp held of John de Bella aqua 6½ carucates in Rughford[b] by the service of half a knight's fee, of which the same William holds 4 carucates in Rughford in demesne, worth £20 a year; and of the residue the heir of William, son of Henry, holds one carucate and two bovates in Merston,[c] worth 50s. a year; Everard Prodom holds half a carucate in the same vill, worth 20s. a year; and Henry, son of the said Everard, holds six bovates in Merston, worth 30s. a year.   Sum, £25.

Richard de Malebys held of John de Bella aqua 3 carucates of land in Coupmanthorpe in demesne, by the service of the fourth part of one knight's fee, worth £10 a year.   Sum, £10.

The heir of William, son of Thomas, held of John de Bella aqua 9 carucates in Merston, by the service of half a knight's fee, of which the heir holds six carucates in demesne, worth £12 a year, and of the residue the abbot of Fountains holds one carucate (*sic*) in frankalmoign, worth 40s. a year.   Sum, £14.

[a] Wilstrop in the parish of Kirk Hammerton, Tocwith, and Hutton Wansley.
[b] Rufforth.
[c] Long Marston.

William *le Vavasour* and Richard *le Walays* hold of John de Bella aqua five carucates in Bylton, by the service of the fourth part of one knight's fee, of which William *le Vavasour* holds a carucate and a bovate in Bylton in demesne, worth 45*s.* a year, and Richard *le Walays* holds a carucate and a bovate in the same vill in demesne, worth 45*s.* a year. Of the residue William *le Vavasour* holds of the prior of Helagh Park a carucate and a half and a bovate, which the said prior formerly held in frankalmoign, worth 42*s.* a year; and the prioress of Synithwayt holds in frankalmoign a carucate and a half and a bovate in Tocwyth, worth 42*s.* a year. Sum, £8 15*s.*

Simon de Kime held of John de Bella aqua seven carucates in Neuton Kyme in demesne and service, by the service of half a knight's fee, of which the same Simon holds in demesne four carucates and two bovates, worth £8 10*s.* a year. Of the residue Robert de Elkyngton holds two carucates, worth £4 a year; Elyas de Neuton, clerk, 2 bovates, worth 10*s.* a year; and Alan de Catherton, four bovates, worth 20*s.* a year. Sum, £14.

Henry, son of John of Hamerton, held of John de Bella aqua 12 carucates in Hamerton, Monketon, Wythington, and Quixlay,[a] in demesne and service, by the service of one knight's fee, of which the said Henry holds in demesne 5½ carucates and one bovate in Hamerton and Quixlay, worth £11 5*s.* a year. The abbot of Fountains holds of the same Henry 7 bovates in frankalmoign in Hamerton, worth 35*s.* a year. Alan de Cranelay (?) holds of the same Henry in Hamerton 2 bovates of land, worth 10*s.* a year. Henry Moye holds of the same Henry 3 bovates in Hamerton, worth 20*s.* a year. Robert, son of Hugh, holds of the heir of Richard de Normanville 3 bovates in Hamerton, which the same heir held of the said Henry, worth 15*s.* a year. Isabella, daughter of John of Hamerton, holds 3 bovates in Hamerton of the same Henry, worth 15*s.* a year. Agnes, daughter of Henry, holds of the same Henry 3 bovates in Hamerton, worth 15*s.* a year. Roger de Merkyngfeld holds of the same Henry one carucate in Monketon, worth 40*s.* a year. William *le Walays* holds of the same Henry a carucate of land in Wythington, worth 40*s.* a year. John, son of Alexander of Quixlay, holds of the same Henry one messuage and 5 bovates in Quixlay, worth 26*s.* 8*d.* a year. Robert, son of John, holds of the same Henry a toft, worth 6*d.* a year. Nicholas Clerk, of Quixlay, holds of the same Henry 2 bovates in Quixlay, worth 10*s.* a year. Thomas Waydelove

---

[a] Green Hammerton, Nun Monkton, Widdington, and Whixley.

holds of the same Henry 3 bovates of land in Quixlay, worth 15s. a year. Robert de Gaviesthorp holds of the same Henry 2 bovates of land in Quixlay, worth 10s. a year. Thomas Ingebald holds of the same Henry 2 bovates in Quixlay, worth 10s. a year.   Sum, £24 2s. 2d.

John Mauleverer held of the said John de Bella aqua, of the inheritance aforesaid, 14 carucates in Allerton, Clarton, Lynlandes, Dunseford, Little Useburne, Hoperton, Horseford, and Raudon,[a] in demesne and service, by the service of one knight's fee and the sixth part of a knight's fee, of which the said John Mauleverer holds in demesne 7 carucates of land, worth £14 a year. Richard le Walays holds of the same John (Mauleverer) 3 carucates of land in Dunsford, worth £7 a year. Robert the chaplain holds of the same John 4 bovates in Hoperton, worth 20s. a year. John Skot holds of the same John 2 bovates in Hoperton, worth 10s. a year. Robert, son of Nicholas of Hoperton, holds of the same John a messuage and 2 acres of land, worth 3s. a year. Geoffrey le Normand holds of the same John a messuage, worth 3s. a year. Richard de Hoperton holds a messuage in Hoperton, worth 18d. a year. Henry Morel holds 2 bovates in Hoperton, worth 10s. a year. Thomas de Botlesford holds two bovates in Hoperton, worth 10s. a year. Thomas de Horsford holds a carucate in Horsford, worth 40s. a year. The same Thomas holds of the same John a carucate in Raudon, worth 40s. a year. Richard le Walays holds of the same John 2 bovates in Little Useburne, worth 10s. a year.   Sum, £28 6s. 6d.

Sum of sums, £154 9s. 8d.

John de Bella aqua had no advowson of any church of the said inheritance.

[m. 9]

Extent of knights' fees and advowsons of churches which John de Bella aqua held of the inheritance of Laderana, late his wife, made at York on 6 Feb., 31 Edw. (1302-3), by John de Neuby, Robert Oliver, Peter de Kilvington, Peter at the spring (ad fontem) of Dalton, Hugh de Carleton, William de Norton, John de Boyville, John de Iselbeck, Thomas Maunsel, Richard Wygot, John de Wellebergh, and Edmund Carbonel. Robert de Furneaus and Maude, his wife, held of the said John de Bella aqua six carucates in demesne and service in Bordelby, Herlsay, Sithill, and Salcock,[b] by the service of half a knight's fee, of which the

---

[a] Allerton Mauleverer, Clareton, Lylands, Dunsforth, Little Ouseburn, Hopperton, Horsforth, and Rawden.

[b] Mount Grace, East Harlsey, Siddle, and East Sawcock.

said Robert and Maude hold in demesne two carucates in Bordelby, each carucate worth 30s. a year; also half a carucate in Herlsay in demesne, worth 15s. a year. The prior of Gysburne holds of the said Robert and Maude two carucates in Herlsay, worth 60s. a year. Michael de Upsale holds of the same half a carucate in Herlsay, Sithill, worth 15s. a year. Thomas de Salcock holds of the same one carucate of land in Salcock, worth 30s. a year.

Sum of the whole extent above, £9. No advowsons of churches.

[m. 10]

EXTENT of the knights' fees which John de Bella aqua, deceased, held of the King in chief, beyond Trent, of the inheritance of Laderana, late his wife, and which on the occasion of his death were taken into the King's hand, that is:—

Half a knight's fee in Wyvelsthorpe, Tocwyth, and Hoton, held by Robert of Pontefract, extended at £20 a year.

The thirteenth part of one knight's fee in the same vill of Tocwyth, held by John de Kirkeby, etc., at 50s.

Half a knight's fee in Rughford, held by William de Bugthorpe, etc., at £20.

The fourth part of a knight's fee in Coupmanthorpe, held by Richard de Malebys, etc., at £10.

Half a knight's fee in Merston, held by the heir of William son of Thomas, etc., at £12.

The fourth part of a knight's fee in Bylton, held by William *le Vavassur* and *Richard le Walays*, etc., at £4 10s.

Half a knight's fee in Neuton Kyme, held by Simon de Kyme, etc., at £8 10s.

One knight's fee in Hamerton, Monketon, Wythington, and Quixlay, held by Henry son of John of Hamerton, etc., at £11 5s.

One fee and the sixth part of one knight's fee in Allerton, Clarton, Lynlandes, Dunseford, Little Useburne, Hoperton, Horseford, and Raudon, held by John Mauleverer, etc., at £14.

Half a knight's fee in Bordelby, Herlsay, Sithil, and Salcok, held by Robert de Furneaus and Maude his wife, etc., at 45s.

Sum of the said fees, 5 fees, the sixth and thirteenth parts of a knight's fee.

Sum of the value of the same, £105, and the value of half of the said fees is £52 10s.

[m. 6]

PARTITION[a] of the knights' fees which were of the inheritance of Laderana, late wife of John de Bella aqua.

Sir William *le Vavesour* and Sir Richard *le Waleys* hold the fourth part of one fee in Bilton, extended at £4 10s. a year.

Henry son of John of Hamerton holds one fee in Hamerton, extended at £24 a year.

Richard de Malebys holds in Coupmanthorpe the fourth part of one fee, extended at £10 a year.

John Mauleverer holds in Alverton and elsewhere one fee and the sixth part of one fee, extended at £14 a year.

Out of this partition let Aucher choose which part he likes, and if this partition does not please him, let Aucher divide these fees, and let Miles choose.

Robert de Furnews and Maude his wife hold half a fee in Bordelby and elsewhere, extended at £9 a year.

Robert of Pontefract holds in Wylstorpe and elsewhere half a fee, extended at £28 a year.

William de Bugthorpe holds in Ruchgford half a fee, extended at £25 a year.

The heir of William de Merston holds in Merston half a fee, extended at £12 a year.

Simon de Kyme holds in Newton Kyme half a knight's fee, extended at £8 10s.

John de Kyrkeby holds in Tokwyth the third part of one fee, extended at 50s.

[m. 11]

> Writ directed to Master Richard de Haveringes, ordering a new extent of the knights' fees and advowsons of churches and abbeys which were held by John de Bella aqua in chief, by the law of England, of the inheritance of Laderana, his wife, as there was an error in the extents and partition already made. Notice to be given to Aucher, son of Henry, to be present in Chancery on the morrow of the Ascension (16 May). Dated at Westminster, 23 April, 31st year (1303).

[m. 12]

LETTER, partly destroyed, certifying that the writer (Haveringes) had made inquisition as to the knights' fees and advowsons of churches of the inheritance of Laderana, and of what is further to be inquired about he does not know.

[a] This partition is entered on the *Close Roll* (32 Edw. I., 13*d*). The first half, assigned to Nicholas de Stapleton, was valued at £80 5s.; the second, assigned to Aucher, son of Henry, and Joan, his wife, was valued at £52 10s.

[m. 13]

THE HEIR'S PART, who is under age.

HALF a fee in Wyvelesthorpe, Tocwyth, and Hoton, held by Robert of Pontefract, extended at £20.

Half a fee in Rughford, held by William de Bugthorpe, extended at £20.

One fee in Hamerton, Monketon, Wythington, and Quixlay, held by Henry, son of John of Hamerton, extended at £11 5s.

Half a fee in Bordelby, Herlsay, Sithill, and Salcok, held by Robert de Furneaus and Maude his wife, extended at 45s.

Sum of fees, 2½.

Sum of the value of the same, £53 10s.

[m. 14]

PART OF AUCHER, SON OF HENRY.[a]

HALF a fee in Merston, held by the heir of William, son of Thomas, and extended at £12.

A fee and a sixth part of a fee in Allerton, Clarton, Lynlandes, Dunseford, Little Useburne, Hoperton, Horseford, and Raudon, held by John Mauleverer, and extended at £14.

The thirteenth part of a fee in Tocwyth, held by John de Kirkeby, and extended at 50s.

The fourth part of a fee in Coupmanthorpe, held by Richard Malebys, and extended at £10.

The fourth part of a fee in Bilton, held by William *le Vavassur* and Richard *le Waleys*, and extended at £4 10s.

Half a fee in Neuton Kyme, held by Simon de Kyme, and extended at £8 10s.

Sum of fees, 2½, and one sixth and one thirteenth of a knight's fee.

Sum of value of the same, £51 10s.

This part exceeds the other part in the number of fees by a sixth part and a thirteenth part of a knight's fee, but is less than the other in money value by 40s.

[m. 5]

Miles de Stapelton,[b] father of Nicholas de Stapelton, who is in ward to our lord the King, prays the Chancellor of our lord the King, that the knights' fees, which have descended

---

[a] This partition is embodied in a notice to the Escheator, dated at Langeleye, 10 February, 1302-3, with the following note at the end :—Postea fuit particio feodorum predictorum aliter facta ad prosecucionem Milonis de Stapelton pro rege, prout patet in dorso rotuli clausarum de anno xxxij (*Close Roll*, 31 Edw. I., m. 16).

[b] Miles (*Milis*) de Stapelton, in another petition (*Ancient Petitions*, E. No. 451), claimed twenty marcs rent in Treske and Hovingham, which had been granted to him and his heirs by Sir Roger de Mountbray, and of which Roger and his bailiffs

to Aucher, son of Henry, and to the said Nicholas, of the inheritance of Ladereyne, who was the wife of Sir John de Belewe, may be partitioned between the parceners, so that no prejudice or disinheriting . . . . and to the infant, inasmuch as he is in the ward to our lord the King. That as the assignment which has been ordained of these fees . . . . the fees and the marriages which may arise in the time of wardship, which have been assigned to the said Aucher for his purparty, are worth . . . . . double or more than the fees which have been assigned to the infant, who is in ward to the King. And because the great lords, ...

Sir William *le Vavasour*, Sir Richard *de* (*sic*) *Waleys*, Sir Simon de Kyme, Sir John de Kyrkeby, and John Mauleverer, who have their lands near the manor of Torp,[a] which is the head (*i.e.* of the barony), to which the fees are appendant, and which are convenient to the manor, have been assigned to Aucher and the lesser people, and (the lands) which are farther away, have been assigned to the infant's purparty; and they are not equally extended, for the lands of John Mauleverer, which amount to a fee and a half, and to which wardship and marriage belong (the which John has in one manor a hundred marcs and more), are counted in this assignment for one fee, and the sixth part of a fee, and are extended only at £14, and according to this extent have been assigned to Aucher; and the other fees which have been assigned to Aucher from the other tenants named above, have been extended in the same manner. The fees, assigned to the infant, his parcener, have been extended much higher than the lands are worth, and are far away, and the marriages from those fees poor and of less value than the others, and so the King perchance may be a loser during this wardship, and the infant disinherited. Wherefore the said Miles prays that this matter may be set right, so that right and equity may be done between the parceners in making this partition, and the infant may not be disinherited, or the King a loser.

had disseised him, whilst he was at the war in Gascony (*Garscoyne*) with his lord, the Earl of Lincoln. Miles could have recovered, had not the land whence the rent came been in the King's hand, by reason of the death of the said Sir Roger, so he prayed the King that he might recover his freehold. The King gave him leave to bring an action of novel disseisin against his disseisors, but judgment was to be respited until the King's pleasure should be known.

ª Thorp Arch.

INDEX OF NAMES AND PLACES.

The small figures over the number of the page indicate that the *name is repeated* that number of times in the same page. The letter "n" indicates that the name is in the notes to the page.

A.

Abbitoft', 124
Abbot, Roger, 139
Abby, Rob., 28; Will., 29
Abel, Will., 166
Aberbroth', 42n
Aberbury, Alberbirs, Mr. Thos. de, 108
Aberconewey, 5, 5n, 6, 14n, 16
Aberford, 138n
Absolon, John son of, 9, 76, 101, 112, 139
Acaster Malbis, Acastre, 132n
Acharde, Adam, 56
Ackelom, Rob. de, 100
Aco de Flixton, 66
Acre (*ultra acram*), Thomas beyond the, 63
Adam, Adam fitz, 13n; Cecilia dau. of, 173; Elyas son of, 157; Ralph son of, 128[2]; Ric. son of, 128
Addelstene, Stephen, 91
Adlingfleet, Athelingeflete, Athelingflete, Athelingfleth, 4, 158, 160, 161
Adwick-on-Dearne, Addewyck, 97; Rob. son of Nich. of, 97
———— -le-Street, 84n
Agillon, Geoffrey, 141
Agnes, Will. son of, 4, 170, 171
Ainsty, Aynsty, Hainsti, Wapentake, 15, 16
Ake, Will. Marshall of, 99
Alaintoftes, Aleintoftes, 73, 74
Alan, Adam son of, 166; Brian son of, 158, 162; John son of, 30; Ralph son of, 128, 130; Ric. son of, 128, 130, 167; Roger son of, 86
Albemarle, barony of, 144; earldom of, 145n, 146n; fee of, 96[2]; honour of, 37[2], 90n, 91, 149; countess of, 32; Alina de Fortibus, countess of, 109n; Avelina dau. of Will. de Fortibus, earl of, 72n; Avicia dau. of Will. le Gros, earl of, 145n; Hawisia, countess of, 145n; Isabella de Fortibus, countess of, 7, 47, 56, 56n, 125, 136; earl of, 6, 26, 110; Will. earl of, 46; Will. de Forz, Fortibus, earl of, 7, 96n, 145n, 147; Will. le Gros, earl of, 145n

Alblaster, Roger son of John the, 24
Albo Monasterio, Ranulph de, 157, 161, 165
Albus, *see* White
Aldborough, Vetus Burgus, 126; (Holderness) Aldeburgh, 47; Rob. de, 2
Aldelote, John, 144
Aldfield, Aldefeld, 155, 160, 163; Jollan de, 21; Will. de, 20, 21, 77, 79, 155, 160, 163
Aldwark, Aldewerke, 115; Thos. de, 45, 114
Alexander, Thos. son of, 71, 128; Will. son of, 30
Alger, Alan, 103
Alice, Adam son of, 113; Hugh son of, 134; Robert son of, 94, 149, 171; Thos. son of, 94; William son of, 170, 171
Alinote, Will., 114
Allerston, Alverstain, Alverstan in Pickerynglyth, 51, 52
Allerthorpe, Arlaththorpe, 69
Allerton Mauleverer, Allerton, 156, 164, 176–179
Almer, 89
Alneburgh, 123n, 125n
Alverton, Thos. son of Will. of, called Page, and Ric. his brother, 63
Alwaldecotes, 17n
Alwaldetoftes, Allerwartoftes, 17, 45
Alwoodley, Alewodeleye, Alewoldeleye, 31; Roger de, 31[2]; Alice, his wife, 32; Alice, Anabil, Joan, Margaret, his daughters, 31, 32
Alwy, Robert, 88
Amand de Ruda, 91; Serjaunt, 90n; de Surdevale, 4
Amia, 168
Amice, Amys, Robert, 114, 134
Ammory, Thos., 136
Ancelin, Hancelin, Adam, 48; Roger, 48, 82
Anderby, Hugh de, 135
Andrew, Rob. son of Rob. son of, the younger, 166; William son of, 166[2]
Angrom, 38
Appelby, John de, 46; Simon de, 55

F.

Faber, *see* Smith
Fadymor, 164
Fairfax, John, 167, 168, 169, 174
Falsgrave, Wallesgrave, Whallesgrave, 92, 93; Thos. de, 92; Thos. son of Matilda of, 88
Fancurt, Fanecurt, John, John de, 15, 43, 94
Farnham, Farneham, 43, 132
Farnlaye, Rob. de, 168
Farwath, Farewath, Elias de, 167, 169
Fassham, Will. de, 27
Fatting', Alice, 152
Faucomberge, Faucumberge, Faucunberge, Faukunbergge, Henry son of Will. de, 5; John son of Will. de, 5; Peter de, 5; Rob. de, 5; Walt. de, 5, 14, 124; Will. de, 4; Will. son of Will. de, 5
Faucuner, Will., 66, 67
Faukes, Will., 174
Fauuel, Fauvel, Adam, 154; Constantine, 12, 106, 110; Everard, 12, 146; Ric., 154
Fauuelthorpe, Ric. de, 146²
Faxflete, John de, 3
Fayceby, 117*n*
Fayrhehe, Will., 78
Feckenham, 23
Feetham, Fyton, 80*n*
Fellesclife, 131
Felton, Will. de, 52
Fennonoyr, 16*n*
Fenton, 63, 67; Ric. de, 11, 44, 119; Rob. de, 142; Stephen son of Rob. de, 142; Warin de, 63, 107; Will. de, 125
Fenwick, Fenewyke, 103
Ferlington, 17
Fermesona, 104
Ferrars, earldom of, 72*n*
Feryman, Eustace, 111
Feryngesby, 131
Fethirstan, Ric. de, 87, 103; Will. son of Elias of, 87
Feugers, Andrew de, 114*n*
Fewston, Foston, 131
Fikais, Walter, 104
Fimmer, Fynmer, Adam de, 109; Will. de, 141
Finkehale, prior of, 138
Finningley, Fynyngleye, 161
Fisker, Thos., 145
Fiskersgate, Fyskergat, Ric. de, 8, 105
Fisschebourne, Thos. de, seneschal of the Earl of Lincoln, 103
Fitling, Fittelinge, Fyttelyngge, Henry de, 90; John de, 4, 27, 37², 47, 91, 124, 149
Fitoun, *see* Fyton

Fivile, 67
Flanders, 52, 75, 77*n*; Ghent, 76*n*
Flasceby, 154, 160, 162
Flaundres, Will., 172
Flaxby, Flasceby, 2
Flaxton, 61
Flemenge, Flemyng, Flemynge, George le, 106; Henry, 3; James le, 106; Roger, 172
Fletburgh, 122
Fletham, 135; Adam son of John of, Adam Webster of, 135
Flettewyke, 41*n*
Flinton, Walter de, 4, 26, 27
Flixton, 88; Aco, Aso de, 66, 68; Thos. de, 74
Flouer, Gaceus, 106
Flynthull, John de, 103
Folejaumbe, Thos., knt., 103
Folifait, Alan de, 167, 168, 174; Elena his wife, 168
Foliot, Folyot, Beatrice, 10*n*, 26*n*; Jordan, 10*n*, 26*n*, 102*n*; Margery wife of Jordan, 102*n*, 103; Ric., 10*n*, 26*n*, 102, 155, 163
Folke, Thos., 92
Folketon, 74, 88, 139; Geoffrey de, 111; Simon de, 89, 91, 111
Folkingham, 80*n*
Forbrace, Forbrase, Rob., 65, 146
Foreman, Forman, Prepositus, Adam, 97; Alice dau. of Will., 169; Alice wife of Henry, 169; Ric., 166²; Ric. son of the, 127; Rob., 100; Will., 133
Forester, Forster, Forestarius, Henry, 1; John le, 133; Rob., 76, 112, 173; Roger, 171
Foreward', Rob., 134
Forfar, 35, 40*n*
Forge, Elena, 92
Forland, 16, 78, 169
Fornas', *see* Furneux
Forne, Henry, 89
Fossard, Will., 99, 132
Fossur, Gervase le, 152
Fosteton, Rob. de, 55
Foston, Thos. de, 25, 151
Fountains Abbey, 76*n*; abbot of, 155, 163, 175
Fox, Adam, 53; Alan, 136; Rob., 15, 38, 155
Foxholes, Foxholt', Ralph de, 66, 139; Rob. de, 77, 133
Fraght, 129
Fraisthorp, Fraysthorp', 118², 119
Franceys, Fraunces, Fraunceys, Fraunsays, Henry, Henry le, 15, 113; Isabella, 152; John, 133*n*, 152; Rob., 34
Franckelain, Fraunkeleyn, Geoffrey, 35; Godfrey, 42; Rob., 30; Will. le, 25

Skeurus, Joan de, 42n
Skewsby, Schouseby, Shouesby, Scowes-
by, 10, 25; Elyas son of Ralph of,
61; Walt. de, 25, 76, 140, 151
Skidby, Schiteby, 96
Skipse, castle guard of, 37[a]
Skipton-in-Cravene, 12, 65, 107, 110,
146n; barony of, 146n; castle, 106,
109n; honour of the castle, 12, 147;
court of, 109n; knights' court of, 48;
bailiff of, John de Totenhou, 47;
Will. de, clk., 106, 110
Skipwyth, 143; John de, 143
Skirne, Skyren, 36, 140; Ric. de, 140;
Steph. de, 55
Skutterskelfe, Scothershelf', Scother-
skelf', 116, 119; Rob. de, 116, 119
Skyrewyth, Adam de, 125n
Skyteby, Ric. de, 125
Sledmere, Sledemer, 41, 159, 160, 162
Sleght, Sleht, Will., 21, 53, 54, 136
Slette, Will., 109
Slexte, Will., 41
Sleye, Peter, 23
Slingsby, Slengesby, 151-153, 156, 160,
162
Smale, Will. le, 63
Smarber, Smerbergh, 80n
Smith, Faber, le Fevre, Laurence, 29;
Ric., 166, 168; Rob., 111; Will.,
23, 28, 124
Smytheton, Will. de, 119
Snaynton, Christiana wife of Will. de,
149
Snayth, 171; Henry le clerk of, 170;
John son of Thos. of, 171; Ric.
de, 170; Thos. de, 171; Thos. son
of Adam of, 171
Snel, Steph., 15
Snou, Henry son of Peter, 173
Snoute, Walter, 186
Snyttiby, Rob., 34
Sokeburne, 142; Eliz. lady of, Will.
parson of, 142
Solihull, 64n
Solio, Thomas in, 89
Somer, Adam, 173; Rob., Rog., 172
Somersetshire, see Ashton
Sommonur, John, 99
Southants, 86n
Southburn, Suthbrunne, Suze Brune,
99, 167
Sowerby (Thirsk), Soureby, 159, 163
Spakeman, Will., 128, 130
Spaldington, Sir Osbert de, 102
Specer, see Especer
Spencer, dispensator, Roger, 66; see
Steward
Spiche, Geoffrey, 93
Spinis, Simon, 34
Sprotborough, Sprotteburg', 84

Sprotle, Sprottele, 47, 150; Geoffrey de,
98; Simon de, 26, 37, 47, 124, 149
Sproxton, 101; Maude wife of Rob. de,
102; Peter de, 101; Rob. de, 9,
100; Will. son of Rob. de, 102
Spruisty, Sprotesby, 131
Spry, Reyner, 53
Squier, see Esquier
Stabler, Stabeler, Adam, Adam le, 36,
99, 140; John le, 45; Will., 140
Stacy, John, 111
Stallage, 129
Stampe, Adam, 71
Stanforde, 58
Stang, 28, 29
Stanleye, Kirke, 131
Stapleton, Stapelton, Stapilton, Isabel,
Sibil, wife of Miles de, 165n; Miles
de, Milis de, 135, 157, 164, 178,
179, 179n; Nicholas son of Isabel,
Sibil de, 165n, 167, 170, 178n, 179;
Roger de, 78, 158
Statherne, 161
Staveley, Stavelay, Stayveley, 43, 131,
132; Will. de, 44, 98
Staxton, 139
Stayncliff, Staynclyf', Steyncleve, wapen-
take, 14, 109, 154
Stayncros wapentake, 138
Stayneley, Hugh de, 68, 71
Staynemore, 77
Staythorpe, Starthorpe, 161
Stede, Will. del, 40
Stephen, Henry son of, 130; John son
of, 128; Ralph son of, 130; Rob.
son of, 86[a]; Will. son of, 93, 117
Stepney, Stebeneth, Stebenhethe, 102,
103, 124
Steresby, 158, 162
Steward, Stiward, dispensator, Alan, 1;
John, Rob., 36; see Spencer
Steyntone, Ralph de, 91
Steynwegges, 90
Stikebuc, Walter, 44
Stirling, Stryvelyn, 86
Stivelington, 17
Stockeld, John de, 2
Stodlay, see Studley
Stokesby, Walter de, 17
Stokesley, Stokesle, Stokeslee, 11, 44,
100
Stoketon, Margaret wife of Rob. de,
Ric. de, Rob. de, 125
Stonegrave, Stangreve, Stangrewe,
Stayngrif, Stengreve, Steyngreve,
9, 11n, 25, 157, 164; Ida wife of
John de, 10n[a]; Isabel dau. of John
de, 10, 11n[a]; Jo n de, 9, 76;
Rob. Forester of, 101
Stonesdale, 80n
Stopham, Will. de, 130

PRINTED BY

J. WHITEHEAD AND SON, ALFRED STREET, BOAR LANE,

LEEDS.

ND - #0207 - 211122 - C0 - 229/152/12 - PB - 9781332066100 - Gloss Lamination